ATE DUE

D0801496

HUMILIATION *and* CELEBRATION

HUMILIATION
and
CELEBRATION

Post-Radical Themes in Doctrine, Morals and Mission

by GABRIEL FACKRE

Sheed and Ward : New York

65823

To
D. J. T. A. F.

© *Sheed and Ward, Inc., 1969*
Library of Congress Catalog Card Number: 72-82605
Standard Book Number: 8362-0040-3
Manufactured in the United States of America

CONTENTS

PREFACE

What happened to the "death of God"? So goes the coffee break chatter at the laymens' retreat and the clergy conference. The topical "future of God" has elbowed aside the funereal. Theologies of secularization are making way for theologies of hope. Or so it seems to those eager for the au courant. One publishing house has already commissioned a manuscript on post-future developments in Christian thought.

Theological innovation comes and goes with such haste and fanfare, often courtesy of a sales-oriented media, that the professional task of sorting and sifting gets short shrift. Are we really done with the secular theologies? Even if the flamboyant has discredited itself, have the learnings from the radical theology been rescued so they may be preserved in whatever new directions we move?

The transition from a theology of the secular to a theology of the future has been an awkward one because those anxious to move on have not always done their homework carefully. Before the resources of the theological community are harnessed to a full-scale inquiry into the new eschatology, there must be a more serious settling of accounts with radical thought. One fundamental undone task is the careful relating of talk about the death of God to declarations about the death of code and cult.

That is one thing we are about in this study, a look at the ways in which radical theology, morality and mission represent a first nervous response to secularization from which we can learn something.

What this book attempts to do, therefore, is to hear out the radicals critically, and to dig some post-radical footers for the futurist theology abuilding. Some of the seed thoughts appeared in a *New Theology No. 4* essay, "The Issue of Transcendence in the New Theology, New Morality, and the New Forms." An Oxford sabbatical, made possible by an American Association of Theological Schools grant, gave the opportunity to develop them. The writer is grateful for that stimulating scene and its influence on organizing these thoughts. But the real incubator has been a running exchange of ideas with American radical theologians, moralists and missioners. From that association has been born the conviction that we must move beyond them. But there are no shortcuts. The route to the next point on the pilgrimage—a theology of promise—is through radical thought, not around it. The road to the future is by way of the secular city. We shall try to follow that route so the turn can be made at the right cloverleaf.

GABRIEL FACKRE

INTRODUCTION

Donald Michael maintains that responsible institutions need a critic-in-residence. An era of incredibly rapid change demands its "self-imposed disruptors." How else can soundings be made and imaginations stretched to grasp the fresh alternatives required by the vast shifts taking place?[1]

Quite frankly this study began several years ago as a critique of radical currents in modern thought and practice. Here was to be a defense of the faith against the disturbers of our peace in theology, morality and mission. In the process it became something else. The need for Michael's boat-rockers began to dawn on the writer the more he grappled with the specifics of radical teaching. Yes their perspective still must be critically assessed, but in a different way and with a different spirit. They ought not to be dismissed as the enemy to be read out of the party posthaste. They are the scouting parties who are casing unfamiliar ground.[2] They are the research teams carrying on bold experimentation. They are our critics-in-residence.[3]

What this study has become is the attempt to interiorize the findings of the church's scouts. We ask ourselves what they have to tell us about the secular land into which we are moving. Are the trails they have explored and find negotiable for their small party also manageable for a larger company? After their reports are in and digested, what is our next move?

This last question is really the nub of the matter here. We are less interested in distributing bouquets or brickbats for the excited reports of those who range ahead than in asking what we ourselves, as the community of faith, are to do now in making tracks on secular terrain. How can both the insights and short sights of the radicals be used as stepping-stones on the church's pilgrimage?

This study therefore is an exercise in liaison theology. It attempts to bring the reports of the scouting parties of the church as data for the policy and planning of the larger Christian community. But liaison means as well a serious enough listening to the outrider to begin to redraw the community's maps and charts in the light of his reports. And this we try to do in terms of a set of themes and images that begin to take form in the struggle to come to terms with secularization and the radical response to it.

In the final analysis, therefore, it is a household struggle that we attempt. It is an inquiry within the Christian community, for the Christian community, not a survey of modern theology for the general reader, or apologetics in the usual sense. Of course, Thielicke may be right about such in-group talk—that it is the most interesting and salutary kind of approach to "the outsider" precisely because there is a little of the "sidewalk superintendent" in us all.[4] For example, those looking in at the Vatican II updating and its agonizing aftermath have probably learned more Roman Catholic theology—and gained a greater appreciation of it—than all the energetic and self-conscious official sallies in communication put together could have achieved. Be that as it may, the main concerns of this study are "from faith to faith."

A household meeting means that the "fathers" and "brethren" will be invited in. By fathers we mean the community inheritance of thought and practice. The Christian past is a partner in the conversation on where we go from here. So is the Christian present, the brethren. And it can be no select present (or past) in ecumenical times. To open the conversation to the brother involves the readiness to put the radical reports down in front of companions that range from Orthodox spirituality to the new eschatological lefts and old eschatological rights. It even means a place at the table for the "popular piety" held in such widespread academic disdain which is, but for all that, the working faith of multitudes who do not read the books about themselves. A real welcome mat at the household door is pretty hard to manage, let's face it. In spite of our good intentions there will be some left out in the cold, and for that we apologize. Also, invitation to join the conversation does not mean monopolizing it, and it may mean rebuttal. So we are not saying that one must "buy" each partner's tale told, only listen to it as a friend and brother.

There is one tale, however, that is not a "perhaps, yes, perhaps no" matter in these pages. It is the Story that stands at the center of all the smaller stories of fathers and brethren. We take the Christian drama as a fundamental reference point for our reflection. Couched in ancient idiom and in need of drastic updating and bold translation, yes. That is the whole point of the inquiry, how to do just that. But at the center, the historical dialogue between God and man with its focus on one Man is the premise of Christian identity that makes this a conversation within the faith-community. What that Story is, and how its framework bears on the reconceptualizations needed in theology, morality, and mission, we hope to show as the themes and images of the inquiry are unpacked.

Who are these "radicals" we choose to view as our critics-in-residence? Why this trio and not others?

We shall explore the particulars of their positions in Part I and make reference to them throughout the study. The bond that links them is not only nomenclature chosen or conferred but a thread of commonality in assessment of what it is the community must pay attention to, secularization. Shared as well is a way of dealing with it that incorporates in "radical" fashion the secular sensitivities themselves, proclaiming the demise of old commitments. Hence the tags that are, or could be, variously used: new theology, new morality, new forms; radical theology, radical morality, radical mission; secular theology, secular morality, secular mission; the death of God, the death of law, the death of church.

Linkages among the particular trinity we examine have been noted in commentary that runs from Robinson in *Honest to God* and *The New Reformation?* to Rubenstein's *Playboy* remarks.[5] From time to time partisans have acknowledged their fellow revolutionaries. Thus William Hamilton can speak of hard and soft radicals, racial, sexual and institutional as well as theological radicals.[6] Joseph Fletcher can applaud the new mood that expresses itself in the alliance of new morality, new theology and new evangelism.[7] And the study in which radical missionaries played an important part can note parallel "new" developments and conclude: "We are only at the beginning of evolving . . . a 'pilgrim theology,' and in the years ahead major attention will need to be given to working out the implications of this historicity."[8] Those of a more critical turn of mind have also pointed to parallels in the perspectives, with varying degrees of perception.[9]

Of course, these three developments are not the only ones that can be found in the harness of the new, the radical and the secular. There is "new hermeneutic," experimentation in radical liturgies, and so on. We chose this set of partners and not others for several reasons. For one, hermeneutics and liturgics are not in the area of the writer's competence. For another, there is something to be said for focussing on what grips the household if it is housecleaning we are after. There is little doubt that the clergy exodus and excitement about new forms, lay-wrestling with the questions of a new style of morality in issues ranging from war to sex and slick magazine obituaries of God, are signs of a deep-going restiveness in the church. Radical theology, morality and mission both give voice to this ferment and contribute to it. And below it all, we believe, is the earth tremor of secularization. These are the factors that have led to this kind of exploration.

But it is not, as we have said, first and foremost an assessment of the radical currents. The radical perspective is very much there in the analysis, but more as a building block than as a target. We are primarily interested in how to get on with the post-radical job of thinking and doing in church and world. The "news" are a serious step along the way, but the way is ahead. However, it is through radical thought, not around it, that we must go, hence the pause to examine its findings before the pilgrimage continues. Pilgrimage beyond means the developing of some sort of charts for the road up front—based on the impression of the scouts, but not captive to them. We are talking, therefore, about guidelines—modest, tentative, exploratory, but still guidelines.

We are passing through a time of theology that is largely pre-guideline in both form and content. Structures are ad hoc, task-oriented, little-(but not necessarily low-) keyed. Tomes outlining systems in theology, ethics or mission are hard to find. We have a light paperback style that chooses to deal with specific issues or to outline a method for dealing with them, or sees its task as "raising the right questions" but is reticent about drawing any big conclusions. Theological modesty is a good thing when the old formulas are cracking and new ones have yet to appear. The case by case approach also becomes an empirical era that moves inductively through its data, wary of speculative pretension.

The fragment notion of Christian reflection has its roots as well in the very perspectives that use it. Where there is reluctance to deal in the large idiom of "God-talk," it is not surprising to hear William Hamilton defend a theological style of "bits and pieces."[10] And a situation ethics that works case by case without the benefit of encompassing mandates finds itself naturally at home in the pocket-size, best-selling reader and is content to describe itself as a method.[11] Again, the mission mood that stresses the ad hoc and calls into question the given institutional continuities (the local church pre-eminently) does its work in the tentativities and explorations of a mimeographed forum[12]— the newsletter of a missionary model, a study guide on the methodologies of renewal, a popular blast at the establishment.

This work is not in that idiom. One reason is the conviction that we have had sufficient experimental probing at the ad hoc level to give us data for some working opinions on direction. Not blueprints, not a system, but nevertheless the beginnings of an overview, or at least some *themes* and *images* that are ingredients of it. That there are grounds for moving beyond the raising of questions and the ad hoc sortie there are such signs as the efforts in ethics of a Winter or Sellers[13] and the movement within the World Council inquiry on missionary structure toward planning for more embracing mission.[14] The press beyond the spare task orientation has its counterparts in secular phenomena signalled by restlessness in the Movement with a piecemeal reform and toward some new ideological inquiry, and by metropolitan renewal efforts that are inching away from one-by-one preoccupations to planning for umbrella renewal of the city.[15]

But it is more than changing times and baskets of data that lie behind the guideline-making this study represents. The quest for overview and continuities rises out of the perspective itself. Let us admit that it even may be the "ideology" of the post-radical phase, as radical thought was the epiphenomenon of a time of the dissolution of old concepts and norms. Hopefully it is a fighting ideology that brings to self-consciousness new vitalities at work rather than a smokescreen for reaction. We do attempt here something beyond fragments of thought because theology, morality and mission are not understood to be essentially ad hoc endeavors. They are community-oriented and connectional in the way representative democracy and responsible supra-parochial polity attempt to preserve the integrity of the individual unit, yet acknowledge the communal bonds that transcend political or ecclesiastical occasionalism. The continuities are modest, this in contrast to the architectonic ambitions of an era properly indicted by radicals. But the bonds are there. Our post-radical thematic medium is a post-radical message.

And style itself cannot be separated from perspective.[16] As opacity appeared to fit the laboriously profound system builder, so the critical Kierkegaard opted for another mode. Today's ad hoc mind seems to be at home in pithy near-journalistic utterance.[17] Those who veer away from both system and fragment have their task cut out: a style neither ponderous nor impressionistic. Whether they can manage both clarity and flavor is an open question. At least they must work at it.

There are some structural aspects of the study that require preliminary explanation. One is the uneven weighting of the three constructive sections Parts II, III, and IV. The opening discussion of post-radical theological motifs is more detailed because it introduces and expounds ideas that thread their way through the whole study. To duplicate and triplicate this material in the succeeding parts would be tedious. Thus the imbalance is no indication of the relative importance attributed to each of the three areas. In the writer's judgment the persons of this trinity are co-equal.

On the boundary between style and structure is the manner in which we have handled chapters that deal directly with radical thought. If we mean what we say about really listening to what is coming in from the church's laboratories, we had better treat them in a way that befits responsible research. Review of the data ought to be precise, detailed, and from the experimenter's own reports. That is the reason for the heavy documentation. In the rest of the book there is a minimum of direct quotation, for we are trying on new sets of wings that require their own sort of test flights.

The perceptive reader may find what he considers to be an anomaly in the kind of data to which reference is frequently made. Will he wonder why, in a book that purports to be about secularization, there are not more citations of secular material? Why all this church-talk? A good question. The frame of reference must be kept in mind. It is (1) a book in theology that is (2) for the members of its household and (3) from a point of view that seeks to preserve the integrity of the community's interests within the celebration of secularization. While secular sources do make a regular appearance, particularly those of a scientific and a political-social kind, they serve to illumine not control what is fundamentally a conversation in the faith-community's universe of discourse. There is a certain gamesmanship about these days that tempts secularization theology. "Come let us see your credentials in this-worldliness. Show us your finesse in literary criticism, command of the scientific vocabulary, sociological penetration."

Indeed those who work on these frontiers must have that kind of passport. In fact we need a recovery of "orders" so that the church practitioner and theoretician is knowledgeable in one secular discipline (perhaps several) and can both represent the church in and be a gadfly to the church on this specialized area. But for the work of theological overview, it does not become the theologian or enhance the work he is doing to major in his minors. He makes his contribution when he plays his own language game with eyes open, of course, to the scores in other ball parks.

A final word of introduction about the tone of the book. To immerse oneself in the issues of secularization is to experience a mounting excitement about these days of human maturation. Of all the signs of coming of age, a spurting science-technology represents the most dramatic expression of man's new ability to "construct himself," as brain researcher José Delgado has put it. What incredible possibilities are now man's portion! To survey these prospects is to taste the heady wine of celebration. And this exhilaration is caught in the notes of a hope born of the conviction that it is the God of adulthood at work by secular grace, notes that resonate as well to the developing eschatological theologies.

But the tone is not a gay one. Hope is sobered by the horror everywhere manifest in the uses to which an advancing technology is already put, and can yet be put. Within the theological framework here sketched, it is well within the possibility of man to "blow it." That's what adulthood means. The father gives his son the freedom to make or break himself. And worse, the sheer process of secularization increases the chances of hurt as well as of healing. The situation is summed up in another of Donald Michael's observations. Science-technology with its effect on the increase of population and its accelerating interaction maximizes the possibilities and effects of disaster:

While the percent of disrupting events may not be any larger than it even was, the number of times they happen becomes greater. And even though an event may be extremely unlikely, there are more occasions when the unlikely can happen—a power blackout in the Northeast, one of the world's largest tankers breaking up in an unlikely place and ruining southern Britain's recreational area, a presidential assassination, or other strange and outrageous crimes. They don't have to become frequent; but there are more of them just because there are more people and circumstances in which they can happen. This is a particularly important aspect of complexity that we haven't had to deal with in the same way before, and from the way we talk we still don't know how to deal with it.[18]

That is why celebration cannot stand alone.

But the risk and the promise are what makes this "a great time to be alive." The misery and grandeur of man come clear and stretch faith to find a meaningful response. It should know

something about these things, born as it is in crucifixion and
resurrection. And that is why it must speak of humiliation and
celebration.

Footnotes

1. Donald N. Michael, "Twenty-first Century Institutions: Prerequisites
for a Creative and Responsible Society," *Human Values and Advancing
Technology,* compiled by Cameron P. Hall (New York: Friendship Press,
1967), pp. 103–104.
2. George Mcleod, *We Shall Rebuild* (Glasgow: The Iona Community
Publishing Dept., undated), p. 21.
3. While the radical theologians frequently dissociate themselves, and
the doing of theology, from any connection with institutional Christianity,
there are times when they come close to understanding their role in these
terms, as when Hamilton speaks of the death of God theologians as "speaking out of a community to a community." Cf., Thomas J. J. Altizer and
William Hamilton, "The Death of God Theologies Today," *Radical Theology and the Death of God* (Indianapolis, Indiana: Bobbs-Merrill, 1966), p.
28 (hereafter referred to as *RT*), copyright © 1966 by Thomas J. J. Alitzer
and William Hamilton, reprinted by permission of the publishers, The
Bobbs-Merrill Company, Inc.; and Paul van Buren's observation that "theology is carried on by a fraternity," "Straw Men and the Monistic Hangover—A Response," *Religious Education,* Vol. LX (January-February, 1965),
p. 42 (hereafter referred to as *RE*).
4. Helmut Thielicke, *The Trouble with the Church,* translated by J. W.
Doberstein (New York: Harper, 1965).
5. Richard E. Rubenstein, "The Playboy Panel: Religion and the New
Morality," *Playboy* (March, 1967), p. 60 and *passim.* See also his book
After Auschwitz: Essays in Contemporary Jewish Theology (Indianapolis,
Indiana: Bobbs-Merrill, 1967).
6. William Hamilton, "The Shape of Radical Theology," *The Christian
Century* (October 5, 1965), p. 1220, and Altizer and Hamilton, *op. cit.,*
pp. 5–6.
7. Joseph Fletcher, "Situation Ethics Under Fire," in *Storm Over Ethics.*
John Bennett et al. (Philadelphia: United Church Press, 1967), pp. 152–
153.
8. North American Working Group, *The Church for Others and the
Church for the World* (Geneva: World Council of Churches, 1967), p. 95.
9. See Henlee H. Barnette, *The New Theology and New Morality* (Phi-

ladelphia: The Westminster Press, 1967); Kenneth Hamilton, *What's New in Religion?* (Grand Rapids: Eerdmans, 1968); Gabriel Fackre, "The Issue of Transcendence in the New Theology, the New Morality and the New Forms," and Max L. Stackhouse, "Toward a Theology for the New Social Gospel," in Martin E. Marty and Dean G. Peerman, editors, *New Theology,* No. 4 (New York: The Macmillan Company, 1967), pp. 178–194, 220–242. A work that relates the areas of thought dealt with here to the "new hermeneutic" is Frederick Herzog's *Understanding God* (New York: Charles Scribner's Sons, 1966).

10. William Hamilton, *The New Essence of Christianity* (New York: Association Press, 1961), pp. 13ff. Hereafter referred to as *EC*.

11. Joseph Fletcher, *Situation Ethics* (Philadelphia: The Westminster Press, 1966), pp. 11ff. Copyright © 1966, by W. L. Jenkins. Used by permission.

12. *Concept,* a collection of mimeographed papers circulated periodically by the Department on Studies in Evangelism of the World Council of Churches is an example.

13. See Gibson Winter, *Elements for a Social Ethic* (New York: The Macmillan Company, 1966), and James Sellers, *Theological Ethics* (New York: The Macmillan Company, 1966).

14. See "Church Structures in the Zone Humane," in *Concept,* VIII (November 1964), pp. 2–12; Western European Working Group, *The Church for Others and the Church for the World,* pp. 38–41.

15. See Harvey Cox, *The Secular City* (New York: The Macmillan Company, 1965), pp. 160–161.

16. As Larry Shiner points out in his appreciative study of Carl Michaelson, "Carl Michaelson's Contribution to Theology," *Religion in Life,* Vol. XXXVI, No. 1 (Spring, 1967), pp. 81ff.

17. With some notable exceptions, such as Altizer whose anti-system posture expresses itself in language and style, "exciting . . . logically imprecise, calculated to make empiricists weep." Altizer and Hamilton, *op. cit.,* p. 31. For a less sympathetic evaluation see Robert MacAfee Brown, "What Does the Slogan Mean?" *The Meaning of the Death of God,* introduction by Bernard Murchland, ed. (New York: Random House, Vintage Books, 1967), pp. 179–184.

18. Michael, *op. cit.,* p. 97.

PART I

SECULARIZATION AND
RADICAL RESPONSE

1

SECULARIZATION: COMING OF AGE AND THIS-WORLDLINESS

Current conversation on the secular begins with a certain hesitation. An awesome array of research has made the concept a meeting ground for a variety of disciplines, historical, sociological, philosophical, and theological.[1] To this richness of data is added the fact that theologians, "obsessed with the attempt to pin down the meaning of 'the secular,'"[2] have either written it on their banners as a new fighting word, or used it as their favorite pejorative. The ambiguity and abuse of the term has led some to consider the possibility of its abandonment.[3]

Theology has no corner on the market of semantic confusion, however, as Talcott Parsons and other sociologists reminded us in a memorable plea several decades ago for "a common language in the social sciences." Moreover, *secular,* and its somewhat more prim sister, *secularization,* have "made the scene." They are crucial developments with which the Christian community must come to terms. Rightfully, we ought to ask for the same kind of clarity and agreement within the theological fraternity on the meaning of these words as the social scientists sought for *status* and *role.* In our more sober moments, however, the plea of Larry Shiner in his careful review of six types of

15

definition appears to be a more realistic goal: "let every user say what he means and stick to it."[4] We shall attempt to do that with the concept of secularization.

Since the word is the eye of a theological hurricane, it is most difficult to arrive at a definition that is not loaded with value overtones or premises. Better then to just say what they are, or what they appear to the definer to be.

The frame of reference in which we do our business with secularization is the conversation with the three radical perspectives of theology, morality and mission. In wrestling with them, one is drawn back time and again to a factor which threads its way, explicitly and implicitly, through their work. What is this thing that we meet peering at us around corners of radical theology, morality and mission, leading them on their chase? It is a process any theology responsive to the modern task must sooner or later hunt down. Thus the radical quest for this elusive modern sprite and the discovery of its footprints in our own pilgrimage give shape to the characterization used here.

There is one more preliminary consideration dictated by the audience to which the study is aimed: the empirical church as it expresses itself in men and women who take the trouble to keep pace with the intellectual and action issues of the day and yet must at the same time serve a constituency unmoved by theological subtlety and "turned off" by its mystifications. Is it too much to ask that a definition of secularization come somewhere in range of common discourse—dare we even say, of *secular* idiom? To be faithful to our intention, therefore, the searching but somewhat circuitous reasoning which calls the deideologizing of Marxist thought secularization[5] or describes pious megalomania as "secularization"[6] must be shelved, at least for our purpose here. True, the common sense world is not the last word on reality, as even tough-minded moderns have shown,[7] but communication must at least build its launching pad there.

Out of respect for this communication line to the modern constituency, and to keep in range of historical usage, we place our understanding of secularization within the secular-religious tandem. And we define "religion" in the homeliest of terms. It has to do with the words, ideas, behavior and institutions of what is generally understood to be the religious community; Jewish, Christian, Buddhist, Moslem, etc. We leave it open-ended as to whether this more or less visible collective entity is good or bad, or a little of both. And further we resist the temptations to rescue the word for some pure quality that is above or underneath all this institutional ordinariness or to use it as the whipping boy for the more authentic, faith. Why faith itself may come in the humiliating garb of "religion" we shall explore later. For the time being we simply want a handle to get a hold of this provocative phenomenon, secularization. We find it in a commonplace definition of empirical religion.

What then is secularization? It is an historical process with two components, human maturation—"coming of age," and this-worldliness. Let us examine them.

Coming of Age

The connection here with the thought of Bonhoeffer is obvious, as his prison diaries have given currency to the concept and phrase.[8] The world's coming of age means that over the past centuries—with beginnings variously located in the late Middle Ages, the Renaissance, the Enlightenment—and at an accelerated pace in our own era of a rapidly advancing science-technology, the human race has been in the process of learning to do things formerly thought to be the special province of religion. And it has not only found its own key to presumed mysteries guarded by the religious communities but has shouldered aside the priestly sentinels and literally opened the doors of life. Did the gods or God control the storms in the sky or the soul? Did the holy men and their incantations have a way of coping with these miseries? Well, now things are different. Even the most pious rural church puts a lightning rod on its steeple, as Walter Kaufmann observes, and men make their own bolts in the laboratory and rain in the fields. And as for the spiritual clouds, there are fewer and fewer that depend on the sunshine of the gospel song or pastoral prayer, and more and more who find peace and new life through the ministrations of pharmacology, psychiatry, sociology, and perhaps soon in more dramatic ways through biochemistry and physics.

The general disengagement of religion, sometimes described as "differentiation" by sociologists,[9] admits of various refinements. We might distinguish between more visible institutional relinquishment in which the functions of clergy, religious organizations, or religious practices disappear as going methods of getting things done (entertainment which passes from the rural Sunday night prayer and song meeting to the urban weekend TV evening, education dominated by divines re-emerging in the science-oriented university, healing arts which transfer from sanctuary and church hospital to the mass medical center, etc.), and the changing ideational patterns characterized by autonomous sciences no longer beholden to a theological queen. Or we might isolate the kinds of religious posture that are displaced, notably religion functioning as either a *controller* or a *support*, the father with a whip or a mother with the crutch. Thus secularization sweeps aside Galileo-restricting religion as well as the more benign version whose offers of security seemed to beguile men from taking their own destiny in hand. We shall pay particular attention to this last duality in our treatment of the radical response.

Secularization as the passing of both religious authority and dependency and the emergence of a mankind in charge of its destiny is comparable enough to the developmental process of individuals to be described as "coming of age." It is macrocosmic maturation, self-emergence writ large.

The use of figures like "maturation" and "coming of age" admittedly has its booby traps. A common one is the misunderstanding introduced by importing value judgments associated with the words as they are used in some other contexts. Thus it is assumed that "the world come of age" means that men are now morally grown up and ascending the escalator of progress.

And to this we hear the predictable retort, "oh yeah?" and brace ourselves for the homilies on man's "immaturity" (sin, evil). Bethge has carried on an unending struggle to clarify Bonhoeffer's usage of the coming of age vocabulary in the light of this common misreading.[10] The coming of age of the race is no different from the arrival of a citizen at voting age. Upon reaching twenty-one he can choose to cast his ballot for some neo-Nazi candidate. There is no inherent guarantee that his new physical, mental and social powers will be harnessed to the purposes of humanization. Coming of age is a time of great peril and promise for both the individual and the race. There can be no naive belief that advance in prowess means inevitable progress. That is what Bonhoeffer meant, and that is what we mean here.

Another misunderstanding is the assumption that man's new freedom and choice to "go it on his own" means, ipso facto, the elimination of religion as such: the gods or God must pass if man is to seize his own destiny as an adult. That is, of course, one way to respond to the process of secularization (as in the radical theology we shall examine), or one meaning of which it is accused by those, for example, who run scared from it on religious grounds. But it is by no means integral to the process itself. It is possible to view God otherwise than as the deus ex machina who solves the problems that man cannot solve for himself, and to interpret the "gap-filling" role of religion in quite another way than is traditionally done. But that is the burden of our study. For the time being we simply note that coming of age does not by definition exclude God any more than the maturation of a human being requires the death of the parent who served at one time or another as controller or crutch.

Time in the Aging Process

When we speak about coming of age, we are dealing implicitly with the functioning of time and an attitude toward its dimensions: past, present, future. Aging touches all these bases as it passes through what has been into what is and will be. In the radical commentary on coming of age, we confront regularly a certain view of each of these segments of the historical process through which mankind moves toward adulthood. As we shall see, for the radical, maturation means an emergence that cuts loose from a past viewed as inimical to a responsible life that can only be lived freely in the "now." And along with that there is some radical reflection on the operation of the future on the present. Our sifting of the radical data prompts, therefore, the inclusion of sections in our study that deal with the function of the time dimensions. It might well have been considered in a category separate from secularization, such as the "relativity of structure," or the "modern sense of historicity." It is all these things, but as a perspective on aging it also falls within the compass of our analysis of the race's maturation vis à vis religion. As such, we have chosen to include it as an important sub-category of coming of age.

This-Worldliness

Only faintly distinguishable at first sight from the coming of age process, but in fact a separable motif in secularization, is what we shall identify as "this-worldliness." William Hamilton disentangles the two threads in his description of the movement from cloister to world as the passing of religion, on the one hand, and the movement into the world on the other.[11] Or we might put it another way. In the process of cultural disengagement from the complex of attitudes and behavior patterns of empirical religion, there is the fading of the reference point of most of that complex, "transcendence." This "atrophy" (Mascall) of the religious sensitivity, of the passing of the sense of absolute dependence into a sense of absolute independence (Daniel Williams), is reflected in what makes our pulses beat faster, how we spend our time, and how we use our words. Compare the meaning of "minister" when it appeared on the tongues of our grandfathers with its function in the front pages of the *New York Times* or the London *Times* today. Weigh the time spent in the practice of piety in the farm home a century ago with the visceral interests of the modern suburban family. Within organized religion itself, we have traversed quite a distance from the time when "the Movement" had reference to the battle against rationalist incursions and a recovery of churchly orientation to the transcendent in nineteenth century England, to "the Movement" that means quite naturally, even within the church, the struggle for human rights. It's a long way from Oxford, England to Oxford, Mississippi.

Horst Symanowski has summed up the shift from transcendent to immanent orientation in his familiar graphic description:

The question of previous ages, such as, e.g., Luther's question when he was in and even after he left the monastery: "How can I find a gracious God?"—this was the question that drove men, was the motor of their behaviour in the world, unleashed crusades and started wars. It drove man and wouldn't let him sleep. But how many people today are awakened to rise and seek an answer to this question? Most of us sleep on it pretty well. Either we don't ask it, or it appears to us as a mere historical, antiquated question. But another question does drive us around, unsettles us, agitates whole peoples, and forces us into anxiety and despair: "How can I find a gracious neighbor?" How can we still live together? Man and wife, superiors and subordinates, colleagues in competitive struggle, and finally, one people with another, East and West? Here we become excited, ask questions and seek ways. The question of a gracious neighbor has become the cardinal question of our industrial society.[12]

Symanowski's connection of the horizontal preoccupation of modern men with "industrial society" points up not only the science-technology factor that has bent human attention toward the earth, but also points to some of the qualities invariably associated with contemporary this-worldliness. The empirical mind adopts the style that has given science-technology its success. It is pragmatic, asking "what works" rather than pursuing the more elusive questions of Why? Whither? and Whence? It is case-oriented, proceeding by little steps to modest conclusions, content with "little keys" to unlock manageable doors. It is data-conscious and most at home when it is dealing with concretions.[13] The methods of the laboratory and the shop floor have formed the habits of our this-worldly temper.

A Definition and some General Comments

Let us now try to weave our threads together into a working definition. Secularization is an historical process, accelerated in our own time by rapidly advancing science-technology, in which man turns his attention to this world, able and willing to shape his life in it without control of or dependence upon religion. It is a mature this-worldliness that seizes from religion the responsibility for making life livable.

Our working definition needs several clarifying footnotes. One raises the distinction between secularization and secularism. Celebrators and denigrators of secularization have introduced some confusion by not making careful distinctions between these.[14] Secularization we have described as a *process*. But that we mean (a) something that is happening in men's psyche and public history and (b) something that is going on right now. Secularism is to secularization as a product is to a process. Secularism assumes that the basic bend of the process is definitive of reality itself. It holds that the way things are now is the way things really are. It is the transformation of a secular sensitivity into a dogma that declares itself to be an exhaustive and closed reading of the human situation. In short it is a canonizing of the premises and sensitivities of this age which excludes openness both to depth and future dimensions. It is a product in a second sense as well, for it believes that what is now a process in motion in this slice of history is of absolute value for history as such. It would like to see our age's visceral commitment to this world drive toward its logical conclusion, a world denuded of any transcendent referent. Secularization, as we have described it, is a more modest phenomenon than the ideology of secularism. It refers to an historical momentum in our age. There is no pontification about it exhausting the depths of what is or what will be. It does not preclude the possibility of this enigmatic statement: "The God who makes us live in this world without using him as a working hypothesis is the God before whom we are ever standing. Before God and with him, we live without God."[15]

There is another qualification suggested by this fertile Bonhoeffer remark. To allow for the possibility that faith may affirm secularization does not of necessity entail the claim that the process has been put in motion by, or can only be secured with, the help of faith. The historical connections between the Judeo-Christian tradition and the process of secularization deserve the most thorough study, and there are some impressive pieces of research already to show in this enterprise.[16] However, it does not follow that the theological significance of secularization lies in either its religious ancestry or need. There is a vestige of "god of the gaps," if not triumphalist thinking, that clings to some of the most astute commentary on secularization when it feels the urge to demonstrate the debt the process owes to its biblical or churchly roots, or makes a case for faith as the one perspective that can truly help it along.[17] In fact it would be in harmony with the thesis of this study to find that secularization was the fruit of secular factors, and today does not need our guidance about how to protect it from going astray. For our purpose at the moment, however, it is enough to note that there are no religious strings attached to the source or completion of the process.

The question we now confront is: Given the massive presence of this process in our time, what response is appropriate to it from within our community of faith? The first step towards an answer is the careful examination of the reports from those within our community who have made the most daring sorties into this land of promise and peril. We turn to the radicals. We are not concerned with every sheaf of data they have filed. We listen for those overt and covert reactions and proposals for the pilgrimage of faith that have arisen directly from what they have seen and felt of the contours of maturation and this-worldliness.

Footnotes

1. Important recent work in the fields (some of which overlap) include historical: Arend Th. Van Leeuwen, *Christianity in World History,* foreword by Hendrik Kraemer, translated by H. H. Hoskins (New York: Charles Scribner's Sons, 1964); sociological: Bryan R. Wilson, *Religion in Secular Society* (New York: International Publications Service, 1968); philosophical: Hans Blumenberg, *Die Legitimität der Neuzeit* (Frankfurt am Main: Suhrkamp Verlag, 1966). The explosion of commentary in the theological field on secularization makes the selection of the most valuable, or a listing of all the relevant, material most difficult. The best we can do is cull out those which have seemed to the writer to be of particular importance for secularization scholarship, confining the list to the most recent vintage: Ronald Gregor Smith, *Secular Christianity* (New York: Harper, 1966); Leslie Dewart, *The Future of Belief* (New York: Herder, 1967); Gregory Baum, ed., *The Future of Belief Debate* (New York: Herder, 1967); Albert van den Heuvel, *The Humiliation of the Church* (Philadelphia: Westminster, 1967); Larry Shiner, *The Secularization of History* (New York: Abingdon Press, 1966); Martin E. Marty and Dean Peerman, eds., *New Theology,* No. 4 (New York: The Macmillan Company, 1967); Charles Davis, *God's Grace in History* (New York: Sheed & Ward, 1967); Bernard Meland, *The Secularization of Modern Cultures* (New York: Oxford University Press, 1966); Colin Williams, *Faith in a Secular Age* (New York: Harper, Chapel Books, 1966); Arnold B. Loen, *Secularization,* translated by Margaret Kohl (London: SCM Press, 1967); Robert L. Richard, *Secularization Theology* (New York: Herder, 1967); John Macquarrie, *God and Secularity,* "New Directions in Theology Today," (Philadelphia: Westminster, 1967), Vol. III; John Vincent, *Secular Christ* (Nashville: Abingdon Press, 1968); Donald Bloesch, *The Christian Witness in a Secular Age* (Minneapolis: Augsburg 1968); John Cogley, *Religion in a Secular Age* (New York: Praeger, 1968); Kenneth Cauthen, *Science, Secularization and God* (Nashville: Abingdon Press, 1969; J. B. Metz, *Theology of the World* (New York: Herder, 1969). Mention should also be made of recent illuminating interpretations of the theology and life of Dietrich Bonhoeffer, including especially the definitive biography by Eberhard Bethge, *Dietrich Bon-*

hoeffer (Munich: Christian Kaisar Verlag, 1967); the helpful series of essays edited and introduced by Ronald Gregor Smith, *World Come of Age* (Philadelphia: Fortress Press, 1967), and the penetrating and carefully documented study of the development of Bonhoeffer's thought by John A. Phillips, *The Form of Church in the World* (London: Collins, 1967).

2. Marty and Peerman, "Beyond the Secular: Chastened Religion," *op. cit.*, p. 10.

3. See Shiner, "The Concept of Secularization in Empirical Research," *The Journal for the Scientific Study of Religion*, Vol. VI, No. 2, 1967, p. 219. Note also the essay by David Martin, "Towards Eliminating the Concept of Secularization," *Penguin Survey of the Social Sciences*, Julius Gould ed. (Baltimore: Penguin Books, 1965), pp. 173–176.

4. Shiner, "The Concept of Secularization in Empirical Research," *op. cit.*, p. 219. See also Shiner's companion piece on types of theological interpretation, "Toward a Theology of Secularization," *The Journal of Religion*, Vol. XLV, No. 4 (October, 1965), pp. 229–295.

5. "An Interpretation of Secularisation," Western Working Group in *Planning for Mission*, Thomas Wieser, ed. (New York: U. S. Conference for the World Council of Churches, 1966), pp. 90–91.

6. Winter, *The New Creation as Metropolis* (New York: The Macmillan Company, 1963), pp. 45–53.

7. See Frederick Ferré's criticism of van Buren's "descriptive metaphysics" taking off from Whitehead's observation that "the 'common sense' of one century is almost always the simplified remainder of the creative and advanced thought of the preceding century or two." Van Buren's "A Theology of Christian Education," *RE*, Vol. LX (January–February, 1965), p. 22. The common sense world of some linguistic analysis and its ideological possibilities (in the Marxist sense) is examined by Herbert Marcuse in *One-Dimensional Man* (Boston: Beacon Press, 1964), pp. 170–199. Reprinted by permission of the Beacon Press, copyright © 1964 by Herbert Marcuse.

8. Dietrich Bonhoeffer, *Prisoner for God: Letters and Papers from Prison*, Eberhard Bethge, ed., translated by Reginald H. Fuller (New York: The Macmillan Company, 1967), pp. 122–125, 142–143, 145–149, 156–160, 162–164, 166–169, 177–183. Copyright, The Macmillan Co., 1954. As Bethge notes, beginning particularly with the letter of April 30, 1944. Bethge, *op. cit.*, pp. 959ff.

9. Joachim Mathes, "Sociological Comments on the Theme World-History-Eschatology," *Planning for Mission*, *op. cit.*, pp. 82–88.

10. A point made often in Bethge's lectures and discussions in his recent stay in the United States. See also Bethge, *op. cit.*, pp. 958–1000, *passim*.

11. Altizer and Hamilton, "The Death of God Theologies Today," *RT*, *op. cit.*, pp. 33–41.

12. Horst Symanowski, *The Christian Witness in an Industrial Society*, translated by George H. Kehm, introduction by Robert B. Starbuck (Philadelphia: The Westminster Press, 1964), p. 50. Copyright © 1964, W. L. Jenkins. Used by permission. For a more careful review of the phenomenon in sociological terms see Wilson, *op. cit.*, which examines it in overt British and covert United States terms. The this-worldly focus of even the most vocally religious can be documented by an examination of the words and ideas of the "gospel song" which are interested essentially in how people can find rest, peace, happiness, courage, etc., for their life on earth. The same thing can be discovered by a word count of the radio talk of such fundamentalists as Carl McIntire, who are preoccupied with the eminently this-worldly matters of fluoridation, the United Nations, civil rights, law and order, Communism, and sex.

13. See the discussion of this in Cox, *The Secular City, op. cit.*, pp. 60–78.

14. Thus both van Buren and E. L. Mascall tend to blur the lines between the two, van Buren, *The Secular Meaning of the Gospel* (New York: The Macmillan Company), pp. 13–14, 20 (hereafter referred to as *SMG*), copyright by P. van Buren, 1963; E. L. Mascall, *The Secularization of Christianity* (New York: Holt Rinehart & Winston, 1966), pp. 8, 40–105. In a later work, *The Christian Universe*, Mascall refines his earlier pejorative use of secular, and instead suggests that the historical process of secularization leads ineluctably to the retrograde secularism, pp. 40–50. However, there are still the remnants of the earlier equation of secularization with the atrophy of the religious consciousness and the organization of life without acknowledgment of the transcendent dimension.

15. Bonhoeffer, *Prisoner for God, op. cit.*, p. 164.

16. Especially van Leeuwen, *op. cit.*, and Blumenberg, *op. cit.*

17. See the interesting observation by Kurt Luthi, "We should clearly recognize that there are two sources for the stream of secularization. On the one hand, with the Renaissance, the world of antiquity; on the other hand, with the spread of Christianity, the world of the Bible. There is too little differentiation in the position which presents the modern world as secularized Christianity. We emphasize the well-known theological fact for the following reasons. A theological 'triumphalism' could reinterpret the consequences of antiquity by means of the concept of secularization in the spirit of Christian integration. Integration through interpretation! We have however so much respect for antiquity as a legitimate foreign structure standing over against Christianity that we decline this move of Christian

or theological triumphalism. In order to see the world of antiquity and of Greece as real partners of Christian faith, we refuse to let the concept of secularization be used in an undifferentiated way." Luthi, "Sakulare Welt als Object der Liebe Gottes," *Evangelische Theologie,* Conzelmann, ed., Gollwitzer, March 1966, cited in *Secularisation,* doctoral dissertation at University of Melbourne, J. Vandermark.

2

RADICAL THEOLOGY

Who are the radical theologians? An exhaustive review would include such varied thinkers as Herbert Braun, John Wren-Lewis, and Richard Rubenstein. We shall limit our exploration, however, to the three theologians most often associated with a radical critique of transcendence, William Hamilton, Thomas Altizer, and Paul van Buren. In doing so we work with a manageable body of data and also follow the precedent of Hamilton in his *Christian Scholar* overview, "The Death of God Theologies Today," and also Thomas Ogletree's sensitive commentary in *The Death of God Controversy*. Our intent in this chapter is not to summarize the radical position as such but to trace the lines of its response to secularization.

WILLIAM HAMILTON

With an acknowledged debt to Bonhoeffer,[1] it could be expected that Hamilton would view our era as a "world of the radically accelerating pace of secularization, of the increasing unimportance and powerlessness of religion, of the end of special privilege for religious men and religious institutions."[2] Secularization is not a speculative subject for Hamilton, nor one that is examined with laboratory dispassion or artistic finesse. It is "something that has happened" to a person, a "gut" experience that is almost as datable as a tent meeting conversion and expresses itself in the same spillover of personal testimony and empathy with others who have shared it.[3]

What Bonhoeffer's prophetic sensitivities perceived in impressionistic patterns, Hamilton has grasped with the further clarity made possible by positioning in the exploding science-technology world of the 1960's. In an illuminating *Concilium* essay, he ascribes the rise of present radical thought to

what we are coming to understand as the technological revolution of our time, and particularly because of the impact of technology on our sensibilities, our language, our feeling. Modern technology is taking on the whole world, the whole dedivinized cosmos, and as the moralists often say, man is the lord of things. It is improving on creation, making alterations in our world and in our bodies (one has only to think of the pharmacological revolution and the new attitude to the body this entails—both the psychedelic and birth control drugs come to mind). It is this that has annihilated our sense of piety and awe and thus our capacity to speak to or about God. There is still a world we do not know, but we are not afraid of it. There is still mystery and ignorance and wonder and awe. But we can't mythologize it, we can't trust these experiences of "not knowing" as being able to point to the meaning of God. This new relation to the world, it seems to me, is the central fact of our time, and it is the decisive spiritual event that enables us more clearly to understand the experience of the death of God. . . . Wallace Stevens has called this new situation "walking barefoot into reality."[4]

The secularization defined today by the new science-technology has evoked the "death of God theology" of which Hamilton has been a chief exponent. We shall not follow down the many interesting language trails that have shot off from this phrase in the last few years, or enter the debate as to whether the movement that goes under that banner has itself passed away— under the cloud of being declared a fad by "the theological establishment" or having given up the ghost as a good experiment that has done its work.[5] We are examining radical theology as an option within the Christian community that has set itself a task: "We are trying to see if it is possible to live and think as Christians without God, and we see this experiment as both a practical-political and theoretic-theological task."[6] Since there is semantic unclarity about the phrase "death of God," and ambivalence among those who have put it into circulation or have accepted it at one time as descriptive of their position,[7] we use here the broader umbrella, "radical theology."[8]

With the typological dexterity of which Hamilton makes regular and effective use,[9] the radical position is characterized as a two-pronged movement "from cloister to world"—toward the world and away from religion. As these correspond to the two components of secularization, we shall use them as the framework for the response of radical theology to secularization.

Coming of Age

Following Bonhoeffer, Hamilton declares that we have entered a time in which "religion" has come to an end. He understands this to mean the demise of

any system of thought or action in which God or the gods serve as a fulfiller of needs, a solver of problems. Thus I assert with Bonhoeffer the breakdown of the religious a priori and the coming of age of man. . . . There is no way, ontological, cultural or psychological, to locate a part of the self or a part of human experience that needs God. There is no God-shaped blank within man. . . . He (God) is not necessary to avoid despair or self-righteousness. . . . This is just what man's coming of age is taken to mean. . . . It is not true to say that there are certain areas, problems, dimensions to life today, that can only be faced, solved, illumined, dealt with, by a religious perspective.[10]

This is more than a description of an historical process. It is the normative judgment that men can and ought to try to "make it" without the supports of religion: "God must not be asked to do what the world is fully capable of doing: offer forgiveness, overcome loneliness, provide a way out of despair, break pride, assuage the fear of death. These are worldly problems for those who live in this world, and the world itself can provide the structures to meet them."[11] The end of religion is not only a curtain rung down on the ancient assumptions that religion was man's protection against sin, evil, and death, or the popular piety that believes peace of mind and positive thinking are the rationale for religion, it also is a bell that tolls for the existentialist theologies that justify faith in terms of its ability to aid men in coming to terms with universal diseases of the spirit, the questions of brokenness, despair, meaninglessness and death.[12]

In some of his earlier reflections on the disappearance of religion there were faint hints of another motif. Hamilton wondered out loud whether there might not be another role that God played, one in which he came to us not as gap-filler, but as a Reality to be honored for his own sake.[13] He declared himself to be "interested in the search for a language that does not depend on need or problem. Perhaps the Augustinian distinction between *frui* and *uti* will prove helpful. If God is not needed, if it is to the world and not to God that we repair for our needs and problems, then we perhaps may come to see that he is to be enjoyed and delighted in."[14] These remarks, however, were tentative, and even "eschatological" ("faith is a hope").[15] Thus Hamilton speaks about a ministry of waiting until more meaning can be breathed into what are at best only sparse hints: "Part of the ministry of waiting for God is found in this attempt to understand what delighting in him might mean."[16]

As Ogletree notes, Hamilton has apparently abandoned this line of inquiry.[17] Perhaps it is more correct to say it has become secularized, for there is still modest comment made on the theme of "for its own sake," but in the area of play and the new kind of optimism which delights in the world for its own sake. The music of John Cage represents a turn to a celebrative style which

believes that "the end of artistic creativity is not order or value
but purposeless play, a play that affirms life and invites other
men to wake up to the ordinary life around them that can be
lived here and now. . . . Cage represents an attack on the whole
Renaissance conception of self-consciousness and an adoption of
a kind of secular-mystical idea of the self as an enemy that must
be removed before one can delight in the world for its own
sake."[18]

The Time Factor in Coming of Age

In his early essay, *The Essence of Christianity*, Hamilton ponders
the role of tradition and the past for the work of the American
thinker:

Is there something basically antitraditional about the American, even
the American man of faith? If so, such a man must begin to speak, as
if no one had ever spoken before, about that tradition, and how he is
bound both to take it and to leave it. This native relation to tradition
may be a weakness; it may, for instance, make it especially hard to be
a novelist, Christian, or even a theologian. But it is there, surely, and
it cannot be eliminated by a conscious decision to ignore it.[19]

Some pages later, he returns to the subject of our relationship
to the past with the same mixed feelings, speaking of the dialectical relation of both rebellion and resignation that is needed, in
fact defending the note of resignation that is muted in the usual
talk of the American spirit of rebellion. However, it is interesting
to see that he associates the past with the figure of the father,
conceived in Hamlet-style as the vengeful autocrat. Commending
the rebel Cordelia, he says: "King Lear . . . is really a study in
how the present must always break with the past in order to become conscious of itself. We must repudiate 'the father': the past,
authority, because it has sinned against us."[20] Nevertheless this
rebellion must be balanced by the final conciliatory act of

Cordelia, for "we must learn, after the rebellion, to forgive and to love, for this past is what has given us our lives."[21]

While honoring the dialectical relationship, Hamilton still notes, following Harold C. Goddard's interpretation, that the tragedy of Hamlet does in fact consist of the "resignation and conformity to the father."[22] And this assessment of tradition is enlarged upon in the succeeding paragraphs that weave together paternity, the past and Deity:

We must rebel against the father, and against everything for which the father is a symbol: the past, tradition, authority as coercive, even religion and the church. . . . Some of us may even need to rebel against God, to accuse him of injustice or impotence or irrelevance, in order to come to know who he is. Rebellion of this kind may be the only way of being honest with ourselves, and for many in our time it will be the only way religious faith can come, if it can come at all. Rebellion against the father can be a means both of self-knowledge and of knowledge of God.[23]

In some later writing, the repudiation of the past is reaffirmed, without the lingering ambivalence of rebellion and resignation, in some powerful words about faith, hope and love. Associating each with a dimension of time, Hamilton says: "Taking faith, hope, and love together, the feeling is that the American theologian can really live in only one of them at a time, perhaps only one in a lifetime. If this is so, and if it is also so that as an American he is fated to be a man without a sense of past or future, then it follows that the theologian today and tomorrow is a man without faith, without hope, with only the present, with only love to guide him."[24]

The radical present-orientation in the Hamilton perspective is qualified nonetheless by moods of both wistful longing and whetted expectations. In fact he anticipates some of the notes sounded in the more recent explorations in eschatological theology. In the category of wistfulness may be placed the hope earlier cited that we may come to know someday what the Augustinian *frui* might mean for our age. The same thing may be expressed as the redefinition of faith as "hope," faith in God as a possibility for the future, something that now is "purely eschatological"[25] and the effort to "pray for God to return."[26] But more often the future-orientation is found in a "new optimism" which anticipates the possibility of real historical improvement. Echoing the notes of "We Shall Overcome" and Beatle music, discovering the sounds of expectation in Johnson's Great Society, a Saul Bellow rebuke to the sour mouth of existentialism and McLuhan's delight in the new media,[27] bending an interested ear to the Marxist-influenced "socio-political optimism" of Hanfried Müller,[28] with allusion as well to the "eschatological optimism of the synoptics,"[29] Hamilton can say: "We trust the world, we trust the future, we deem even many of our intractable problems just soluble enough to reject the tragic mood of facing them.[30] . . . What it [optimism] really means in this context is a willingness to count on the future and a belief in its real improvement."[31]

This kind of hope does not speak, of course, of a future which holds promise because there is "One out ahead" or "One who comes." The promise emerges within the present itself as the eyes of the Now pick out signs of better things to come. The hinge of tomorrow's door is firmly fixed on the post of today.

This-Worldliness

The movement from cloister to world includes a second motif related to but not to be confused with its coming of age partner: the "movement into, for, toward the world, worldly life, and the neighbor. . . ."[32] The radical effort to interpret Christianity without God is an attempt to affirm and celebrate unambiguously the public, neighbor-drenched life of man and his cosmos. "The combination of a certain kind of God-rejection with a certain kind of world-affirmation is the point where I join the death of God movement."[33]

The world to which a "Protestant 'yes'" is said is Luther's "bustling middle class world of the new university of politics, princes and peasants."[34] The comparable climate today is the terrain on which men "affirm the value of the technological revolution, the legitimacy of the hopes and claims of the dispossessed, most of all, of the moral centrality of the Negro's revolution in America today."[35] To participate in the secular ferment is to come with no agenda except a listening, broken love, and the will to take up one's place in the struggle for justice, and among "poets and critics, psychiatrists and physicists and philosophers."[36]

And one moves in such a world with an appreciation and use of its tools: an empirical spirit that is awed no longer by the esoteric, a concentration on specifics and concretions, a reluctance to deal with big generalities,[37] work in the idiom of fragments rather than systems,[38] an at-homeness with the visible, public, historic, and restlessness with the introspective and private,[39] a stress on the possibilities rather than the impossibilities of this world and this time,[40] and a movement of the center of gravity of theological thought and Christian life from the academy and temple to the street.[41]

A fundamental fact about this press toward the world that rescues it from being "sheer atheist humanism"[42] is its Christological underpinning. Life in the world for and with the neighbor is life alongside the Jesus who is present where the hungry are fed and the naked clothed (Matthew 25:34ff). We minister to him and "unmask" his incognito life in the world when we are about our task of discerning and following his secular footfall.[43]

This-worldliness and coming of age, the secular facts of our time, cry for Christian response. Answer comes from the radical theology of William Hamilton who has mapped these contours with rare sensitivity and has determined to find his way over this ground without doing violence to it. For him it means a pilgrimage that "has no need for religion and no need for God." This means that we refuse to consent to the traditional interpretation of the world as "a shadow-screen of unreality, masking or concealing the eternal which is the only true reality."[44] To honor the integrity of this world and the adulthood of the race, Deity must die.

THOMAS ALTIZER

"Must Christian witness inevitably speak of the glory and the sovereignty of God?"[45] This opening query in Altizer's *The Gospel of Christian Atheism* sets the author's sights on the Autocrat whose lordly power comes to crush and enslave his vassal, man. The answer "No!" is at the center of a determined effort to restate Christian faith in consistently immanent terms. Although he rarely refers explicitly to the process of secularization, its celebration is much in evidence in Altizer's attack on divine tyranny. However, we would be unfair to his thought if clear distinctions between coming of age and this-worldliness were made. His trumpet call to maturity and affirmation of the profane constantly merge into each other, and we shall therefore treat them as one, recognizing the hints of distinction where they appear.[46]

While the coming of age formula is not the language tool Altizer uses, he does speak of an epochal man-oriented change that has taken place in modern times, "the challenge of a world which has lost or abandoned all sense of the reality of the transcendent."[47] We have moved into a period in which the religious sense has atrophied. Man's will to live in an immanentist frame of reference is the "portal to the twentieth century."[48] While the temptation is great to flee back into the securities of transcendence from this "totally profane world," there is no road back. Moreover, the passing of the old certainties is an open door beckoning toward the liberation of man. But the death of old certainties is no festive occasion. It is "dark," threatening, sad, chartless, uncertain terrain.[49] In fact it may lead to some new nihilist horror.[50] Yet the only way to new life is through death.[51]

The seismograph of this earth-shift in human consciousness Altizer locates in the visionaries of the nineteenth century. Blake, Hegel, Nietzsche, Dostoevski, and their spiritual kin, understood the bubbling reality of the human world, the fulness of its pains and joys. They are heralds of "the new man." They exposed as well the culprit that diverts men's eyes from his true home and drains from them the sparkle of life. That "bloodsucker" is the God of traditional religion. From the Nietzschean rumination about the passing of the "spider-God," the imagery of Blake's assault on the "God afar off," the conceptual tunnelling by Hegel into the divine self-alienation, Alitzer draws together his own unique version of God's death and man's life.[52]

Who is this tyrant? He is the God who dwells in aloof glory, an "impassive," "awesome," "distant," "transcendent" Lord who works in the idiom of "naked and absolutely sovereign power." This possessive, "wholly other God . . . demands a total submission to his numinous and judgmental power."[53] To persist in the belief in the present reality of this God is to give in to the mean resentment against the vitalities of life, the "refusal of the life and energy about and within us."[54]

But maturity demands that we do not give in. In fact, it is at the heart of faith to see and exult in the fact that this "God is no more."[55] What has happened? the transcendent God has negated himself. The divine self-sacrifice is enacted in Jesus ("God is Jesus, "not" Jesus is God"),[56] beginning at birth and finalized on the cross.[57]

Conventional church-talk of self-emptying has left transcendent residues: "An understanding of a fully kenotic Christ continues to elude the theologian."[58] The consistent attack on the tyrant, a conviction at the heart of Christian faith itself, demands a God who is completely and irrevocably dead.

But death must be understood in the Christian framework illumined by the Incarnation and the Holy Spirit. The death of God in Jesus is not dissolution but "metamorphosis."[59] Indeed, while there is no more oppressive man-demeaning transcendent "out there," there is "a real change or movement in God himself"[60] (from transcendence into immanence) into the vitalities of man's world, one that "continues to occur wherever there is history and life." Thus the divine experiences "epiphany" in the profane as the "Incarnate Word," that pulsing grace that is found in "the pain, joy, the fullness of existence."[61]

Altizer makes use of the concept of *coincidentia oppositorum* to interpret the holiness of the profane. Enlarging on a motif in Oriental mysticism that brings together sacred and profane in a coincidence which evacuates secular reality of luster and meaning by retreat to the "primordial," he asserts that the uniqueness of Christian faith lies in a union of the two poles in which the reverse is true: the profane becomes the sacred. In this dialectical movement, the sacred makes itself available only when men resist the diverting mesmerism of the transcendent and turn to find Christ present in the "brute reality of the world."[62] Then the "life and movement" which is man and his cosmos come into their own, and the Incarnate Word shares itself with those who have the courage to participate "wherever there is life and energy," who are ready to make the "wager," to be the yea-sayers to the profane.[63]

The Time Sequence

One of the most powerful deterrents to man's union with the Incarnate Word is the devious work of "the past."[64] The past does its treacherous business in the disguises of ontology and historical structure.

Oriental mysticism again provides the foil for the ontological analysis. In its search for the sacred, it leads the believer back away from the profane present to primordial depths, thus severing contact with the living present. "God" is found in the paradisal totality and therefore can be reached only by involution, the return to the untainted origins.[65] But Oriental mysticism's *coincidentia oppositorum* is but an expression of a universal element in religion. Thus its thirst for return into a primitive origin recurs in the Christian tradition's location of the truth in an originative transcendent that invites "the Christian Word to recede into an impassive and primordial form."[66]

Captivity to the past also expresses itself in the identification of theology, cult and morality with bygone events. To canonize the Bible, ecclesiastical tradition, or even the message of Jesus, is to enslave the Incarnate Word. We cannot "expect the new revelation to be in apparent continuity with the old."[67] Crystallization of the living Word appears with raw ugliness in the identification of Christ with the visible Christian community. "If we were to confine Christian witness to those communities claiming to be churches, we would in effect be denying the presence of an active or transfiguring Word. . . ."[68] This is not simply a case of the Incarnate Word being in both church and world. Rather "ecclesiastical tradition has ceased to be Christian, and is now alive only in a demonic and repressive form."[69] While the visible church is lost, there are signs of the appearance of a new, rough-hewn community of those who affirm the profane and thus participate in the pulsing life of the Incarnate Word.[70]

Altizer makes some use of Joachim of Floris' periodization of history to spring faith loose from the past. Thus he views the present as the age of the Spirit, in which something new is breaking into the now which claims our final allegiance.

Thus it is the "now" which commands the attention of faith. A living Word by definition is one that shatters what has gone before. Because its very character is "forward-moving," it leaves in its wake the death of all original forms.[71] The only way to honor its flowing reality is to be free of "even the memory of transcendence." In so doing faith will lose all sense of bondage to the past, and with the loss of that bondage will be freed from all the nay-saying which turns us away from the immediacy of an actual and present "Now."[72] The only Christ there is to know is "the contemporary Christ . . . moving . . . into the depths of life and experience"[73] that fill this moment which is before you.

Altizer sometimes makes use of the category of the future to give expression to the "forward-moving" thrust of the Incarnate Word.[74] The eschatological impulse is the pressing forward of the Spirit to find its end in union with the flesh. This apocalypticizing of the *coincidentia oppositorum,* however, ought to be recognized for what it is, a way of expressing the urgency of commitment to the ever-claimant call of the Word in the Now. While, in more recent Altizer commentary, there is some point of contact with current Christian futurology,[75] in most contexts the eschatological means the New Age that is now breaking in (Joachim of Floris), a forward movement of the Spirit that disengages faith from past concretions, a "horizon of faith" that "lies in that future which extends into the present,"[76] a "form that is present or dawning in the immediate contemporary life of faith."[77] The eschatological Word is a call away from the Beginning that entices men from the life of deep immersion in the immediacies.[78]

In these mystical expostulations, sometimes repetitious, turgid, incoherent and rambling, we have a powerful declaration of human independence. Christian atheism is the report of a soul's struggle with an emerging mutation in man's psyche and public history. It is a response to humanity's reach to defend its own reality and disentangle itself from formulas and entities that have shackled the freedom to be a man. We are offered a passport to the risk of living in a new land in which there is no transcendent Yonder, and invited to say "Yes" to a Word that stretches the threshold of human awareness. "The 'good news' of the death of God can liberate us from the dread of an alien beyond, releasing us from all attachment to an opposing other and freeing us for a total participation in the actuality of the immediate moment."[79]

PAUL VAN BUREN

The problem of secularization is explicitly at the center of Paul van Buren's exercise in radical theology. His *The Secular Meaning of the Gospel,* in fact, was near the head of the decade's parade of enquiry into the impact of the secularization process on Christian faith. As with the other radical theologians, the question is not an academic one, or an issue of apologetics in which a confident evangelist deals with a once-removed target "out there," but an autobiographical concern for "'the modern man' who is inside the church, more or less . . . wondering what he is doing there."[80]

While van Buren has disassociated himself from some of the ideas developed in *The Secular Meaning of the Gospel*, and is working on a "prolegomenon to a prolegomenon" to theology,[81] there are common threads of thought bearing on the secular and the Christian response to it that make their way through most of his work in the past five years. We shall follow them as they appear in his major book, and in essays and lectures since then.

This-Worldliness

While van Buren makes reference to the coming of age theme from time to time, by far the greatest stress is on the secular understood as an orientation to the time-space arena in which we live out our lives. Therefore, our examination of his response to secularization will begin with what we have called the "this-worldly dimension" of secularization.

If faith and theology are to live and work in the twentieth century, they must breathe the same air as "empirical, industrial, Western man."[82] The common sense ethos, "somewhat empirical, pragmatic, somewhat relativistic, somewhat naturalistic, but also somewhat aesthetic and somewhat personalistic,"[83] sets the boundaries within which the language of faith moves. This world of human experience—pragmatic, experimental, data-oriented— we accept as "our limiting terms . . . the theological limits against which we live and speak."[84]

The work of a theology in a secular empirical idiom is done with a modesty that befits its method. No claims are made for either the finality of its judgments or the everlastingness of the perspective itself. Conclusions are "fragmentary" and "tentative."[85] The effort to begin with "a descriptive metaphysics" of common sense experience is not necessarily a permanent assessment of the way theology is to be done, or a definitive explanation of the way things really are. It is unexplored territory which invites probing. "My interest . . . is to see, experimentally, just how far theology can go on this basis, and what happens to it when we proceed along these lines. We cannot say we have actually tried this and shown that it will not work."[86]

The tools and mind-set of a technological society are very much in evidence in this perspective on the world and the leads it gives for the theological enterprise. Science-technology has made its home, in particular, in the Anglo-Saxon world. "Our English-speaking culture has an empirical tradition, and . . . the world today is increasingly being formed by technology and the whole industrial process. Whether this is to be regretted or applauded, it is nevertheless the case."[87]

It is quite natural, therefore, for van Buren to acknowledge links with the spirit and methods of British empiricism,[88] and to discover in one of its expressions some fundamental clues for the reconstruction of theology. It is to language analysis, especially as it has been nursed in British settings, that he turns for assistance in the refinement of the empirical posture and its implementation in the work of the theologian.[89]

Van Buren puts the limiting terms, language analysis tools, to a double use by way of a "modified verification principle." In the first instance it bears upon the boundaries of meaningful talk. Human language is about human reality. It "goes on a holiday" if it makes claims to describing a world beyond our experience, "the presence of entities (such as gods or God) lying beyond the general framework of the descriptive metaphysics of our time and place."[90] One way he develops this theme is by reference to the famous Wisdom-Flew parable of the gardener in which modern God-talk ("qualified literal theism") is shown to be translatable without remainder into man-talk, having no "cash value" and thus rendering its function as language dubious: "Whatever ancient man may have thought about the supernatural, few men are able today to ascribe 'reality' to it as they would to the things, people, or relationships which matter to them. Our inherited language of the supernatural has indeed died 'the death of a thousand qualifications.' Flew's point is that the Believer has said no more than the Sceptic about 'how things are.' His implied question, then, is reasonable and straightforward: Can the Christian today give any account of his words?"[91]

Van Buren has devoted not only his writings but his work in the religion department of an urban university to an attempt to answer that question.[92] What indeed is the function that religious language and perception perform? It is at this point that the second use of the linguistic and empirical conceptual apparatus makes its contribution. Bringing together Hare's notion of "blik," Ramsey's idea of a "disclosure-situation," and more recently data from Wittgenstein and Schleiermacher, van Buren is exploring a use of religious language that does not pretend to identity supra-empirical entities, but does serve important human purposes, and functions within the rules of responsible language games.

To say that John loves Mary may not tell us anything that is verifiable by laboratory techniques, but it is nevertheless meaningful language. It describes a perspective that takes form in particular behavior and bears witness to an experience that enriches life, thus operating within the boundaries set by empirical limiting terms.[93] Again, the story of the Pilgrim Fathers as it is embellished in American lore may not be susceptible to strict verification, but it does express and celebrate a certain way of looking at life, and this illumines reality for those who are caught by the tale.[94] The language of love, poetry, literature, art, duty, and music, therefore, perform the crucial functions of adding lustre and life to a world that would be drab and lifeless if open only to the language of the laboratory.[95]

Religious language, and faith itself, is of this genre, "a human posture, a commitment, a way of seeing some people and things

. . . and it entails certain actions."[96] The stories associated with the biblical faith, therefore, are to be understood as angles of perception on human reality that disclose a quality and evoke a response that enriches life.[97] The story of Jesus has a special role: his life, death and resurrection tell of a genuinely "free man" unfettered by anxieties that cripple care for other human beings.[98] As the disciples had a new vista of freedom and humanness opened in the resurrection experiences, so men today can share in that fresh horizon as they confront the man for others at the center of the biblical tale.

God-language itself is worth reexamining in the light of the vehicle of "imaginative act," although the difficulties here are especially great insofar as talk about Deity has been tied historically to the belief in the existence of supra-terrestrial reality. However, the Schleiermacher of *The Speeches on Religion* offers some clues as to the understanding of "God" not as a behind-the-scenes "explanation" of the world but as the expression of a human sensitivity and openness to the universe around us. God as the "whence" of our existence was not for the early Schleiermacher a being outside the time-space world, but "a word to characterize the sensitivity itself, and to characterize all awareness of phenomena as being one aspect, the immediate aspect at the time of the universe."[99] "God" might then be "a way of speech about the universe" that is not in competition with the explanations of science but a spilling-over of the religious sensitivity that enriches our relationship to the world. The prosaic mind of the "sectarian secularist," who operates in the narrow confines of positivist language, and of the religious traditionalist, both of whom insist that "God" can refer only to "an entity of some sort," will resist this reconceptualization of religious language. But this "God" who might better be a "little god" cannot so easily be dispensed with. Talk about him will not soon be stilled, for "He has been able to rock men back on their heels, open new vistas on life, and send men to glory without any such prosaic power."[100]

It should be noted in passing that while van Buren is now

exploring new uses for the word "God," his theology still operates within the this-worldly context of other radical perspectives. With the qualification that "God" or "god" may be a helpful imaginative construct, the intention expressed several years ago still holds true: "I . . . am aware of the historical fact that 'the fundamental contention of Christian theology' has ordinarily, if not always, been expressed by the doctrine of God, but the point that I should like to explore is whether it must be so, whether in an age of the dissolution of the absolute, Christianity has an alternative course to that of nursing the monistic hangover."[101]

Coming of Age

The Secular Meaning of the Gospel begins with a tribute to Bonhoeffer. In a poem by Auden in memory of his martyrdom, and in the opening pages of the introduction, the coming of age motif is underscored as a rationale for the interpretation to follow. Bonhoeffer "as a citizen of this modern adult world, (was) as much inclined as the next man to consult the weather map and the meteorologist for the answer to a question about a change in the weather, rather than to 'take it to the Lord in prayer.' "[102] As Bonhoeffer tried "to find an appropriate way for a Christian in a 'world come of age' to confess his faith in Jesus Christ,"[103] so van Buren seeks to work at the task of contemporizing.

Implicit in this judgment is agreement with the historical analysis of Bonhoeffer. Coming of age, therefore, is a descriptive statement. That is, religion has offered itself for the deus ex machina function, " 'filling in the picture' of the world of human affairs,"[104] and now it is being edged out of this role. "God, however he may have served as an explanation for men in other ages, has been serving less and less well in recent time as an explanation for anything from natural phenomenon to and including religious faiths."[105]

But coming of age is understood by van Buren normatively as well as descriptively. An adult faith puts away its former childishness and tries to find a new frame of reference in a world in

which man can do the things formerly considered divine prerogative. If religious language cannot make this adaptation, it will be
repeating the error of traditional religion which made the mistake
of accepting this focus (using God as "explanation"). "They
tried to argue that God was the prime factor of the real, a factor
whose efficacy necessarily had to be limited, in the face of the
growing competence of prosaic investigation and explanation of
the real, manifested in the rise of modern science."[106] Man's
ability to control his own destiny and solve his own problems is
an advance that must be affirmed, worked with, and celebrated
as a liberation. "If man is slowly learning to stand on his own two
feet and to help his neighbor without reference to the 'God-
hypothesis,' the Christian should rejoice, even if he may not over-
look the danger of pride in this new freedom compared to the
humble freedom of Jesus of Nazareth."[107]

The affirmation of coming of age is embodied in the style of
Christian life and the practitioner aspect of the church as van
Buren sketches them in the last section of the book. Coming of
age means, for example, to look for the "secular meaning of
prayer." As prayer for rain seemed the natural expression of
neighbor love for a drought-ridden farmer in ancient society,
now, in a time when technology replaces the God of the gaps,
compassion will mean a visit to the neighbor to "study the situation with him, and see what can be done to get water on the
fields by irrigation or other means."[108] A faith come of age in a
world come of age will attempt as well to restate the meanings
of faith so that it will not abort human development. The task of
translating religious language into secular idiom we have dealt
with under the rubric of this-worldliness.

The Time Sequence

The past is not the unqualified enemy of van Buren's radical
theology, as it appears in Altizer. In fact, he carries on a running
debate with the existentialist interpretations of Ogden and Bult-

mann which assert that "to 'exist authentically' is to be free from one's past and open to one's future."[109] In the interest of his double loyalty to "the historical aspect of the Gospel" as well as to "the secular empirical spirit of the age," he resists the collapsing of faith into a moment of internal decision. Faith requires the serious acknowledgment that "certain events to which there were witnesses took place at certain times in the past,"[110] eminently the life and death of Jesus, and the resurrection excitement of the disciples that launched the church. Theology as well, "should be carried on in conversation with its own past."[111] He also points out how the past shapes our very evaluation of it, and that common experience is rife with illuminating disclosure situations.[112]

While there is, especially in van Buren's earlier formulations, a strong commitment to the historical conversation and a repudiation of an existentialized "nowness," the honoring of the present is a fundamental premise of his theology. He makes explicit reference to this in some comments on religious education seen as reading the stories of faith through the eyes of the present,[113] and frequent observations on the discontinuity between the understandings of the first century and our own conceptual and linguistic frame of reference.[114] The definitive commitment to the present is most evident, however, in the operating assumption of van Buren's theology that faith must be fundamentally restated in the universe of discourse of modern, empirical man. The commitment to a world whose reference limits are human experience, and how the past must find its place in such a context, is summed up in van Buren's comment on the Wittgenstein description of language as comparable to an old city that continues to live and grow in the modern world. For van Buren the city as a whole is the human world that defines the limits of reality. With Wittgenstein, he sees it made up of the ancient inner ring with its narrow streets and old houses, and beyond it the mushrooming suburb with its trim modern design and straight highways. As we have both the ancient and modern in a rich urban mix, so we have both the old words "to be and to have and to know" as well as the language of science and technology. To Wittgenstein's city van Buren adds a "quaint little ghetto," the language world of religion, the Bible. "Out of that ghetto . . . a man once wrote that God is love."[115] Now we can take that to mean a description of some kind of life outside the city, a dialect that is appropriate to another world, thinking of "God as a being who loves."[116] But at its deepest level this dialect is the city's own voice, "an imaginative reading of ordinary experience."[117] The personification and hypostatization is an act of the imagination that is an expression of deep conviction about the way things are in the one world of human life, a commitment to the belief that "it is better to give than to receive, to love than be loved. . . ."[118] Thus the past ought no more to be erased than the picturesque old towns torn down, for both give character to the city. Yet the ancient religious language must understand that its true home is that secular city, and make no pretensions about offering guidebooks to other lands.

We have in the theology of Paul van Buren a carefully worked out attempt to come to terms with secularization. It is a "secular Christianity" which believes "that it is possible today to be agnostic about 'otherworldly' powers and beings, but that people matter. . . . We have done this by exploring the empirical footing of the language of the Gospel and Christian faith, its function as it is used by men to express and communicate their understanding of the world in an age in which statements about 'how things are' are expected to have some sort of relationship to men's experience of each other and of things."[119]

Footnotes

1. Hamilton was asked by *The Nation* to introduce Bonhoeffer to its readers on the occasion of the anniversary of Bonhoeffer's death. See "Dietrich Bonhoeffer," *The Radical Theology and the Death of God, op. cit.,* pp. 113–118 (hereafter referred to as *RT* and without special identification of the essay except as needed).

2. *RT,* p. 114.

3. See comments in *Playboy* (August, 1966).

4. Hamilton, "A Note on Radical Theology," p. 44. From *Opportunities for Belief and Behavior,* edited by Christian Duquoc, O.P., Volume 29 of the Concilium Series. Copyright © 1967 by Paulist Fathers, Inc. and Stichting Concilium. Reprinted with permission.

5. Hamilton suggests as early as 1966 that the death of God movement "can now be decently retired." See footnote reference by Robinson to letter from Hamilton, J. A. T. Robinson, *Exploration into God* (California: Stanford University Press, 1967), pp. 50–51. He reaffirms the end of the movement, insofar as it was "a journalistic pseudo-event," in his *Concilium* article. However in April, 1967, he takes a somewhat different line calling for direction and clarity in the developing "theological revolution." "This is not to say that 'death of God' was useful for journalistic and offense-giving purposes and should now be put to pasture," "A Funny Thing Happened On the Way to the Library," *The Christian Century* (April 12, 1967), p. 469.

6. *Concilium, op. cit.,* p. 44.

7. In addition to the reservations of Hamilton about the continued use of the death of God lexicon, there is the oft-noted uneasiness of van Buren with the phrase and his occasional attempts to dissociate himself from "the movement." However, it should be noted that he has aligned himself with both the phrase and the thrust it represents in his essay significantly entitled, "Christian Education *Post Mortem Dei,*" *RE,* Vol. LX, No. 1 (January–February, 1965), pp. 4–10, especially page 10; also his response to symposium, "Straw Men and the Monistic Hangover—a Response" in the same volume of *RE.,* pp. 40–42, 48.

8. Put in circulation particularly by Hamilton.

9. See, for example, his analyses of Oedipus and Orestes, Prufrock and Ringo, etc. In spite of the various farewells he has said to his teacher Reinhold Niebuhr, Hamilton has been influenced by Niebuhr's typological mind and method.

10. *RT,* p. 40.

11. *Ibid.,* p. 116.

12. See *RT,* pp. 116, 92, 44, 47.

13. *RT,* p. 41.

14. *RT,* p. 41.

15. *EC,* p. 63.

16. *RT,* p. 41.

17. Thomas Ogletree, *The Death of God Controversy* (Nashville, Tenn: Abingdon Press, 1966), pp. 29–46.

18. *RT,* pp. 162–163.

19. *EC*, pp. 22–23.
20. *Ibid.*, p. 140.
21. *Ibid.*, p. 140.
22. *Ibid.*, p. 140.
23. *Ibid.*, pp. 140–141.
24. *RT*, p. 87.
25. *EC*, p. 64.
26. *RT*, p. 47.
27. *Ibid.*, pp. 162–164.
28. *Ibid.*, p. 42.
29. *RT*, p. 165.
30. *Ibid.*, p. 168.
31. *Ibid.*, p. 156.
32. *RT*, p. 37.
33. *Ibid.*, p. 41.
34. *Ibid.*, p. 36.
35. *Ibid.*, p. 37.
36. *Concilium, op. cit.*, p. 44.
37. *RT*, p. 46.
38. *EC*, pp. 13–20.
39. *RT*, p. 44.
40. *Ibid.*, pp. 159ff.
41. *Ibid.*, p. 3.
42. *Ibid.*, p. 48.
43. *Ibid.*, pp. 48–50.
44. *Ibid.*, p. 47.
45. Altizer, *The Gospel of Christian Atheism* (Philadelphia: Westminster Press, 1966), p. 15 (hereafter referred to as *GCA*).
46. We shall draw our quotations essentially from *GCA*, with parallel ideas in other literature cited in the footnotes.
47. Altizer, "Introduction to the Readings," *Toward a New Christianity* (New York: Harcourt, Brace and World, 1967), p. 7.
48. *GCA*, p. 22.
49. *Ibid.*, pp. 22–23.
50. *Ibid.*, p. 146; See also *RT*, p. 19.
51. *Ibid.*, p. 28. Sometimes Altizer speaks about the death of God in more recent terms, *RT*, pp. 11, 95.
52. Other influences include Altizer's work in the history of religious discipline especially under the influence of Joachim Wach and Mircea Eliade, and also kenotic Christology.
53. *GCA*, p. 45.
54. *Ibid.*, p. 145.

55. *Ibid.*, p. 22. This Blake phrase is used by the Pelzes for the title of a lyrical version of radical theology centered on the person of Jesus, Werner and Lotte Pelz, *God is No More* (Philadelphia: J. B. Lippincott, 1964).

56. *GCA*, p. 44.

57. *Ibid.*, p. 54.

58. *Ibid.*, p. 43.

59. *Ibid.*, p. 50.

60. *Ibid.*, p. 44.

61. *Ibid.*, p. 142.

62. *Ibid.*, p. 144. For discussion of the *coincidentia oppositorum* see *Ibid.*, pp. 38–48 and *RT*, pp. 140–155.

63. *Ibid.*, pp. 132–157.

64. *Ibid.*, p. 51. *RT*, pp. 19–20, 110, 123 and "Creative Negation in Theology," *Christian Century*, Vol. LXXXII, No. 27 (July 7, 1965), p. 865.

65. *Ibid.*, p. 134.

66. *Ibid.*, p. 41.

67. *Ibid.*, pp. 27–28; *RT*, p. 18.

68. *Ibid.*, p. 19.

69. *Ibid.*, p. 26; *RT*, p. 15.

70. *Ibid.*, p. 16.

71. *Ibid.*, p. 21.

72. *Ibid.*, pp. 137–138, 154; *RT*, p. 99.

73. *Ibid.*, p. 135; *RT*, p. 126.

74. *Ibid.*, p. 18; *RT* pp. 130–133.

75. "Introduction," *Towards a New Christianity, op. cit.*, p. 14; *RT*, p. 16.

76. *GCA*, p. 18.

77. *Ibid.*, p. 18; *RT*, p. 130.

78. *Ibid.*, p. 40. One enigmatic note that does not seem to fit this description is found in *RT*, p. 19, "A profane destiny may yet provide a way for the return to the God who is all in all, not by returning to a moment of the past, but by meeting an epiphany of the past in the present."

79. *GCA*, p. 145.

80. van Buren, SMG, *op. cit.*, p. 11.

81. In his lecture series and public appearances at Oxford University, 1967–68, and in Paul van Buren, *Theological Explorations* (London: SCM Press, 1968), pp. 4–5, 63. Hereafter referred to as *TE*.

82. SMG, p. 43. See also the essay, "The Dissolution of the Absolute," *TE*, pp. 29–42.

83. *RE, op. cit.*, p. 5. The essay to which reference is made several times in this chapter is reprinted with some minor changes in *TE*, pp. 63–77.

84. Swander Lectures, Lancaster Theological Seminary, Pa., 1966. Mim-

eographed transcript of taped Lecture Two, p. 2. (Hereafter referred to as *SW*).

85. Paul van Buren, "Theology in the Context of Culture," *The Christian Century*, Vol. LXXXII, No. 14 (April 7, 1965), p. 429.

86. *RE*, p. 42.

87. *SMG*, p. 17.

88. *Ibid.*, pp. 13–14.

89. *Ibid.*, p. 99.

90. *RE*, p. 5.

91. *SMG*, p. 4.

92. *Christian Century, op. cit.*, p. 429.

93. *SMG*, p. 106.

94. *RE*, p. 7.

95. *Ibid.*, pp. 8–9.

96. *Ibid.*, p. 10.

97. *Ibid.*, p. 7–10.

98. *SMG*, pp. 121–134.

99. *SL*, pp. 15–16.

100. *SL*, p. 6.

101. *RE*, p. 42.

102. *SMG*, p. 2.

103. *Ibid.*, p. 2. See also his essay, "Bonhoeffer's Paradox: Living with God without God," *TE*, pp. 109–132.

104. *SMG*, p. 82.

105. *SL*, pp. 3–4.

106. *Ibid.*, pp. 8–9.

107. *SMG*, p. 191.

108. *Ibid.*, p. 189.

109. *Ibid.*, p. 74.

110. *Ibid.*, p. 71.

111. *Ibid.*, p. 12.

112. *Ibid.*, p. 112.

113. *RE*, p. 6.

114. *SMG*, pp. 3, 4, 9, 115.

115. *SL*, p. 11. For another use of the city figure, see *TE*, pp. 127–132.

116. *Ibid.*, p. 12.

117. *Ibid.*, p. 16.

118. *Ibid.*, p. 16. See also the discussion of "the duality of seeing the ordinary as the extraordinary . . . the duality of imagination and factuality." *TE*, pp. 180, 169–181.

119. *SMG*, p. 195.

3

RADICAL MORALITY

"A breakthrough has occurred—a breakthrough that should be recognized in a broader context, as a companion piece to the new theology and the new evangelism which reflect the pluralism and empiricism and relativism of 'mature men' in the modern age."[1] Thus Joseph Fletcher links situation ethics with its allies in a common departure from classic ontological commitment and the quest for new categories of thought and action. While there are many able exponents of the radical moral perspective, we shall use Fletcher as representative of the position. As in the case of the other radical positions, our task will not be to expound in a rounded and detailed way Fletcher's conception of ethics but to try to lift out those characteristics that make it a significant response to the process of secularization, especially as they touch upon the question of moral law.[2]

The discussion of radical morality has been plagued with terminological ambiguity. We must, therefore, begin our exploration with an attempt to clarify what Fletcher's attitude to "law" in fact is. That this is no easy matter is evidenced by the variety of opinions among responsible ethicists on what is being said, and the frequent complaint of Fletcher that his position is often misrepresented. The difficulties of interpreting the position are suggested by the comparison of these two comments:

"The situationist, cutting himself loose from the dead hand of un-yielding law, with its false promises of relief from the anguish of de-cision, can only determine that as a man of goodwill he will live as a free man, with all the ambiguities that go along with freedom."[3]

"He says that I absolutize love, which indeed I do, and that I eliminate any place for law, which I most certainly and clearly do not. It is an odd and I suspect revealing myopia. He can read, but he cannot read situation ethics. But how can this common misreading be got rid of?"[4]

While there are many diatribes against "law" in Fletcher's writing similar to the one cited,[5] it is true that even the most casual reading of *Situation Ethics*, as well as Fletcher's other essays, will turn up many protestations that the new morality is not "antinomian," not anti-law in the sense in which that term is usually used. He develops a typology of methodological options in which he distinguishes his view from legalism on the one hand and an antinomian-existentialist ethic on the other: "whereas the legalist prefabricates his ethical choices, and the antinomian or spontaneist acts 'on the spur of the moment,' the situationist or contextualist enters into his decision making well armed with *principles generally valid* but prepared to modify, suspend, or even violate any principle or 'general rule' if in the situation the command to love the neighbor is better served."[6]

While Fletcher, on occasion, uses the word "law" to describe this "social wisdom" with which the situationist is fortified as he enters the decision-making moment[7] (thus giving some ground linguistically for his reply to the critics), more often he prefers the terms "principle" and "maxim." These suggest a tentativity and flexibility that "law," "rule" and "code" do not. They are "guide-lines and maxims to illuminate the situation" not "directives to be followed."[8] He has proposed recently that the situationists might explore further the source and role of maxims: "What do maxims (as distinct from laws) *tell* people? *How* do they illuminate a problem? How are they adduced from experience?"[9]

There is abundant evidence, whatever the semantic confusion, of Fletcher's *formal* disavowal of a rigorously anti-law position, and his attempt to bring the moral inheritance that has normally gone under the label of law as a serious partner into the decision-making context. However, a definitive understanding of the situational position must come in its own terms, that is, situationally. In other words, the meaning of concepts discloses itself in their functioning. As Fletcher puts it, in objecting to abstract inquiries about sundry ethical matters: "Have you a *real* question, that is to say, a concrete situation? If it has to do with pre-marital sex or libel or breach of contract or anything else . . . the reply is always the same: You are using words, abstractions. What you are asking is without substance; it has no living reality. . . . Give me a case."[10]

The meaning and role of law, understood as maxim (and the larger question of the meaning of situation ethics) must disclose itself in the actual operation of the situational method. We have two ways to scale down the abstract discussion of the status of maxim: (1) Analyze the descriptions of the way in which the method is applied to concrete situations and (2) examine the concrete situations themselves. We shall follow both courses.

As a decision-maker (who is a Christian) stands on the threshold of a specific choice, what is the procedure for making up his mind?

He knows the *what;* it is love. He knows the *why;* for God's sake. He knows the *who;* it is his neighbors, people. But only in and of the situation can he answer the other four questions: When? Where? Which? How?[11]

Love plots the course according to the circumstances. What is to be done in any situation depends on the case, and the solution to any moral issue is, therefore, quite relative.[12]

Christian situation ethics, the "non-system" advocated here, has a critically shrewd tactical formula for the strategy of love: *the indicative plus the imperative equals the normative.* Love, in the imperative mood of neighbor-concern, examining the relative facts of the situation in the indicative mood, discovers what it is obliged to do, what it should do, in the normative mood. What is, in the light of what love demands, show what ought to be.[13]

While the typological review (legalism, antinomianism, situationalism) distinguished situation ethics from an antinomian ethic by including within the former the component of "sophia,"[14] the social wisdom, principles and maxims of our heritage, the *procedural* counsel given in these and related comments deals with the only two real ingredients: *agape* and *kairos*, faith and facts, love and the situational data. In the context of working out the strategy and tactics of the situation method, therefore, it does not seem that law, even in the sense of "maxim," makes an appearance.[15]

While some might attribute the over-simplifications of the two-ingredient tactical commentary to the journalistic phrase-making and "verbal pyrotechnics" ascribed to Fletcher, the love-data tandem is a much more serious expression of what situation ethics means as it carries out its work operationally. This becomes clear when the actual concretions in the Fletcher literature are examined carefully.[16] There are one hundred and sixteen anecdotes and examples in *Situation Ethics* used to demonstrate how situational methodology works. Here, case by case, abstraction gives way to "living reality." Through them we get our clearest picture of the status of "law" in the Fletcher perspective. Of the total number of one hundred and sixteen concrete illustrations, there is no single case in which *sophia* is viewed as anything other than an obstruction to, or irrelevant to, responsible decision-making. The same thing is true of the data to be found in the companion volume *Moral Responsibility*, as Fletcher himself suggests in an interesting concluding observation: "If this essay, or the book as a whole, seems, to be more antilegalistic than antiexistential, rather more 'down' on impassive principles than on spontaneous or impromptu decisions, it is because in this age it is more strategic to keep the old morality off balance than it is to try to give balance to the often wild reactions against it. Law ethics is still the enemy by far."[17]

It is moot question whether legalism is as regnant in "moral conduct and social policy" as Fletcher thinks. But the issue at hand is a descriptive not a normative one. We are attempting to see how situational morality deals with law. Judged operationally rather than abstractly, law in any form—whether it be the legalism of traditional ethics or the maxim of more moderate formulations—dies in radical morality, as surely as "God" passes away in the formulations of radical theology. Whether it can be resurrected within the framework of situation ethics by serious inquiry into, and use of, the "maxim" as is proposed by Fletcher, the future only can tell. How the maxim compares to a "counsel" concept of law we shall explore further in our section on reconstruction.

Coming of Age

The modern history of the arts and sciences, and of the technologies that undergird them, makes it plain that they no longer bow down nor cut their cloth to authoritarian principles. Their lifeline is no more handed down in advance or dropped from above by "revelation" or majesty. Men have turned to inductive and experimental methods of approach, working by trial and error, appealing to experience to validate their tentative and loosely held generalizations. . . . Now at last ethics and moral inquiry are doing it too. This is the new turn in the history of Christian ethics. This is the temper of clinical, case-centered, situational "concretion"–to use Bonhoeffer's word.[18]

Growing up morally, like growing up theologically, means a gauntlet thrown down to old tyrannies. In this context autocracy appears in the dress of "authoritarian principles," the definitive word on moral style which has been "handed down" from "above" by imperial and esoteric commanders. The unquestionable *a priori*, the "directive," the "fiat-absolute," in short, the law that

is "laid down," has had its day and now ceases to be. There are
two interlacing reasons for a maturing morality to resist the
legalism that has "hamstrung and corsetted" man, two specifically
coming of age theses, and in addition, of course, other reasons
for the situational protest.

"Life and culture in a technical civilization is becoming increasingly complicated . . . petty moralism is forced to come of
age and to face the complicated facts of life."[19] To struggle
against old moral dictatorships is to defend the integrity of the
decision-making situation, and the persons involved in it, against
the insensitive absolutes that ride roughshod over the particularities of contexts that have become increasingly intricate due to
the technological developments of our era. To follow these impersonal absolutes that urge men to "do the 'right' even if the
sky falls down"[20] is to be innocent of the "variety and complexity" of the data that comprise the setting of choice, and thus
to do untold harm to human beings. Situationism, on the other
hand, seeks to honor the rich and varied circumstances which the
decider confronts. It "repudiates any attempt to anticipate or
prescribe real-life decisions in their existential particularity."[21] It
does not deal in the abstract universalism of what is "right" or
"good" but rather in the careful empiricism of what is "fitting."
To honor man's coming of age therefore means, first, to embody
in moral decision-making the same thrust toward maturity found
in other disciplines by affirming man's own ability to ferret out
himself with the best empirical techniques possible what the
facts are in that situation, and then to decide accordingly rather
than to be the pawn of sweeping generalizations.

There is another kind of protest against the tyranny of law
ethics and another variety of coming of age affirmation. It is suggested by the periodic reference to the Grand Inquisitor. People
who draw back from the ambiguities of ethical relativism "want
the Grand Inquisitor. T. S. Eliot was right to say that people cannot bear too much reality. But there is no escape for them. To
learn love's sensitive tactics, such people are going to have to put

away their childish rules."[22] To grow up, to be "human" is to
seize the right to choose, and not to "cower in the security of
law." In a world come of age "prefab code morality gets exposed
as a kind of neurotic security device to simplify moral decisions."[23]

In his concluding essay in *Moral Responsibility*, Fletcher examines the idea of "responsibility" itself. While he has formerly
taken pains to distinguish his position from existentialist notions,[24] here he speaks appreciatively of their insights, as they
bear on man's freedom from slavery to impersonal tyrants and
benign crutches: "Like material objects, abstract principles are
its, no matter how moral or pious. Situation ethics is close
in temper at least to the existential norms of love, freedom, and
openness which are described for example by John Wild in his
Challenge of Existentialism."[25]

Development out of the childhood stage of dependence on
the comforts of law, foregoing its "false promises of relief from
the anguish of decision," and launching into the risk of freedom
and personal love of the responsible life, is what it means to come
of age. Fletcher's sympathy for the existential struggle is expressed in his fight for the humanity of the decision-maker, just as
his protest against the ruthless abstractionism of law is a defense
of the integrity of the decision-making situation.

We have tried to see the ways in which radical morality speaks
to the coming of age aspect of secularization. However, there is
a special turn given by Fletcher to the maturation themes. While
many attempts in both theology and morality to deal with
secularization treat coming of age in historical and corporate
terms, Fletcher interprets the issues of maturity in the setting of
individual decision-making. There is only minute reference to
the responsibility of the community as community to re-evaluate
old codes and develop fresh responses that employ the best
empirical resources available to enable man to come to moral
adulthood. In the one notable instance in *Situation Ethics* in
which allusion is made to corporate moral inquiry, the effort is

declared to have been an exercise in futility.[26] Again, if one examines the array of concrete situations in *Situation Ethics* that are given to demonstrate the meaning of the method, they are without exception personal decision-making situations.[27] Thus, coming of age in the context of the version of radical morality under consideration has fundamental reference to the maturation of the self in its pilgrimage toward adulthood.

The Role of Time in Decision-Making

The attack on law ethics is by its very nature levelled at the omnicompetence of the *given* laws, and hence is a protest against the heavy embrace of the past. We have noted already some of the grounds for man "cutting himself loose from the dead hand of unyielding law":[28] the freedom of the decision-maker to do the loving act, and the freedom of the data to be fed into the chooser's computer. What is it about the past that reinforces the slavery of law? Its particular tyranny is traceable to the imposition of formulas which emerged in another time and may well have been right for that time on a new situation which requires new kinds of thinking. "What is constructive in one era may not be in another; James Russell Lowell's hymn is right, 'Time makes ancient good uncouth.' "[29]

Technology, in particular, radically changes the setting in which moral styles must function, as for example the passing of the threats of "infection, conception, and detection" which were the underpinning of a former sex ethic.[30] Moreover a twentieth century man knows full well that the cultural relativity of moral laws will not stand still for the overbearing claims of rules hammered out in another place and another time. Therefore a responsible ethic will "meet things here and now, without a romantic focus on the past."[31]

And the future? The references to the eschatological dimension of ethics are sparse and undeveloped. The future is characterized as an "escapist focus"[32] at one point, although it is suggested at

another that the Christian ethic "has its eschatological meaning."[33]
In reflecting on Brunner's *Faith, Hope and Love*, Fletcher puts
the three dimensions of time in situational perspective with characteristic emphasis: "The Christian ethic is a love ethic primarily,
not a hope ethic (although it has its eschatological meaning).
This means it is for the present, here and now. By faith we live in
the past, by hope we live in the future, but by love we live in the
present. Legalism is wrong because it tries to push love back into
the past, into old decisions already made."[34]

This-Worldliness

Radical morality's response to the this-worldly orientation of a
secular society surfaces strongly in Fletcher's critique of "intrinsicalist" ethics, the belief that love is a "property" rather than
a "predicate." "Value, worth, ethical quality, goodness or bad-
ness, right or wrong—these things are only predicates, they are
not properties. They are not 'given' or objectively 'real' or self-
existent. . . . This posture or perspective sets us over against all
'intrinsicalist' ethics, against all 'given' or 'natural' or 'objectively
valid' laws and maxims, whether of the natural law or the Scrip-
tural law varieties. It means too there are no universals of any
kind."[35]

The meaning of this declaration is brought home by illustrating
the intrinsicalist-property tack taken by various ethicists. Reinhold Niebuhr is identified as a representative of the position inasmuch as he "reifies" love: "Reinhold Niebuhr, who is closer to
situationism than to any other ethical method, nevertheless held a
sort of supernaturalistic notion of love as a 'thing' or power that
men lack except in a finite and insufficient measure. He saw love
as an 'absolute' property or capacity or state, rather than a
predicate, a way of characterizing what we *do* when we act in a
concrete situation. . . . We cannot therefore speak with Niebuhr
of the 'impossibility' of love."[36]

John Bennett comes under similar strictures:

When John Bennett pleads, in the spirit of Luther's *pecca fortiter,* that "there are situations in which the best we can do is evil," we have to oppose what he says—much as we admire its spirit. On Bennett's basis, if a small neighborhood merchant tells a lie to divert some "protection" racketeers from their victims, no matter how compassionately the lie is told, he has still chosen to do *evil.* It is, of course, excused or pardoned as a so-called "lesser evil." This has always been possible in the merciful casuistry of the ethical realists or intrinsicalists. But no matter how lovingly such "bad things" may be done they are still evil, still wrong, they still require repentance and forgiveness!— This confused assertion that the shopkeeper's lie is both loving and wrong is an obvious contradiction. It is due to the intrinsic doctrine of value. Because its starting point is an ontological rather than existential conception of right and wrong, it is compelled in this barbarous way to divorce what is right from what is good. . . . For the situationalist what makes the lie right is its loving purpose; he is not hypnotized by some abstract law, "Thou shall not lie."[37]

The insistence that there is no intrinsic value that "stands above" every decision judging it a greater or lesser approximation of an objectified standard and its implication for both counseling and action is sharply sketched in the consideration of decisions that were made during the exigencies of war. Commenting on Alexander Miller's judgment that there were times in the underground movement when lies, theft, and murder seemed necessary to continue the resistance against Nazism, but that these actions could only be carried out "with a profound sense of guilt,"[38] Fletcher says "we should change his 'guilt' to *sorrow,* since such tragic situations are a cause for regret but not for remorse."[39] And again he comments: "Legalistic casuistry could not comfort the British intelligence staff in World War II when they let a number of women agents return to Germany to certain arrest and death in order to keep secret the fact that they had broken the German code. Situational casuistry could easily approve their decision."[40]

Situation ethics, therefore, contributes to a general trend that "banishes all perfectionism from Christian ethics,"[41] for "Gone is the former sense of guilt and of cheated ideals when we tailor our ethical cloth to fit the back of each occasion."[42] This removal of enervating guilt feelings is itself, however, the fruit of a deeper root, the shift from a "realist" to a "nominalist" form, an "ontological" to an "existential" conception of ethics, in which the hypostatization of value is rejected. Love does not exist objectively somewhere "out there" but is to be found in the disposition of the decider and as a predicate that describes action which makes for a maximum welfare in a situation or network of situations. Thus the norm of ethics has been relocated from a transcendent beyond to an immanent process.

Has a this-worldly value perspective then eliminated all aspect of transcendence in the Christian life? On the contrary, the final grounds of Christian ethics are traceable to the nature of God himself. It is because God is love that men are called to love. In fact situationism, in Christian idiom, is a "eucharistic ethic." "Christian love is the love of gratitude, of thanksgiving to God for what he has done for us, for mankind, especially in the life, death and resurrection of Jesus Christ. . . . From this faith follows gratitude, a loving response to God's love, i.e. *agape*. . . . Before we ask the ethical question 'What shall I do?' comes the *pre*-ethical question 'What has God done?' "[43]

At this point we again face a certain ambiguity in the development of the radical morality by Fletcher. If the Christian ethical style rises eucharistically from God's own love, is there not an intrinsicalist rootage of situation ethics? A consistent extrinsicalism would have to maintain, as it does with the radical theologians, that there is no transcendent referent. As soon as "God" is introduced and interpreted in the personalistic frame of reference used by Fletcher, there is introduced as well the "hypostatization" inherent in the intrinsicalist position. Fletcher, in fact, does acknowledge that "Only in the divine being, only in God, is love substantive. . . . Only with God is it a property . . . only God *is* love."[44] It is difficult to see how this differs in any basic way from the intrinsicalism attributed to those who are accused of reifying love. It is the basis for their judgments about the guilt of men claimed and judged as they are by the divine love given human shape on the cross. Perhaps, it is not the intrinsicality of love that is at issue, for it seems in the final analysis to be shared by Fletcher. The difference may lie rather in the definition of what divine love is, and particularly whether it has in its furthest reaches a suffering selflessness. Radical self-emptying appears to play a significant role in the understanding of God's love as it is found in Niebuhr, Bennett, Miller, and others to whom the intrinsicalist error is attributed. Fletcher's rejection of Tolstoyean self-abnegation would seem to suggest that his conception of the "property" of divine agape would not be so understood. We shall return to this question in Part III. For our purposes here, we simply note that Fletcher attempts to gear in with a this-worldly age by way of an extrinsic, predicative ethic.

We have already noted the "case-based" quality of situation ethics. The style of doing ethics, as well as its extrinsic content, is a reflection of its response to an empirical era. "It is empirical, fact-minded, date-conscious, inquiring."[45] As such, it has a certain kinship with "British empiricism."[46]

In the same hard-nosed contemporary vein it is in the debt of the pragmatic tradition. "The good is what works."[47] The American Peirce-James-Dewey school has been particularly in-fluential in radical morality. In fact, in describing *Situation Ethics*, Fletcher says "This book is consciously inspired by Amer-ican pragmatism."[48] The characterization of situation ethics as a "nonsystem" and the wish to have it understood as a "method" are intimately related to the empirico-pragmatic, modern, this-worldly idiom.

The work of Joseph Fletcher is a major contribution to the ongoing conversation in the Christian community on the meaning and direction of its moral style. He has attempted to develop a Christian ethic in response to the facets of secularization, and has done it with verve and firmness of purpose. It represents a significant experiment that has to be taken into account in any attempt to develop a post-radical perspective in morality.

Footnotes

1. Fletcher, Bennett, et al., *Storm Over Ethics* (Philadelphia: United Church Press, 1967), pp. 152–153 (hereafter referred to as *SOE*). While Fletcher acknowledges the relationship to companion developments, the identity of his allies is not altogether clear. Judging from a passing reference elsewhere to the "new theology," it probably applies more to the thinking of James Pike and Leslie Dewart than to the position we have described as radical theology. See footnote 12 allusion, *SOE, op. cit.*, pp. 182–183.

2. It is a very tricky business saying who is and who is not a representative of situation ethics. For example, while Joseph Sittler is often described as a situationist, Fletcher takes pains to distinguish his point of view from the "extemporism" of Sittler. *SOE*, p. 156, and *Moral Responsibility* (hereafter referred to as *MR*), by Joseph Fletcher, p. 34. Copyright © 1967, The Westminster Press. Used by permission. Again, surely one would link Robinson with Fletcher in a common situational position, from the development of his ethical perspective in both *Honest to God* (Philadelphia: Westminster Press, 1963), pp. 103–121, and *Christian Morals Today* (Philadelphia: Westminster Press, 1964), particularly with Robinson's explicit reliance on Fletcher's thought (*Honest to God, op. cit.*, pp. 116–120). However, Fletcher lets it be known that Robinson also falls into the "extemporist," "existential," "transrational" trap, and that Robinson's position must not be confused with a genuine situationism. Ramsey, on the other hand, also distinguishes Robinson from Fletcher, but for exactly the opposite reasons. "Bishop Robinson pays high tribute to the need for law and for the net of a good moral ethos that exhibits and preserves the connecting tissue between moral events and experiences." *Deeds and Rules in Christian Ethics* (New York: Scribners, 1967), p. 148. Again, Fletcher links Gustafson to the situational perspective (*SOE*, p. 152), but it is exceeding difficult to find the grounds for this, especially in the light of Gustafson's critique (*SOE*, pp. 38–67). Bennett has been labelled by Fletcher on some occasions an "intrinsicalist." *Situation Ethics* (Philadelphia: Westminster, 1966), pp. 64–65 (hereafter referred to as *SE*). On other occasions he can say, "It seems to me there is no substantial issue as between Bennett's published view and situationism" (*SOE*, p. 157). The same fuzziness attends Fletcher's characterization of a variety of other

ethicists, including Bonhoeffer, Pike, and Lehmann, who are sometimes included and sometimes excluded from the situational circle. In view of the difficulty of determining lines of demarcation, we shall confine our analysis here to one self-described situationist who has written extensively enough about the perspective to give us both sufficient and manageable data for clarification. We shall confine ourselves as well to Fletcher's more recently published works in which the method is given its most definitive statement.

3. *SE*, p. 135.

4. *SOE*, p. 171.

5. Law comes under attack in *SOE*, p. 170. It is used to describe approvingly *agape* as the law of love in *SE*, p. 27.

6. *MR*, p. 74.

7. Law is used to describe the social wisdom of the race in *SE*, p. 31. Situationism may be described, according to Fletcher, as "modified rules-ethics" in *SOE*, pp. 155–156.

8. *SE*, p. 18.

9. *SOE*, p. 172.

10. *SE*, pp. 143, 142.

11. *Ibid.*, p. 142.

12. *Ibid.*, p. 143.

13. *Ibid.*, p. 151.

14. "We may say that Christian situationism is a method that proceeds, so to speak, from (1) its one and only law, *agape* (love), to (2) the *sophia* (wisdom) of the church and culture, containing many 'general rules' of more or less reliability, to (3) the *kairos* (moment of decision, the fullness of time) in which the *responsible self in the situation* decides whether the *sophia* can serve love there or not." *SE*, p. 33.

15. Law as love of course does. But we are talking here of *sophia*.

16. Ramsey's intricate dissection of Fletcher's illustrations is an effort to do just this, and ought to be studied very carefully for he makes the case that "In actual fact Fletcher's operating ethical method is an extreme and exclusive act-agapism; if not *auti*nomian, it is certainly *anomia*, no matter how he formally defines situation ethics and attempts to locate it between extremes." Ramsey, *op. cit.*, p. 148. The treatment, pp. 145–225, is found in the revised edition.

17. *MR*, p. 241.

18. *SE*, p. 158.

19. *Ibid.*, p. 137.

20. *Ibid.*, p. 20.

21. *Ibid.*, pp. 29–30.

22. *Ibid.,* p. 140.

23. *Ibid.,* p. 137.

24. *Ibid.,* pp. 24ff.

25. *MR,* p. 234.

26. *SE,* p. 151.

27. In some of these situations the persons involved are making up their minds about issues of great social moment and/or are doing it in contexts of public structure, as Truman's struggle about the decision to drop the atomic bomb, or the issues of desegregation. To this extent, Fletcher is right in his response to the criticism that he has ignored social issues. However, it is instructive to note that of the 116 cases with which he deals in *Situation Ethics,* 86 are in the area of private morality, and interpersonal decision-making. Moreover, of these, 36 have to do with sex ethics in one form or another, giving further justification to the observation that situation ethics is more at home in the issues of private morality.

28. *SE,* p. 135.

29. *Ibid.,* p. 141.

30. *Ibid.,* p. 80.

31. *Ibid.,* p. 135.

32. *Ibid.,* p. 135.

33. *Ibid.,* p. 142.

34. *Ibid.,* p. 142.

35. *Ibid.,* pp. 60, 64.

36. *Ibid.,* pp. 61, 62.

37. *Ibid.,* pp. 64, 65.

38. *Ibid.,* p. 124.

39. *Ibid.,* p. 124.

40. *Ibid.,* p. 98.

41. *MR,* p. 27.

42. *SE,* p. 27. It should be noted that Fletcher takes exception to criticism that he has eliminated the factor of guilt from the Christian life. He is more receptive to the idea that he has retained personal sin while rejecting the idea of original sin. See *SOE,* pp. 158–159.

43. *SE,* pp. 155, 156, 157

44. *Ibid.,* pp. 62–63.

45. *Ibid.,* p. 29.

46. *Ibid.,* p. 41.

47. *Ibid.,* p. 42.

48. *Ibid.,* p. 40.

4

RADICAL MISSION

We now come to a sector along the frontier of radical inquiry and action that includes a much vaster sweep of literature and a longer period of experimentation conducted by many more theoreticians and practitioners than either of the other two companion movements. Moreover, there is a richness and variety to radical ecclesiological thought that makes generalization dangerous. It is necessary, therefore, to find some way to delimit the area of investigation, yet include enough data so that the radical position can emerge as an identifiable option in ecclesiology and missiology.[1] We shall, therefore, select a manageable body of thought as the target of analysis: the "Missionary Structure Study" of the World Council of Churches. Under the mandate of the New Delhi Assembly of the World Council of Churches in 1961, the Department of Studies in Evangelism of the World Council has organized working groups in various regions that have been researching since 1962 the modern missionary question. A running account of the conversations has appeared in the mimeographed w.c.c. publication *Concept* (a "red" edition for the public and a "blue" edition of internal reports and minutes for working group members), and major essays and reports have been brought together in the volumes *Planning for Mission* and

The Church for Others.[2] These sources will provide our principal documentation for the position of radical mission.

The selection of this kind of a handle for our analysis has several drawbacks which should be mentioned at the start. One is the elimination of some forceful statements of the radical position that have appeared as popular books, and in the array of fertile pamphlets, articles and booklets that have grown out of concrete missionary activity in the industrial missions, coffee houses, renewal centers, evangelical academies, lay centers, etc. Where it is possible, however, the testimony from these sources will be cited in the footnotes. Another problem is that there are areas of consensus in the Missionary Structure Study broad enough to include views on mission that could not be classified as radical. Furthermore, the version of the radical line that appears in this church-sponsored inquiry is by its very roots in the ecumenical movement sufficiently "churchy" in focus, and even in conclusion, to be short of the left wing in missiology. The North American Working Group has recognized these facts in a typology it includes in its final report in which it distinguishes within its own ranks "reformers—who believe that the biggest task is renewal of the old from within; radicals—who believe a radical reshaping of old forms is needed and the fashioning of new ones as well; revolutionaries—who believe that freedom for the new forms requires the radical death of old forms."[3] While this typology is based on the question of the forms of the church and not the larger issue of ecclesiological response to secularization, it does point to the matter at hand—the difficulty of getting clear signals on a radical stance even from this limited area of inquiry. What we shall do therefore is not attempt a careful review or balanced portrayal of the Study, but rather isolate a thread of thought in the Study that we shall define as "radical," indicating how it shades off on occasion into a "revolutionary" position.

The radical perspective on mission, like its sister positions in theology and morality, locates a target and looses its arrows toward it. Not the tyrant God or tyrant law, but in this case the tyrant church. Rigid, aloof, unworldly, imperialistic, the traditional church and its self-understanding impedes human growth and diverts men's eyes from their true home, the world. Radical mission seeks to re-turn the church so that it will be able to live in secular times with a mature and worldly style.

Secularization is a much discussed subject in the Study. In several reviews of the types of definition current, the Western European Working Group cites three going interpretations:[4] (1) a sociological version, given particular impetus by Joachim Mathes,[5] which views secularization "as a continuing process of social *differentiation* by which also the problem of social *integration* is posed in a special way."[6] Differentiation "not only involves the division of labor and the separation of work and home; it also includes an increasing specialization of groups, institutions and interests throughout society."[7] As it bears on the institutional church, differentiation means the passing of the integration of society from an ecclesiastical focal point to a diversity of centers, and the redistribution of many of the social functions of the church to secular agents. (2) A "psychological climate" which in its "pure type" is expressed in thinking that does not operate with the God-hypothesis, and action that is guided by secular standards and feelings devoid of sacred sensitivities. This earlier formulation is refined in some later reflection by the European Group probably under the influence of further secularization research, notably the van Leeuwen thesis that has had a significant impact in ecumenical circles.[8] A distinction is made between an ideological "secularism" that "represents a closed world view which functions very much like a new religion: it threatens openness and freedom,"[9] and secularization as "a liberation from the control of metaphysics and theology."[10] (3) A posture in which the church seeks "identification with the world, even as the son of God identified himself with man."[11] These three understandings of secularization are at work in one or another of the

issues addressed by radical missiology. They are also implicit in
our own working definition, although we have ordered them differently within the definition. Therefore, allusion will be made to
them contextually.

Coming of Age

The world of the national fathers, of the school father, of the church
fathers, is a passing world. But the more the former hierarchy of
offices loses its useful function because of social changes, the more
urgent is the question concerning man's office in the change of the
world.[12] The patriarchal age, with the established authority of the
father and the obedience of the good son serving as a model for the
structure of church and society, has come to an end. Patriarchy is
being replaced by dialogue.[13]

The son's coming of age means that the life of man and his
institutions are affirmed in a way that has heretofore been impossible under ecclesiastical autocracy. Approving Ronald Gregor
Smith's comment on human autonomy, J. C. Hoekendijk says:
"We recognize honestly and completely, without any ulterior
motives, the existence of the world with all its own principles
of movement, hopes and possibilities . . . and identify ourselves
fully with the things and people of the world."[14] To free it from
a choking churchiness is to serve the God who calls man to be a
man, and to celebrate the work of the liberating Christ himself:
"Where the world is left to be the world . . . the profane left to
be the profane, thus being at the free disposal of man, Christ is
at work."[15]

The indictment of the church and the proposals for encouraging maturation can be divided into two categories: practical
and theoretical, sociological and theological. We shall follow this
distinction in exploring the position of radical mission vis à vis
coming of age.

Secularization sociologically considered spells the end of the
"corpus Christianum," a society both dominated by the church

and one in which it was assumed that all men reached their proper earthly destination when they came within its institutional embrace. While identified in terms of the definition of differentiation cited above and the secular distribution of former church functions, it is nevertheless the passing of a tyranny, "the disappearance of ecclesiastical totalitarianism and the recognition that the ordering of life falls to mankind under God and not by delegation from a religious hierarchy. . . ."[16]

Responsible reaction to the process means acceptance of it and alliance with it, for "to oppose secularization . . . can imply an attempt to restore ecclesiastical dominance over society and a domination of science by theology."[17] In fact, suspicion and rejection represent a disavowal of one's own faith, for "secularization, in this sense, is . . . inherent in the biblical faith in God, the creator of all, the only one who is holy in himself. The world, in the bible, is entirely secular and placed under the mandate of men who are responsible to God for their stewardship."[18] And institutional resistance to the world's coming of age is ignorance as well of the historical connection between faith and secularization as "the modern understanding of the world as world, as not part of the divine being, has . . . its roots in the bible."[19]

The alternative to the "Christian imperialism" of the patriarchal days is servanthood. Whereas in days of domination the church played the master, now it must accept the role of the suffering servant. As Hoekendijk expresses it: "The Church . . . will have to *empty* itself, to practice kenosis (Phillipians 2:5ff., in the *New English Bible*, 'to make itself nothing'), mortifying its ecclesiastical stature and status, in order that it may 'bear human likeness and be revealed in human shape.' In Mission the Church will come closest to being simply a segment of Main Street, Anno 1963; in the esteem of the world it will certainly be the poorest section of it 'without form or comeliness.' "[20]

Servanthood has some very practical implications. For one, it is the opposite of the "Constantinian turn of mind" of the *corpus Christianum* which seeks to get people into the "well-defined corrals of institutional religion."[21] Mission in a secular age, therefore, is not "proselytism." "The proselyting Church conceives itself as the mediating center of salvation and *extra ecclesiam nulla salus:* it takes itself as the *oikos,* to where man has to emigrate completely out of his worldly *oikos;* proselytism is the concomitant of a Church's refusal to accept its *paroikia* status."[22]

While there are some other assumptions at work in this reaction to proselytism,[23] it is a posture commensurate with the lowliness of a church that no longer insists on its own way, choosing to listen and learn rather than shout. And while it does believe it brings a perspectival gift to the world, it shares it with a modesty poles apart from the triumphalist monologues of traditional Christianity.

The acknowledgment of the world's maturity means a cooperative and listening ministry with and to those who do not carry the Christian label. The structure of a missionary congregation itself requires an openness, "because the question at issue is not to extend the Church . . . but solely the service of Jesus Christ in which Christians who know him and pagans and atheists who do not know him, gather for a common task in the service of mankind and in expectation of the Kingdom. In saying this we affirm that the presence of the other, the non-Christian, is just as indispensable to the true life of the Church, as the presence of the Church is essential to the health of the world."[24]

The passing of patriarchy means also a new relationship of units and persons within the life of the church. Thus, as touching institutional direction: "While the two inherited forms of life (characteristics: being cared for [the crutch] and being managed [the tyrant]) still largely determine the picture today, in some places the activities (Veranstaltungen) by and by become gatherings of Christians who have come of age, and who carry themselves the responsibility for all life in the Church and who understand themselves as cooperating communities."[25]

The passing of imperialism and monologue have drastic repercussions for clergy-lay relationships as well: "The monopolistic misunderstanding of the ministry must resolutely be abandoned. The pastor is a member of the body of Christ like everyone else."[26] Lest this be interpreted as a simple division of labor in which the clergy are responsible for the "equipping of the saints" and the laity for involvement in the world, it must be understood that the clergy themselves are equipped also by the laity. "It is rather a matter of *all* members of the congregation mutually equipping one another, contributing to the enlightenment and enrichment of the whole body from their respective angles of vision."[27]

There is also that imperialism that has occupied a considerable portion of the concern of the working groups which we shall examine in more detail in the section on the historicity of church structures: "the local congregation . . . has no monopoly as the bearer of the whole burden of the Church's task."[28] For the radical missionary, "All the basic assumptions, all the basic presuppositions of congregational life are foreign to our lives. And those who feel this way can only join congregational life if they are willing to live inauthentically."[29]

Institutionally, coming of age means, therefore, a new relationship to the world that encourages its emergence, declaring its own need of the world's gifts and a new relationship within the church's own precincts in which autocracy in any form is brought under sharp attack.[30]

God-World-Church

The controversy with the tyrant church receives its sharpest formulation in reflection on new ecclesiological directions. They are launched around the fighting word *missio Dei*, the mission of God. This phrase is not to be blandly interpreted as one way of underscoring the divine source of faithful activity, as "a back-reference to God's prevenient initiative; merely a theocentric preface to an unaltered anthropo- or ecclesio-centric text."[31] It means a radical reassessment of the assumption that the church is the center of gravity for the life and work of God. As the authors of the report of the American Working Group put it: "We quickly saw that the mission is not the church's mission, but God's mission, and the real question for us then became the discerning of the mission of God to and from the world."[32]

The new thesis is rooted in the divine "sending-economy" with its landmark action in Jesus Christ:

> God's redemptive mission culminates in the coming of Christ, the true man, the head of the new humanity. His coming and presence is the advent of the acceptable year of the Lord; it brings liberty to the captives, sight to the blind, and good news to the poor. In his earthly life as well as in his new existence as the risen Lord, Christ is providing signs of the fullness of humanity, wherever men and women are led to restored relationships in love of neighbor, in service and suffering for the sake of greater justice and freedom.[33]

Jesus Christ is the embodiment of "the Humane," the new human existence set forth into history.[34]

Christ is at work in the world. The signs of his presence are the same as those that marked his life, death, and resurrection, and the eschatological goal he announced. The biblical word *shalom*—peace, healing, wholeness—expresses the purpose of God's mission and is the mark of his renewing historical activity. "In trying to define the *purpose* of the Mission, we must disregard all religious categories. We might use the keyword in the messianic pattern: *shalom*. A *secularized*(!) concept taken out of the religious sphere (= salvation guaranteed to those who have strictly performed the prescribed rites) and commonly used to indicate all aspects of the restored and cured human condition; righteousness, truth, fellowship, communication, peace."[35] *Shalom* therefore is horizontal healing, "humanization," visible, public, corporate. "*Shalom* is a *social happening*, an event in inter-human relations, a venture of co-humanity."[36] Hoekendijk notes that "*shalom* can never be reduced to a simple formula to be applied in all occurring instances . . . it must be found and worked out in actual situations."[37]

And death as well as life is at work in the worldly processes, making none of them unambiguous bearers of mission. Nevertheless it is possible to point to movements, events, and tendencies in contemporary society that are setting up "*signs of shalom.*" Thus: "One may consider examples like: The emancipation of coloured races, the concern for the humanization of industrial relations, various attempts at rural development, the quest for business and professional ethics, the concern for intellectual honesty and integrity. So God, as he moves toward his final goal, is using men and women, both inside and outside the chuiches, to bring signs of *shalom.*"[38]

It is because men have come to a new appreciation of the secular working of God in the *shalom*-embodying currents in the world that a new understanding of the three components of mission must be put forward. The old conception, beholden to "ecclesiastical positivism," understood the route of divine action to be God-church-world. The new understanding of the divine route is better expressed as God-world-church.

In the past it has been customary to maintain that God is related to the world through the Church. When we sharpen this view into a formula the sequence would be: God—Church—world. This is to understand that God is primarily related to the Church and only secondarily to the world by means of the Church. Further it has been held that God relates himself to the world through the Church in order to gather everyone possible from the world into the Church. God, in other words, moves through the Church to the world. We believe that the time has come to question this sequence and to emphasize an alternative. According to this alternative the last two items in God—Church—world should be reversed, so that it reads instead God—world—Church. That is, God's primary relationship is to the world and it is the world and not the Church that is the focus of God's plan. . . .[39]

To see that the fundamental relation God has to his world is in fact through his world is to call into question the ecclesiology that domesticated Deity in an "ark" into which people had to flee from a world "bereft of the divine presence which is enshrined within and reserved exclusively for the church."[40] This conception is a relic of "presecularized theology" and the "ghetto mentality" that went with it, an understanding of God which treated him as a "Christian Ba'al."[41] It also encouraged a spirituality that related to God in terms of "timeless adoration" rather than from within "historical existence."

If God is at work in the world in its reconciling currents, what then is the status of the church, and what is its relationship to the secular mission of Deity? The church does indeed have a certain singularity. While it must understand itself only as a "postscript" to the world, it is nevertheless "entrusted with God's secret." Its function is "pointing to and celebrating both Christ's presence and God's ultimate redemption of the whole world."[42] It is not a divine lump in secular earth but part and parcel of the world itself. However, it is "that segment of the world which reveals the final goal towards which God is working for the whole world. Herein is the glory of the Church."[43]

But precisely because it knows of a new man and a new mankind, it lives under the mandate not only to be an instrument of *shalom* but to be as well the "vanguard of the new humanity in history."[44] It must therefore live out its life deeply immersed in the "theater of historical responsibility,"[45] and be at those places and times where it is called to "agonize with all men in the bewilderments and struggles of contemporary events and to interpret those events so that they may become for mankind not overwhelming but creative."[46] The church, therefore, brings all its resources of theology, worship and action to bear in the moil and toil of human struggle in order to illumine events as the action of Christ and rescue men from perverse self-understandings such as "idealism and positivism, pantheism and atheism, nihilism and cynicism."[47] In fact the resources of the church are only valid to the degree that they are harnessed to the service of the human task. Thus the life of worship is directed toward a God "who does not claim our worship for his sake but worship for the sake of man who needs it."[48]

What is the status of the church when it fails to live out its *shalom* mandate? Here is the heart of the radical missiology. It is set forth simply in an analysis of the church "reduced to its simplest expression."

The true church does not exist apart from poverty, sacrifice and death. Unseen humility and lowliness are inseparable from the being and mission of the Church. . . . Wherever the God of Jesus Christ *and* the world are taken seriously, there is the Church . . . there is no definite sign, no absolute guarantee that the church(es) is or may become the Church. . . . We can neither guarantee nor possess his presence, but we know that he is faithful—thus in the unceasingly renewed *event* of his epiphany we say: *Ubi Christus ibi ecclesia.* . . .[49]

This proposition born of the fusion of an "event" theology with a secular conception of mission means that the church exists only where those who name the Name also live out the servant style in commitment to, and immersed in, the human issues of the day at the places where *shalom* is breaking into history. The church only *is* in mission.[50] Thus a functional understanding of the church brings together being and doing in such a way that there cannot be one without the other: "It is not a question of two different realms, one the being of the Church and the other its missionary action. The very being of the Church implies its missionary activity."[51] Hoekendijk traces this behavioral ecclesiology to its source in God's mission, and its link with apostolicity understood as participation in mission: "The Church is a function of the Mission apostolate and even that only insofar as it will actually let itself be used in God's sending economy."[52]

The "church" in the God-world-church formula means therefore two things: (1) The visible Christian community is called to participate deeply in the divine mission of *shalom* in the world, taking up its life within the signs it discerns. It therefore is a postscript to worldly grace acting as its interpreter and servant. (2) The visible community of Christians only *is* the church to the degree that it is in living relationship with the divine mission in the world. Wherever the institutional church, even with all its religious language, ceremonial, and life, fails to live out this relationship, it loses its right to be identified as truly the church. The consistent protagonist of radical mission is convinced that large segments of the religious establishment have forfeited these credentials, and for that reason the radical missionary can judge that it is inauthentic to remain within it. He finds his life instead in the world, and his church among those who name the Name but do it from within the boiling points of secular *shalom*. Of such stuff is coming of age made, for it honors the God who is at work in a world that has taken its rightful place in the divine sequence, replacing the former institutional *impedimenta*, "the church."

We have said that the radical mission represented in the Missionary Study thread we are examining is not on the further end of the spectrum of ecclesiological options. There are, some hints here, however, of other positions. One of them is the suggestion that wherever Christians without communal identification are present in the world as instruments of *shalom* in their work or action, there in some sense is the church: "Wherever a man lives in a true relationship with others in the name of Christ, there is the Church."[53] An urban missionary in a secular job puts it in the form of a question that needs further exploration: "Another question that both the gospel and my co-workers ask about the church is, *when?* The theological statement of this question is how Christ's kingdom relates to his renewing presence in city hall. Is each Christian at city hall the church? At what future point will we be able to call ourselves the church in this place? How long will it take?"[54]

The Freedom Movement has pressed this question insistently

on sensitive proponents of radical mission who themselves are deeply involved in its life. Citing the presence of many Christians in the Movement, a Bossey consultation agrees that "These persons are God's People in the midst of the world. They are gathered around the immediate concern or urgent issue, and God gives them the form which their obedience should take."[55]

Others press one step further and give voice to a conception of the church which is fully secular. Here it is not the Name-namers whose presence, either corporately or individually, consciously or unconsciously, establish the presence of the church. Rather the church exists wherever men are for other men, living out the life of servanthood and thus representing "unconscious or latent membership in the New Mankind . . . and [sharing] the apostolate of the Church."[56] P. Vrijhof sums up the possibility of a death of the church toward which radical missiology may be veering:

The church will remain only as a temporary construction, which may gradually merge unrecognizably with the world under certain social relationships and patterns of responsibility (G. Winter and J. C. Hoekendijk). We must see the possibility that religion and the church in their present forms will disappear, or at least fade out as separate phenomena. We would then travel along the road towards a religion which is valid and true for the coming period of our civilization. It would be wise to take this into account when reflecting about the structures of missionary congregations.[57]

Historicity and Radical Mission

"Would it not be more realistic, according to all the information we have, to speak about the congregation mainly in the past tense, indicating that this is a structure we have to move away from so that we may really participate in mission?"[58] Hoekendijk's question is answered by most of the representatives of radical mission with a "yes." The pastness of the church meets us today in the petrified forms of local congregations and a conception of the church which invests them with near divinity and omni-competence. Maturity in mission must therefore throw off this hypnotism with a single ossified social expression, a form that may have been relevant to another age but is not so to ours. The lens through which radical mission views the obsolescence of the congregational form is that of the historical relativity of all social shapes derived from modern social science: "Sociology calls the attention of theology to the relativity of the structures of ecclesiastical life; it formulates the question of the historicity of the life of the church. . . ."[59]

The awareness of structural relativity makes the radical mis-sionary sensitive to the dangers of "morphological fundamental-ism":

In its broadest sense, the combination of the term "morphological" and "fundamentalism" indicates a rigid and inflexible attitude toward the *morphe* (structure, Gestalt) of the congregation similar to the atti-tude prevalent in "biblical fundamentalism." Consciously, or more often unconsciously, the existent *forms* of the life of the Christian com-munity are taken to be fixed once and for all; their historical nature—and that means their changeability—are likely to be ignored. A case in point is . . . the parish system designed at a particular period of Church history for the specific needs of those times, and henceforth very often misunderstood as *the* one *morphe* in which the congregation expresses its obedience in an authentic way.[60]

What specifically constitutes the structural inadequacy of the present parish system and/or local congregation? Obsolescence expresses itself in the failure of the inherited structure to be a vehicle of mission in the matters of people, power, and issues, in the modern world.[61]

The local church is not a structure to serve members of a mobile generation that no longer "live where they live."[62] Tech-nological developments have sundered the former units of hu-man community in which men lived and died, worked and played, bought and sold, were educated and had their ills tended.

Since the local church is tied to the residential sector, it is cut off from the other "worlds" in which men are viscerally involved. In addition to its decreasing access to people, the local congregation is out of touch with the centers of decision-making and the movements of power that shape our society.[63] As a consequence of its distance from vital secular ferment, it is divorced from the issues that anguish and excite modern men.[64]

Its marginal role in society disqualifies it as a living option for mission. While there are other serious failures of this form— its ethical and theological impoverishment as well as its sociological irrelevance[65]—its significance in our present discussion is the example it affords of radical mission's view of the past and its commitment to the present. From within its sociological perspective on the historicity of forms, it puts the institutional inheritance into question. It arose in another time with its very different conditions, and therefore cannot be a fit instrument for mission in an era in which radically changed circumstances require "new forms."[66] Radical mission is an ally of the present.

What of the future? With its close relationship to the ecumenical movement, talk of the future has been familiar in the Missionary Structure Study, inasmuch as the 1954 Second Assembly of the World Council of Churches had as its eschatological theme "Christ, the Hope of the World." In fact the one-time leader of the Study, Hans Margull, in his carefully researched *Hope in Action*, seeks to link the ecumenical conversation with mission. While the inquiry of the 1950's came before the full bloom of involvement thinking and action as well as accent on mission in the world (and the Freedom Movement in the United States and comparable developments elsewhere) and therefore did not have the advantage of the secular soaking that has given the eschatological theologies of the 60's a new lustre, it nevertheless anticipated some of the current themes. As such, the note of hope is prominent in the radical mission thinking found in the Missionary Structure Study.

The radical questioning of the past has its roots not only in the inherited structure's manifest awkwardness relative to present reality, but also in future-oriented bearings. There is a call for "an openness to the future" that hold lightly all past and present baggage so that the unforeseen circumstances of tomorrow may be responsibly met. Suggesting the need for a church futurology, the Western European Working Group says: "With the man of today, the churches must direct their gaze, their thought, their plans to the twenty-first century, which is already dawning in all spheres of life. The decisions to be taken now have to be determined in the light of the future if the witness of service of the churches is to be at all faithful to God's world."[67] Such anticipation means planning, and "planning 'beyond our maps,' "[68] with radical openness toward what lies out ahead.

Whetted expectations are based not only on the wisest strategies of the secular discipline but also on the eschatological orientation of faith. "Mission is a matter of faith. That the end of time has come, and therefore the time for nothing less than mission, that God is calling all nations, that they are reconciled with God in Christ's death and resurrection, that ultimately in their missions the churches are not propagating themselves—all this and more is a matter of faith. . . . Mission is defined only by our hope that God will have the last word in this world."[69] An eschatological perspective which understands that the goal of history has already broken in Christ and moves to completion is the animating center of mission. We are "infected with hope," discerning and working within the signs Christ has promised.[70] Moreover, since the church has a clue about a future which is already at work now, it has "a head start . . . in loving and serving. For only through love and service does it witness to the Lordship of Christ in the interim between 'already' and 'not yet' . . . by living in it as the 'avant garde' of its contemporaries."[71]

A past that is structurally suspect, a present that commands our missionary attention yet is seen through the eyes of the future—these are the meanings of time in the aging process.

This-Worldliness

Most of the response to the this-worldly dimension of secularization has already been spelled out in the coming of age discussion.
The radical mission reacts to the this-worldly temper of the times
by translating mission into secular witness: participating in,
illumining by its faith, and where possible taking pioneering
initiative in the work of humanization. Illustrating the secular
bend of mission are such representative "Types of Missionary
Presence" as those that meet man at "points of secular strength"
among scientists, workers and artists, in the diverse worlds of
work, play and residence, in the crisis situations of the alcoholic,
the aged, and the migrant, in the social revolutions of the black
and the poor, in metropolitan and rural planning and action,
and through the development of disciplined intentional communities such as Taizé and the Iona Community.[72]
    While there are significant "vertical" referents in this list, such
as the worship concern of a Taizé or Iona, the fundamental turn
is toward the visibilities of this world and this time, and the act
of human service in the midst of them. Moreover, while religious
words, concepts and rites are part of a missionary tack that still
believes it important for the church to "acknowledge and celebrate" the One who is at work in the world, it is increasingly
being asked in radical mission circles how and where this can
be done. There is great reluctance to display the code language
of faith in secular engagement, and a kind of working assumption that the place for explicit religious talk is in the bosom
of the committed community rather than in the participative
acts of that community in the world. These directions, doubts
and indications of continued movement surface in the recent
pondering of North American members of the question "Should
we declare a moratorium on 'God-talk?' "[73]
    One proposal for doing justice to both the vertical referents
of the faith-community and the integrity of secular participa-

tion and its secular partners is the development of an understanding of "profane sacraments." "They must be forms of expression which can be understood by those *intra muros* as a theological expression (in a sacramental way) and by those *extra muros* as a human expression."[74]

This-worldliness themes embody themselves also in radical mission in the variety of strategies, tactics and tools for doing the work of *shalom*. Thus the members of the Body that live close to the human ferment become the tip-point for humanization: "the laity is the bearer of mission."[75] Again the secular disciplines, particularly sociology, become necessary companions to theology in the world of mission.[76] Also, missionary strategy proceeds inductively, without benefit of the big blueprint, and is embodied in the ad hoc form.[77] And further, the church honors the integrity of the secular calendar rather than bending it to fit its own esoteric purposes.

Thus radical mission, as it stands up to be counted for present human emergence against the tyrannies and crutches of an overbearing church and ecclesiology and a grasping institutional past, does it in the language and clothing, the word and deed, of an age whose eyes are fixed on the horizontal plane.

Footnotes

1. Although often used to describe different disciplines we shall use them interchangeably, as they are inextricably bound together in much current thought on the nature and mission of the church, and are hardly distinguishable in those positions that assert "the church is mission."

2. Wieser, *Planning for Mission* (hereafter referred to as *PM* with identification of the writer or Group), and *The Church for Others and the Church for the World, op. cit.* (hereafter referred to as *CO* with identification of the Group). For the rich ore we cannot mine by virtue of this narrowing of the range of data, see the bibliography for "The Crisis of the Congregation: A Debate," by Gabriel Fackre in *Voluntary Associations*, D. B. Robertson, ed. (Richmond, Virginia: John Knox Press, 1966), pp. 427–432.

3. North American Group, *CO*, p. 65.

4. Mathes and Western Working Group, *PM*, pp. 88–94, and Western European Working Group, *CO*, pp. 8–11.

5. Mathes, *PM*, pp. 82–88.

6. Western European Working Group, *PM*, p. 88.

7. Western Working Group, *CO*, p. 9.

8. See the World Council of Churches staff discussion in "Secularization and Conversion," *Study Encounter*, Vol. I, No. 2, 1965, pp. 55–81.

9. Western European Working Group, *CO*, p. 9.

10. *Ibid.*, p. 10.

11. Western European Working Group, *PM*, p. 89.

12. Hans Schmidt, *PM*, p. 116

13. Miroslav Heryan in *Concept*, Vol. XII. (December, 1966) *op. cit.*, p. 25.

14. J. C. Hoekendijk, *PM*, p. 47.

15. Walter Hollenweger, *PM*, p. 59.

16. Western European Working Group, *CO*, p. 10.

17. *Ibid.*, p. 10.

18. *Ibid.*, p. 10.

19. *Ibid.*, p. 10.

20. Hoekendijk, *PM*, p. 44.

21. Paul Kramer, *Concept*, Vol. V. (Sept. 1963) *op. cit.*, p. 35.

22. Hoekeddijk, *PM*, p. 47. See also Western European Working Group, *PM*, p. 141.

23. Related to a version of the Barthian position which holds that men are in some sense already in the New Mankind (enlarged Working Group, Bossey, *PM*, p. 54), and to the revulsion against the crass methods of a high-powered evangelism. (Western European Working Group, *PM*, p. 141.)

24. Western European Working Group, *PM*, p. 141. See also, *CO*, p. 12.

25. Eastern European Working Group, *PM*, p. 163.

26. Werner Krusche, *PM*, p. 177.

27. Western European Working Group, *PM*, p. 25.

28. Western European Working Group, *CO*, p. 30.

29. Hoekendijk, *Concept*, Vol. VII, *op. cit.*, p. 6.

30. For a similar ecclesiological tack in other quarters see Charles Davis' comments in *A Question of Conscience, op. cit.*, pp. 220–239; 62–117.

31. Hoekendijk, *PM*, p. 41.

32. North American Working Group, *CO*, p. 62.

33. *Ibid.*, pp. 77–78.

34. Western European Working Group, *PM*, p. 80.

35. Hoekendijk, *PM*, p. 43.

36. *Ibid.* The words are incorporated into the Western European Working Group's final report, *CO*, p. 14.

37. Hoekendijk, *PM*, p. 43. See also Western European Working Group's report, *CO*, p. 14.

38. Western European Working Group, *CO*, p. 15. See also Hoekendijk, *PM*, pp. 51–52 and North American Working Group, *CO*, p. 79.

39. *Ibid.*, pp. 16–17.

40. Western European Working Group, p. 17.

41. Hoekendijk, *Concept*, Vol. VII, *op. cit.*, p. 4.

42. North American Working Group, *CO*, p. 70.

43. Western European Working Group, *CO*, p. 43 and the concept *pars pro toto*. *Ibid.*, pp. 18, 26.

44. Enlarged Working Committee, *PM*, p. 55.

45. Gibson Winter, *The New Creation as Metropolis*, *op. cit.*, and *Concept*, Vol. VII, *op. cit.*, *passim*.

46. Enlarged Working Group, *PM*, p. 55.

47. Western European Working Group, *CO*, p. 37.

48. Hollenweger, *PM*, p. 59.

49. George Casalis, *PM*, pp. 124–125.

50. Casalis, *PM*, p. 124.

51. Western European Working Group, *PM*, p. 126.

52. Hoekendijk, *PM*, p. 44.

53. Casalis, *PM*, p. 124.

54. Theodore Erickson, *Concept*, IX. (July, 1965), p. 6.

55. Enlarged Working Committee, *PM*, p. 166.

56. Winter, *The New Creation as Metropolis*, *op. cit.*, p. 105.

57. *Concept*, IX, *op. cit.*, p. 31.

58. Hoekendijk, *Concept*, Vol. VII, *op. cit.*, p. 7.

59. Hoekendijk, *PM*, p. 131.

60. Hoekendijk, *PM*, p. 134, incorporated into final report of Western European Working Group, *PM*, p. 19.

61. See Fackre, "The Crisis of the Congregation: A Debate," *op. cit.*, pp. 279–280.

62. Colin Williams, *Where in the World* (New York: National Council of Churches, 1963), pp. 7–17.

63. Hugh C. White and Robert Batchelder, *Mission to Metropolis*, Occasional Paper No. 7, Detroit Industrial Mission, pp. 8–9.

64. Mark Gibbs and T. Ralph Morton, *God's Frozen People* (Philadelphia: Westminster Press, 1965), pp. 38, 41–44, 69–74. Weiser, *PM*, p. 12.

65. Fackre, "Crisis of the Congregation: A Debate," *op. cit.*, pp. 279–281.

66. Schmidt, *PM*, p. 137.
67. Western European Working Group, *CO* p. 38.
68. *Ibid.*, p. 39.
69. Hans Margull, *PM*, pp. 33–34.
70. Western Working Group, *PM*, p. 81.
71. *Ibid.* pp. 81–82.
72. Enlarged Working Committee, *PM*, pp. 160–161.
73. Report of the Enlarged North American Committee, Oct. 1967.
74. Hollenweger, *PM*, pp. 60–61.
75. North American Working Group, *CO*, p. 80.
76. Hoekendijk, *PM*, p. 131; J. G. Davies, *Ibid.*, p. 7; Mathes, *PM*, p. 88.
77. Hoekendijk, *PM*, p. 47; Wieser, *PM*, p. 16.

PART II

POST-RADICAL IMAGES OF THE DIVINE-HUMAN RELATIONSHIP

5

GOD AS FATHER

The radical theology repudiates the Oriental potentate of traditional God-talk. Honor accorded to a Deity who keeps his own counsel and benignly orders the course of cosmic affairs means abasement. The freedom of man demands the death of God.

"Big daddy is dead" reads the graffiti wall at the renewal conference.[1] And so he is, not only in styles of church leadership but also in theological formulations. We begin our attempt to work at a response to secularization by agreement with the intent of the radical theologians. There is no room in Christian faith for divine tyrannies or human dependencies in a world struggling to come of age.

The historical context of current protests against divine autocracy is an important factor in their emergence: (1) the political and social ferment of the first half of the century and (2) the thought forms through which many in the Christian community addressed these times. We are thinking, in the first case, of the rise of "isms" of one sort or another which brought the world to the brink of disaster. Out of this matrix rose the second, the response of the crisis theologies. Radical theologians trace their own lineage to the dominant theologians of this period.[2] Some critics find unacknowledged links.[3] There seems to be another kind of interrelationship as well, having to do with the style and claims of the ancestors. That is, radical theology is a reaction against the *fortress mentality* of a church which saw itself in a life and death struggle with demonic forces.

No matter where one looks along the spectrum of yesterday's regnant church thought, there is found a thunderbolt theology. God's freedom was defended against an ugly human reach; man's idols had to be exposed for what they were, and shattered; the kingly Christ ruled even in the face of human pretension and disobedience; grace invaded man's heart and history; God overpowered man in divine-human encounters; divine initiative was honored and human initiative suspect; the church's rock would stand against the heaviest assaults of the world; even the most ardent denials of unbelief could not harm the Deity, for he was present in the very act of doubt. Men of faith spoke little of vulnerability, weakness, defencelessness. The cross itself was the sword of victory. The dialectical theologies with their militant imagery were the response of an embattled church. Divine triumphalism and human frailty were the theological orders of the day.

What is the effect of these assertions about a bold God and a bashful man on a new generation which finds the roles reversed: When science-technology brings man close to the creation, extension and direction of life, functions once assigned to providence? When the thirst for "honesty" and the empirical spirit meet to demand that old authorities have their credentials carefully checked? When men look with hope for the possibilities rather than the impossibilities in history, and see evidences of human creativity as well as destructivity? In the latter half of the century we live with the sounds of men and the silences of God. And they are bound to have their effect on Christian thought.

The kind of impact on theology is almost predictable. When an assertive soteriology speaks about a divine "I" that encounters a human "thou" in an overpowering way, a newer voice asks, "Really? Let's check that out." When the needle of an older theology gets stuck on the "no" God says to a sinful world, a new hand changes the record. When confident claims are made about a resurrection victory, inquiries are set in motion on whether this is in fact so, and translation made from divine to human categories. Perennial human doubts about God, prompted by the fact of massive evil, are joined by candid post-war empiricism and the cutting back of theological claims to fit human reality. The inescapability of God in declamations from Barth to Tillich pass into a "new debate about God."[4] Thus when the affirmations of yesterday's fortress posture meet a new generation with different sensitivities and a new agenda, a theological credibility gap opens. Prophets of the new time now rush to the defense of man and hail the death of his oppressor.

The bold theologies of the previous generation did not, of course, represent an isolated event in the history of Christian thought. They were, truly, *neo*-orthodoxies in the sense that the triumphalism of traditional theology re-surfaced to do battle in the arena of modern totalitarianism. (The crisis theologians, in fact, modified the divine autocracies of conventional thought in significant ways with their accents of witness in the world under the Lordship of Christ, openness to cultural ferment on the left wing of the movement, and later a fresh interest in the "humanity of God.")[5] We do not have to do with an oddity evoked by a period of historical horror, but rather the underscoring of the note that has been a constant in Christian thinking: God is a "winner" and man is a "loser." Therefore, we view the radical theology as more than an unlooked for "side effect" of its predecessor's cures. It is as a protest against a whole era of church reflection. As such, it is an attempt to come to terms with the phenomenon that increasingly marks the boundary of our age, setting it apart from all previous eras, rapid secularization. We address ourselves here, in particular, to the coming-of-age dimension.

The radical theology is intensely aware of man's developing capacity to fashion his own nature and destiny, and challenges any would-be tyrannies that would abort this emergence. It views traditional theology's declaration that man must be submissive to, and dependent upon, extra-terrestrial power and wisdom as an invitation to immaturity. Yes, conventional theology may now be more chastened, granting autonomy to man's efforts to control the physical universe, although fertility deities still reign in the church underworld. But the divine imperialism is still at work in sophisticated existential perspectives which claim that man can cope with anxiety, meaninglessness, guilt and death only by the aid of faith. It is to be found in the modern moralist who holds that personal integrity and social healing are possible only through commitment to a transcendent that rescues from fanaticisms and idolatries, or assures the dignity of personhood, or supports such precious and elusive values as depth and mystery. And in a thousand ways it makes its presence felt in the churches in the guarantees that benefits running from peace of mind to the cure of marital infidelity can be found only in religious belief.

What do these claims mean, asks the radical theology, except that man is still locked into his nursery? Before the God of religion he is still a child who must run to "big daddy" for his allowances. And how is he to grow up and claim his right to be a man? The Father must die if the son is to come into his own.

The Waiting Father

Must God die if man is to live? Can human maturation be celebrated and worked for only if Deity passes away? We shall explore another option. Our major concern is not to mount a shattering attack on the radical theology. The last thing we need at this juncture of the theological enterprise is a new triumphalism. Rather, we see the radical theology as a kind of laboratory experiment conducted in one of the church's research centers. The rhetoric generated within its ranks and that hurled from beyond at it ought not to prevent us from seeing the radical theologians as companions in a common inquiry. They are members of the faith-community who are scouting the new secular terrain on which we are called to live.[6] We have already been deeply influenced by what they have found, however excited and impressionistic their reports have been. The question now is, what do we make of their data? From the perspective of its story, what is to be the church's response to secularization?

We shall take hold of these questions by exploring a central Christian image: fatherhood. We do this for several reasons. First, the figure of father is a target of the protest against divine autocracy. It suggests the childlike dependence of man on a benign and/or tyrannical parent. Second, it is such a pervasive metaphor in the New Testament, in historic Christian reflection on the nature of God, and in the day-to-day life of the church (the Lord's prayer, for example), that any restatement of the concept of God must come to terms with it. Third, the image of fatherhood has within it a powerful clue to a Christian response to secularization. Let us examine it, looking at the historical context, the biblical usage, and its viability as contemporary language of faith.

The Historical Context

As Riesman and others have observed, there is a correlation between the demographic curve and cultural style.[7] Population factors, specifically longevity, are bound to have their influence on cultural understanding of paternity. Thus when the life span is shortened by the toll disease takes on adults, the sibling knows the father essentially in his early relationships of dependency and submissiveness. However, in times of lengthened life expectancy, the father is still actively in evidence after the offspring has come "into his own." Thus in modern societies characterized by increasing life spans, new sets of post-maturity parent-child relationships must be honed.

The dependency concept of paternity is, of course, particularly true of patriarchal societies. Here, even after maturity, the sibling tends to stand in a submissive relationship, awaiting the death of the father before genuine emergence can be attained. And emergence brings with it the assumption of some prerogatives of the now deceased authority figure. Intra-cultural dynamics often resemble the family pattern. Thus in patriarchal settings the class and race structure, teacher-student, man-woman, governor-governed relationships tend to follow the authority-submission design.

Theology and popular belief borrowed the sociological categories. God the Father became the benevolent sovereign who presided over the affairs of the human family and over the table of the household of faith. The role of both the man of faith and the man of the world was the submissiveness appropriate to an obedient child. Although the term "father" did not come into wide usage as a description of the clergy until the nineteenth century[8] (it appeared very early, of course, in the title "pope"), nevertheless the authority-submission pattern was a long-time characteristic of the clergy-lay relationship. The church's self-understanding of its role vis-à-vis society as the parental figure (more "mother" than "father" in this case) guarding its children's spiritual, moral, and sometimes political welfare is further illustration of the power of the cultural mold.

Who is "father" today? Longevity contributes to new dimensions of paternal identity. The son knows the father in a bond that extends far beyond the period of early nurture. In the lengthy span that stretches beyond post-maturity, the father must come to terms with his progeny in a role that is "without authority." He can neither force his will on the "child," nor is he called upon regularly to "bail him out." And the offspring now has the opportunity to come to know the father in the relationship free of the agendas of need or obeisance that determined the pre-coming of age bond.

Woven into the changing age patterns in our own culture are the massive sociological shifts taking place that affect the family.

Thus, with the passing of the family's productive, educational, recreational and medical functions, absorbed as they are by public and other private institutions, the mass media, peer groups, etc., the parent exercises less and less effective power in the shaping of his or her offspring. Adding to this are the strong democratizing currents signalling the emergence of youth as partners in the cultural enterprise. Thus the young are consumers to be reckoned with. Again, the new technology puts into their hands tools to break out of the prisons in which old authorities have kept them locked; the car and motorcycle, the mass media, the music cults provide instruments of expression and resistance against inherited behavior and value patterns. Further, youth no longer stands still for directives from the political or educational establishments, as evidence the protest movements against the war and the draft, and the surge forward to gain a voice in the decision-making processes of higher education. In the midst of all this, the father as a controller of his children's destiny wilts as a symbol of parentage. Divested of his role as source, will the modern parent re-emerge instead as *resource?* Will the father see his role now as friend and counsellor? We cannot here go into the new sociological twists and turns that may lay around the next corner. Our concern is rather to explore tangents in human experience that offer clues to re-conceptualizing divine paternity.

Dietrich Bonhoeffer has stirred a generation to reflect on secularization. He has also offered some tantalizing suggestions on Christian response to it. An understanding of divine fatherhood played an important part in his effort to interpret man's coming of age. In fact his biographer and friend, Eberhard Bethge, believes that his wrestle with the filial cry of dereliction (Mark 14:15)is a key to his struggle.[9] It is not our business here to try to ferret out what Bonhoeffer "really meant."[10] It is enough to say that his brooding over the themes of crucifixion, human and divine, have deeply influenced what follows.

The cross has meant many different things to the church at

different times. It has been a call to suffering and martyrdom, the sword by which Christ mortally wounds the powers of sin, death, and the devil, the sacrifice and substitute for guilt-laden man. Is there another facet of its truth that can be seen from our fresh angle of secularization? One that, in turn, has a word to speak to it?

Good Friday, and in particular its mournful closing cry, illumines the meaning of divine fatherhood and filial maturity. This moment of dereliction tells us of Christ's willingness to share the very depths of our own human estrangement from God. But, like the parable of the prodigal son, does it not also tell us something crucial about the Father?

It is a word about a "waiting Father."[11] In striking parallel to the father who remained at home while his son struggled in freedom in a far country to "come to himself," here on the cross we learn of a kind of paternal love which "only stands and waits" in the moment of filial misery. "My God, my God, why have you forsaken me?" But how else could the son's messianic task have been fulfilled except that it be an act of a ripened freedom? The cry of desolation meant more than a son expecting to be relieved at the last minute of the mandate of crucifixion. (Although that is a possible interpretation consonant with Christ's full humanity, it would seem that the struggle over accepting the mission was fought and won at Gethsemane.) The anguish on the day of execution is bound up with the absence of the Father. Where was the supportive "abba," the "daddy"[12] whose never-failing presence gave its paternal assurances in the most critical hours? The tellers of the Christian story are saying in this brutally honest passage, which weathered all the editorial softeners, that the Father had indeed chosen to absent himself in the time of testing. Faith offered no cushion or consolation. Here was to be the demonstration of adulthood. Thus along with the experience of the estranging wrath of God against human sin that Christ underwent in his torment (this older interpretation is not necessarily cancelled by the present attempt to see Good Friday from the perspective of secularization), there is the call to the son to accept his mission for himself, unsupported by the Father's everlasting arms. The cry of dereliction was the agony of freedom.

The love of God is a fatherly love precisely because it granted this fearful freedom to the son as he faced his vocation. The mission of the cross had to be lived out in the autonomy of adulthood if it was to be "freely laid down." We are concerned here, however, to underscore the fatherly luster disclosed on Good Friday, a compassion manifesting itself in its power and will to withdraw the helping hand at the critical moment. Robinson draws attention to a searching comment by Kierkegaard on the character of divine omnipotence:[13]

The greatest good which can be done to any being . . . is to make it free. In order to do that, omnipotence is necessary. That will sound curious, since of all things omnipotence, so at least it would seem, should make things dependent. But if we rightly consider omnipotence, then clearly it must have the quality of so taking itself back in the very manifestation of its all-powerfulness that the results of this act of the omnipotent can be independent. . . . Omnipotence alone can take itself back while giving, and this relationship is nothing less but the independence of the recipient. God's omnipotence is therefore his goodness. For goodness means to give absolutely, yet in such a way that by taking oneself back one makes the recipient independent. . . . It is only a miserable and worldly picture of the dialectic of power to say that it becomes greater in proportion that it can compel and make things dependent. . . . It is to him who makes me independent, while he nevertheless retained everything, that I owe all things.[14]

While Kierkegaard is speaking of the fatherly love at work in creation, Simone Weil relates the divine creativity to the passion, sketching as well on the broader canvas of universal faith:

On God's part creation is not an act of self-expansion but of restraint and renunciation. . . . God accepted this diminution. He emptied a part of his being from himself. He had already emptied himself in this act of his divinity; that is why St. John says that the Lamb had been slain from the beginning of the world. . . . God denied himself for our sakes in order to give us the possibility of denying ourselves for him. This response, this echo, which it is in our power to refuse, is the only possible justification for the folly of love of the creative act. The religions which have a conception of this renunciation, this voluntary distance, this voluntary effacement of God, his apparent absence and his secret presence here below are true religion. . . . The religions which represent divinity as commanding wherever it has the power to do so are false.[15]

We have a picture on the cross of one who waits while another struggles and dies. What kind of Deity can this be? Yes, he may seek a fully human decision from his son. But are there not here the contours of a cruelty that is worse than the indulgence of an overprotective parent? We do not have to do here with a common act of coming of age, such as starting one's own bank account, or choosing a mate, or a first ballot cast. A son's life is at stake. How can a father stand by and do nothing when the last breath is being torn from his own flesh and blood? What an abomination is this passivity! The comment of the mission field inquirer on the loud preaching of a penal theory of the atonement that propitiates an angry Deity by the suffering of innocence seems appropriate here as well: "I love Jesus, but I hate God."

As if this weren't bad enough, there is further doubt about this paternal reticence when it comes to the devotion appropriate to a God so portrayed. What is the response to a God who does nothing, whose highest quality is the will and power to let men be? It would seem that we have come up against a "still-life deity" whose benign withdrawal can only evoke an abstract contemplation or even an awed horror.[16] Or perhaps such a God deserves only the "so what" appropriate to one who, in his own Good Friday way, has died the death of a thousand qualifications.[17]

The Serving Father

The chasm between the heart of the Father and the work of the Son cleft by uncritical substitutionary thinking, to which Aulen has pointed,[18] could well reappear in a theology of the waiting Father. But the biblical data will not let it be so: "God was in Christ reconciling the world. . . ." (2 Corinthians 5:1). It is God himself who is present in the free decision of Christ to live out the adult choice of a full humanity. The Father was one with the Son, not only in unity of purpose but co-incidence of being, "without confusion, without change, without separation, without division."[19] The Father was no grandstand spectator to this anguish. In the Son's cry can be heard the Father's own voice; Christ's perfect freedom was God's service.

There is a weak analogy to the co-presence of the cross in human father-son relationships. Thus, it is possible to see the lineaments of paternal character in an offspring's thought and behavior, traceable to heredity or family environment. "Like father like son." But in the final analysis there is no neat sorting out of the anomaly of mutual penetration. The difficulty of coming to terms with it is abundantly illustrated in the Christological debates of the early centuries of the church. Could Christ be both God and man and yet one? Of course not, said men who sought to be faithful to their experience and reason. He's got to be one or the other, or perhaps a melting down or parcelling out of each. As the long line of Ebionisms, Docetisms, and their heirs, passed in review, the faith-community agonizingly concluded that something was missing in each. The richness of the biblical data was impoverished. Either the full humanity or the divine reality were called into question by the clever formulations. The mainstream of the church had no neat solution of its own, but it could recognize what was no solution.

The best it could do was to affirm the ingredients of God-language and man-language, fully honored and living in union with one another: Christ truly God, truly man, truly one.

To take this strange duality seriously is to see it at work on the cross as well as in the crib. The earthing of God at Calvary as well as at Bethlehem means that without ceasing to be free from man he is also for and in man. And that means for and and in this desolated, deserted, and crucified human being. Father and Son are one in freedom and service.

The Suffering Father

What is the service rendered in and through the Son? It is the self-gift of crucified love. Men of daring piety have not hesitated to see it so. From Tertullian's dramatic paradoxes of divine humiliation to Georgia Harkness' poetic reflection on "The Agony of God," Christians have pondered the meaning of God's self-effacement. Bernard speculates: "Just as pure truth is seen only with a pure heart, so a brother's misery is truly felt with a miserable heart. But in order to have a miserable heart because of another's misery, you must first know your own; so that you may find your neighbour's mind in your own and know from yourself how to help him by the example of the Saviour who willed his passion in order to learn compassion; his misery to learn commiseration."[20] The language of devotion, sometimes with the underpinning of a theory of the "communication of idioms," has pressed to the very border of the semantic world of death of God theology, although not its universe of meaning. Thus Eckhart can say that "God . . . passes away," and Tertullian speak of the divine demise on Calvary. Even the most orthodox are not so restrained that a Gilson cannot point to "A God dead on the cross,"[21] and in a famous hymn Isaac Watts puts into a thousand mouths, "When God the mighty Maker died for man the creature's sin."[22] And it was left to Johann Rist's passion hymn, some maintain, to provide food for Hegel to introduce the phrase "God is dead" into the stream of modern Western religious thought, to be appropriated later by Nietzsche, and now the radical theology.[23]

Bonhoeffer himself brings together the strands of devotion and reflection in moving lines on both the suffering and death of God:

> Men go to God when he is sore bestead,
> Find him poor and scorned, without shelter or bread,
> Whelmed under weight of the wicked, the weak, the dead:
> Christians stand by God in his hour of grieving.
>
> God goeth to every man when sore bestead,
> Feedeth body and spirit with his bread,
> For Christians, heathens alike he hangeth dead:
> And both alike forgiving.[24]

What now have we done to the God of faith? Some will surely demand to know. Are we accepting the ancient modalist heresy of patripassionism? Are we putting the "god-ness" of God in doubt by questioning his "impassibility"? Our impulse may be to turn aside such inquisitors by scoffing at the over-subtle intricacies of another era of theology. However, it does no harm to "read the minutes of the last meeting." In fact there are errors identified by other ages which fresh efforts to work at thinking about God cannot lightly dismiss.

Modalistic patripassionism was seen as a blind alley because of the sequential trinity it presupposed. God's suffering was that of a Father who had disappeared into the Son in a metamorphosis that erased his freedom to continue as Father. Any reformulation that speaks of divine suffering must honor the integrity of both Father and Son, neither being subject to dissolution or reduction. The contemporary relevance of this theme may perhaps be seen, apart from the specific issue of divine suffering, in the light it sheds on the position of Altizer. The passing of transcendence into Jesus and the presence in the world now of the Incarnate Word appear to be a kind of modalism of the second

Person (or third Person, if the Joachim of Floris lead is followed).

At the heart of the church's classic defense of God's impassibility is the conviction that God cannot be toppled as God by activity on earthly terrain, nor can his purpose be deflected by human happenings. He is an unswerving God whose being and will are steadfast love.[25] That note surely cannot be muted in any reconsideration of the question of divine suffering.

The intellectual structure used for many centuries to preserve these insights about the integrity and steadfastness of the Christian God, however, shows signs of decay. Its continued housing of Christian beliefs will not stand the strain of the remodelling that must be done in the light of secularization and other new developments. One form now suspect is the Greek value of passionless detachment. This agenda is hidden in classic talk of God as impassible. How could he be subject to the pain of involvement in the transient, when the highest good was an invulnerability to the moil and toil of the passing world? To suggest that there was resonance in God to human anguish was to call his deity into question. Goodness *is* the eternal serenity of disaffiliation with temporal decay. So it was maintained.

Another time-bound vehicle of faith is the ancient conception of fatherhood. If patriarchal autocracy was the order of the day in family relationships, could the understanding of the heavenly Father remain uninfluenced by this style? It evidently did not, for the church could no more conceive of alongsidedness and vulnerability in Deity than it could in the head of the human household.

Our problem then is to disentanagle the perceptions of classic thought from the form in which it took shape, and also to ask whether there might not be a new glint of truth that shines through the event of Calvary when viewed from the perspective of twentieth century coming of age thought forms. And even as we now use patterns of thought generated in a time of secularization, we must be prepared to recognize their relativity and keep them open to future corrections, enlargements, and displacements.[26]

To believe that the Father suffers in and through the desolation of his Son does not mean the extinction or metamorphosis of God. That is, not if we take seriously the paradoxical distancing of Father from Son that must be affirmed with passion equal to the affirmation of his presence on Calvary. God remains free to be himself even as he bends to participate in the action on the cross. Modalisms old and new which call this "freedom from" into question in the interests of asserting God's "freedom for" man in Christ cannot do justice to the integrity of the Father.[27]

But in what does this "freedom to be himself" consist? Is it some serene aseity at the center of his being which remains untouched by the cross of his Son, or the thorns and burdens of his other sons? The only way into the being of God is through his doing. The central act is there for the eye of faith: suffering and crucified love. What happened on a hill happens as well in the divine depths, as is expressed in the idiom of Christian devotion, "there is a cross in the heart of God." It is not an aloof, walled-in power that we find at the center of things but an open, vulnerable "powerlessness." Or more exactly the character of the divine power is its strength to expose its nerve-ends to human abrasiveness. God is love.

Does this kind of open relatedness to the painful changing scene jeopardize divinity itself? If the sorrows of the world really make a difference to him, in particular if they penetrate to the further reaches of his life in the suffering of Jesus, do these relationships not then control his very destiny, making or breaking him? "The suffering of God does not make any difference to his being God. . . . Fully personal love and fully loving personalness might be absolutely capable of being completely open to all the effects resulting from any relations whatever without making any difference at all to the nature, pattern, purpose, and effectiveness of this love."[28] If the inner character of God were autocratic, detached power, openness would indeed be an invasion of Deity. But it is not autocracy with which we have ultimately to do. Love is not hurt by vulnerability; it expresses itself through it. In fact, love cannot be what it is meant to be without it. Suffering participation in the woes of men is the enfleshment of God's own deepest Self.

Will this love conquer? The questioners of God's passibility knew the risk of talk of divine vulnerability and drew back. But the Story does not end on Good Friday. The eyes of faith saw, and see, a vindicated love. And sometimes even the eyes of sight discern here and there broken traces of the victories of suffering compassion. But there are no guarantees, and the evidence is strong that total self-surrender will not be repaid in kind in this world; that perfect love remains nailed to a tree. In the final analysis, it is the resurrection-faith alone which anchors the celebrative conviction that the divine love can neither be quenched nor defeated.

"Man's extremity is God's opportunity." Those are true words if their usual meaning is reversed. God does not exploit human weakness; he does not wait until man is beaten to his knees and then arrive with marine-like gusto to rout the oppressor. He comes himself, as the desolate One. His power is revealed in the weak things of the world and the despised that find their paradigm in the man Jesus, spit on, nailed down, forsaken, dying. Tokens of the way of humiliation are found in the fragile vehicles of his love, lowly water, wine, and bread for his sacraments, flawed human literature for his Book, a restless, incurved company for his church.

Vulnerability is to be found in the conceptual tools of faith, as illustrated in the idea of fatherhood we have been examining. Some will be offended by the analogical movement from the dynamics of human growth and paternity to the life of God himself. Is it not the other way around? Does not God's fatherhood provide the pattern for a man, instead of the divine relying on this finite, sinful form? Yes, God's fatherly love is the model and mandate for his human counterpart. But the term "father" does not exist in the New Testament essentially to provide an object lesson for family relationships. It is an image used to illumine the heart of the gospel. That is not the blasphemy but a marvel. Baptized and cleansed it must be, but for all that borrowed from the raw data of human affairs. This daring vulnerability is consonant with the willingness of God to risk his glory in the frailties of man. It is the humiliation theme enfleshed in language.

Another thorn of vulnerability, especially for the triumphalist temper which is always busy securing the battlement of faith, is the historical rootage of the gospel. Long ago Kierkegaard reflected on the offence of resting the whole edifice of Christian conviction on the belief in a happening so susceptible to the acids of historical doubt and inquiry.[29] Imposing efforts have been put forth to secure the truth of Christianity against the assailability of this base, conceptions of faith that lay claim to validity quite apart from the actual nature or existence of the historical Jesus. But is not the genius of Christian faith that it *does* stand or fall with the reality of a scandalous particularity? If it could be demonstrated that we have to do with a fairy tale at the center of the Story—that there really was no Jesus—then the game would surely be up. Faith cannot armor-plate itself against this contingency. Its truth is bound up with its willingness to live out in the open, unprotected from the risks of temporality.[30]

The same acceptance of the weak things of the world as *modus operandi* is at work in the nature of faith itself. The tender shoot of belief takes roots and lives in the ambiguities of time and space. The strong and well-fed may insist that faith can flower in the most inhospitable soil. However, as Feuerbach has said, man thinks differently depending on whether he lives in a hut or a palace. Faith takes the same risks. A mind and body distracted by the cares of the world, the hurts of hunger and poverty, the wounds of the battlefield, the scars of slavery and hate, or the sophisticated bio-control of 1984, will not bring forth a hundredfold in Christian belief. Faith is not exempt from the rules of history's playing field.

Humiliation is the way of the Christian God who discloses his forsakenness on the cross. And here there is a point of meeting between the suffering Father and the waiting Father. The Father whose withdrawal from the Son when every support from heavenly arsenals seemed to be called for is the same Father who comes not in might but as the powerlessness of a suffering Son. And should it not be so? It is the one Father who in both concealment and disclosure turns the face of love to men.

A Preliminary Comment on Ethics

It would seem natural to draw the conclusion from our discussion of the suffering of God that the Christian is called to a like vocation. Is it not logical for commitment to the divine crucifixion to find expression in the literal embodiment of cheek-turning, second-mile self-abnegation and the disavowal of the use of any power but that of exemplified suffering? It would seem that Bonhoeffer, at one phase of his development, moved toward visible humiliation and Ghandian non-violence as the implicate of his own "condescension-theology." While it is true that his participation in the plot to overthrow Hitler and other underground involvement shows a departure from an absolute pacifism, there is still a question whether his "man for others" ethics does not lend itself to an interpretation of "a life of worldly powerlessness."

Alisdair MacIntyre links Bonhoeffer's convictions concerning the divine suffering to an ethics of powerlessness, and raises an acute question:

So the distinction between secular, atheistic man and Christian man is that the latter acknowledges his powerlessness in his concern for others. But what would it be like to do this in the world of today, of the welfare state and of the underdeveloped countries, facing the patterns of world revolution? One gets from Bonhoeffer's writings no clear picture of what type of action he would be recommending now in 1963, but one gets the clearest picture of what Bonhoeffer means if one sees it in the context out of which he wrote. For in Nazi Germany in the Europe of the thirties, the Christian role was at best one of suffering witness. The Nazi regress to gods of race made relevant a Christian regress to a witness of the catacombs and of the martyrs. There was available then a simple form in which to relive Christ's passion. Bonhoeffer lived it. And in all situations where nothing else remains for Christians this remains. But what has this Christianity to say not of powerlessness, but of handling power? Nothing; and hence the oddity of trying to reissue Bonhoeffer's message in our world.[31]

MacIntyre blurs his point by some later caustic references to how the suffering theme could apply to the church's relationship to power, such as chaplains for the West German army and the Anglican Church's switch from "gilt-edge to equities." The church's stewardship of its own institutional power is, of course, a crucial question, but the heart of the matter is the style appropriate to worldly power and its employment in "the patterns of world revolution" earlier noted in the quotation. This question comes home in the current struggle for human rights in the United States and throughout the world. For example, it has been difficult for proponents of ideological non-violence to come to terms with the "black power" motif. After initial resistance, many have indeed accepted it in the sense of economic and political pressure and as a symbol of dignity in the face of white stereotypes. However, they have drawn the line at physical power, rejecting violence in any form, including self-defence. Others who hold to a total ideology of powerlessness reject any endorsement of pressure, interpreting it as an expression of destructive self-assertiveness.

The problem with a simplistic translation of divine suffering into human behavior is that at this juncture of the freedom revolution power appears to be a crucial agent of humanization.

Segregationists are not moved by moral suasion but do respond to economic, political and social power. Hence the emergence of economic sanctions, voting blocs, public demonstrations and the encouragement of black solidarity and identity. Even though these are non-violent weapons, by no stretch of the imagination can they be called an exercise in powerlessness. They are rather the wise use of power by minorities in a mass society.

And what of the defense of innocent life and limb? And further, what of those countries in which the totalitarian structures forbid the redress of grievances through the processes of law and by the non-violent use of power? Is force to be ruled out *a priori* in faithfulness to the Christian accent on humiliation? We shall have to give sustained attention to the issues buried in these questions in the section that deals with ethics. Suffice to say, at this point a straight line cannot be drawn from the divine defencelessness to an absolute mandate that human power of any and every kind be disavowed in any and every circumstance. The functional difficulties of an ideology of powerlessness, however, do not discount the theme of God's suffering or even the final vision of a world in which cheek-turning love is the standard of human behaviour. It means that the relationship will have to be explored and stated with a care that avoids packaged formulas being exported neatly from heaven to earth. Such an inquiry we will attempt in chapter ten.

The Waiting Father and His World-Come-of-Age

"We believe in God . . . the Father of our Lord Jesus Christ, and our Father."[32] So declares a contemporary statement of faith. The fatherly love for the Son reaches toward other children. The believer, yes, but those as well who do not acknowledge their paternity, who also stand in relationship with One who waits, serves, and suffers. In exploring this Fatherhood we work at a response to man's coming of age that seeks to do justice to both the facts of secularization and the faith in the Christian Story.

The Father whose patient love withholds its presence and support on Calvary is the same Father who refuses to control or "bail out" mankind on his pilgrimage toward maturity. God's silence is his consent to man's quest for self-determination. The Father wills humanity to grow up, to take responsibility for its own life and future. He wants a man to be a man!

For those who honor a waiting Father, secularization is a time for celebration. Man has reached his majority. And what are the signs of twenty-one? They are the powers man now has to seize and shape his own nature and destiny. Modern science-technology gives him the ability to do the things formerly assigned to fate or providence, from the raising of crops to the cure of disease, and now to come within range of the inner circle so long reserved for divinity: the creation, extension, direction and definition of life itself.[33] With this new human creativity, as the radical theology rightly asserts, man must cease to cringe before, or run for solutions to, a Deity in whose jealous hands the reins of history are thought to be held.

But this new human ferment and call to liberation is not the death knell of God. No more so than is the silence of the Father at the Son's moment of decision on the cross. No more so than the reticence of a human father encouraging his offspring to take the first steps into maturity. It is the Father's own will to let his child the world come into its own. In its press forward to maturity it is called to follow in the steps of Christ, the pioneer of coming of age, the first of a new race to go that way. He knew the agony of withdrawal and accepted his vocation to freedom and the Father who beckoned toward it. Maturity in Christ for the man of faith come of age is to "grow up into him" to a "mature manhood" in which freedom and Fatherhood are seen not as competitors but companions.

A maturity in sonship which honors both the call to manhood and the Father who is its source is a difficult pilgrimage. Whether it is achieved depends both on the willingness of the father to encourage it and the son to seize it, yet in such a way as not to erase the reality of the father. Paternalism and autocracy stunt the son's growth by enchaining freedom and producing a permanent childishness in the offspring. The same authority-posture in the father sows the seeds of a bitter adolescence in more independent spirits. To break out of the tyranny and dependency relations, the eager youth must drive against his benign oppressor so hard that he seems to want to destroy him. The angry face of adolescent rebellion, appearing to cry, "Dad, you're dead!" can be readily forecast.

Traditional theology and piety, and the more contemporary crisis theology, have portrayed the Father as jealous of his authority and continuing to lord it over his creation. It has shown little disposition to reconsider its ascension-submission mold in response to even the dramatic coming of age development of the twentieth century. What else is to be expected from the meeting of a youthful vitality chaffing at the bit for new freedom to use new power with a reluctant parent at home in his role of dominance and treating the thrust toward adulthood as insolence? The death of God theology is the predictable ideology of independence. We have no one to blame but ourselves for its funereal rhetoric. Its intention to deal with tyranny and crutch must be fully honored.

The parallel to struggles against horizontal rather than vertical patriarchies (although often with accents of the latter mixed in with the former) is instructive. Consider the revolts of the VLPs (very little persons) against the VIPs: the press forward of citizen, worker, woman, youth, black, poor, and the aged to come into their own in the face of old despotisms.[34] Sometimes, frustrated by enemies not easily dislodged, the surge to down the old tyranny may turn into something other than the introduction of participatory democracy. Rather than bring the old authority down from his pedestal and into the circle of common partnership, there may emerge the wish to destroy the old tyranny and replace it with another. The VLP himself seeks to become the VIP. Black messianism replaces the goal of reconciliation, the dictatorship of the proletariat is seen as the only way to social democracy, the "now" generation repudiates its ancestry, etc. Again, the intransigence of old establishments does its work in laying the foundations for new hegemonies. A radical turning of the tables is bred by the resistance of our own patriarchies.

But a new megalomania can be no final answer to an old one, be it in the arena of theology or social change. The option we sketch here is not adolescent scorn for the father, or a revolt that cries for the head of the old king only to replace it with a new candidate for the throne. The alternative to tyranny is maturity and partnership. Continuing our father-son figure as it touches on the theological question, we are looking for a post-adolescent growth in which the son acknowledges the father's right to be, and a post-patriarchal maturity in which the father encourages the son's self-determination. This is a union in which each affirms the integrity of the other and seeks to come into a living relationship with the co-partner. It presses beyond imperialism and monologues, old and new, to a participatory life together, a dialogical bond in which the man-ness of man is celebrated in union with the god-ness of God.[35]

We see the battle fought out in the early centuries concerning the integrity of man language and God language in Christology (and its sequels in the soteriological, sacramental, ecclesiological, hermeneutical, etc., debates) reappearing in the church's struggle to come to terms with secularization. And no more here than there can one be collapsed into the other. While exclusive divinization threatens to smother the humanization at work in man's coming of age, the radical excision of Deity by a restless adolescent theology is no more adequate than an early Ebionism in revolt against an overweaning Docetism. We shall examine in more detail the problems for Christian identity raised by calling Deity in question in the section that deals specifically with this-worldliness. Here we are concerned only with lining out the contours of another option. We have used the figure of the waiting Father to express it, and have traced it to the Father-Son relationship on the cross. In that event, and on the larger canvas of modern secularization, we see the reality of a Father who does not intrude on his progeny's growth, but encourages it by a patient withdrawal that foreswears autocracy and dependency so that the future may be shaped in freedom. In such a maturity the integrity of both Father and son is preserved. Can it be that a new kind or relationship of son to Father is possible when the Father is no longer seen as autocrat or crutch? We shall explore that in the succeeding section on God as Tutor. Here we are concerned to underscore both the freedom of man to be man, and the freedom of God to be God, in the Father-son bond for a world come of age.

The Serving Father and His World-Come-of-Age

Classic Christology tells not only of preserving the integrity of God and man but also of their hypostatic union. While not dealing with a comparable human "perfection of nature," parallel doctrines speak also of a divine presence expressing itself through a human church, the earthiness of elements and actions, the exercise of personal decision and behavior, and the literature of men. In each case God intimately winds himself into the bubbling and broken affairs of men on earth. He is not only conjoined to, but makes himself known in and through the worldly.

At the center point of the Christian Story, on the cross, the action of God in and through the action of man reaches its burning point. In the very cry of dereliction, God was in Christ reconciling his world. Even at the place where he makes most evident his distance from the Son, the Father is present. We might add, *especially* where this chasm is deepest, proximity is most real. "The God who is with us is the God who forsakes us (Mark 15:34)."[36] From this presence-in-absence we find a clue to the style of the divine working. God labors in the activity of human maturation. Where men are liberated so they may launch out on their own, and when they seize this opportunity, *there* is his encouraging grace. The Father drew near as the Son was freed to choose his future.

As the Father served his Son through the Son's gift of freedom, so God is a living presence in man's coming of age. Maintaining his identity as God he yet unites himself with, and pours himself into, the secular vitalities of a maturing humanity. Where man seizes the reins of his history, where he no longer cringes before the tyrant or turns over his weal and woe to a Deity called in to grant favors or bail him out of trouble, there the servant God is to be found manifest in human courage and creativity. "The God who makes us live in this world without using him as a working hypothesis is the God before whom we are ever standing. Before God and with him we live without God."[37]

The Suffering Father and His World-Come-of-Age

It is in the figure of divine weakness that both the absence and presence of God come together. Let us lead into an exploration of their unity by examining some alternative views of the meaning of the Christian theme of humiliation as it touches the interrelation of the actions of God and man.

The suffering of God for man points toward Christian suffering for man. The life of commitment is a life for others. To participate in the sufferings of God in the world is to exercise the ministry of compassion to those in need. And this cannot be done by grandstand charity. Self-denial means servanthood in the midst of and to the hungry, the thirsty, the stranger, the naked, the sick and the prisoner, for in their desolation is he to be found (Matthew 25:31–46). The rediscovery of this biblical theme lies behind the struggle of the church today to "turn." Renewal means an end to the self-glorification and incurvedness of institutional Christianity and a self-emptying life for the world. The debt to Bonhoeffer here is manifest.

A further dimension of meaning may be added by others to this understanding of sharing in the suffering of God in the world. As God embodies his love by crucifixion, we are called to a powerlessness that receives in patience the buffets of the world. We have made brief allusion to this conception before and will return to it again.

Do these understandings of the suffering of God exhaust its meaning for the human venture? Do they do justice to Bonhoeffer's reflection on the divine humiliation? We are primarily interested in the first qestion. However, there are some notes sounded in the prison letters which press the inquirer beyond what has become the conventional wisdom about the meaning of servanthood and suffering.

Such a question is posed by secularization, and Bonhoeffer's preoccupation with it in the midst of his struggle with the divine suffering. How does man's coming of age relate to God's humiliation? What can connect the call to honor man's new power and creativity in a world come of age, yes, even of the need to "confront him (man) with God at his strongest point,"[38] with the very weakness of God? It does not seem that the ethical mandate to be a man for others, and surely not the claim that the Christian life is a life of powerlessness, cover all the nuances of this juxtaposition of human strength with divine weakness.

Some light is shed on this dilemma if we pursue our image of paternity-in-maturity. The waiting Father is the one who has withdrawn to allow his sons to shape their own future. Yet paradoxically he is present in their very coming of age. What else is this absence-presence movement than the pouring out of the paternal vitalities into the son's emergence? The Father divests himself of his power. But there is more here than the classic self-emptying theories of atonement. The power is breathed into human history. The glory of God becomes the glory of man. The strength to control human destiny, to bail men out in need, to solve problems, to fill gaps, is now in man's own hands. That is what coming of age means; the Father transferring the prerogatives to create, extend, shape and direct life on the earth to his son.

It is a short step from here to a radical theology which interprets the passing of transcendence into immanence to mean the annihilation of God himself and the appearance of whatever there was of godness only in the shape of the profane. Thus to find the majesty once invested in Deity, we must now immerse ourselves in the secular. Yes, the transcendence has passed into a majestic immanence, the creativity of the maturing man. But God is not synonomous with the lofty reality described in "trans" terms. He divests himself of this quality on the cross and in the sequels of secularization, but he does not thereby evaporate. His freedom to be God is not enslaved by his self-emptying but in the maturing of man takes the form of the suffering Father.

His humiliation consists in the passing of his power. He chose no longer to relate to man as the One who controls his existence, but the One whose power to create and control life is now in the hands of man, and who dwells on the margins of human life. Emptying is suffering in that it is the pouring out of the divine Self's classic power. And this suffering love, this life given for man, this willingness to descend as man ascends, this paternal readiness to decrease as the son increases shines through precisely at the points of human vitality. Man's strong points are the signs of God's self-chosen weakness; man is strong because the power of God has gone out of him into the sinews of a growing humanity.

We do not seek to make a case here for these reflections as faithful extensions of Bonhoeffer's thought on the divine suffering. Perhaps there is no final way to put together the fragments of his thought in the letters, as the various strands may be contradictory in their undevelopedness. But, read in the light of a Father's Self-gift to his son come of age, do not these sentences take on special luster?

God allows himself to be edged out of the world and on to a cross. God is weak and powerless in the world, and that is exactly the way, the only way in which he can be with us and help us. Matthew 8:17

makes it crystal clear that it is not by his omnipotence that Christ helps us, but by his weakness and suffering. This is the decisive difference between Christianity and all religions. Man's religiosity makes him look in his distress to the power of God in the world; he uses God as a deus ex machina. The Bible however directs him to the powerlessness and the suffering of God; only a suffering God can help. To this extent we may say that the process we have described by which the world came of age was an abandonment of a false conception of God, and a clearing the decks for the God of the Bible, who conquers power and space in the world by his weakness. This must be the starting point for our "worldly" interpretation.[39]

The poem about Christians and Unbelievers embodies an idea you will recognize: "Christians range themselves with God in his suffering; that is what distinguishes them from the heathen." As Jesus asked in Gethsemane, "Could you not watch with me for an hour?" That is the exact opposite of what the religious man expects from God. Man is challenged to participate in the sufferings of God at the hands of a godless world.

He must therefore plunge himself into the life of a godless world, without attempting to gloss over its ungodliness with a veneer of religion or trying to transfigure it. He must live a "worldly" life and so participate in the suffering of God. . . .[40]

This is what I mean by worldliness—taking life in one's stride, with all its duties and problems, its successes and failures, its experiences and helplessness. It is in such a life that we throw ourselves utterly in the arms of God and participate in his sufferings in the world and watch with Christ in Gethsemane.[41]

There is surely to be heard in these great passages the call to a life for others, a call that carries with it the possibility of crucifixion "at the hands of a godless world." Such a life of suffering love is contrasted with the expectation of the "religious" that they will receive support from a strong God who will help them when they are "sore bestead." But then can be heard as well the call to joyful participation of the believer in worldly "health, fortune, vigor," at the mouth of the horn of plentiful human creativity, power, exhilaration, in short in the possibilities as well as in the impossibilities of life. These are the fruits of his emptied, paternal glory. To share in this kind of worldly life is also what it means to participate as a son in the sufferings of God in the world. And to blend the two participations—to be a faithful rather than prodigal son—is to learn what it means to steward the power of man for others, and thus, for God.

Footnotes

1. A popular slogan of the United Church of Christ, 1968–69. Emphasis on "The Local Church in God's Mission," referring to the demise of clerical paternalism.

2. See Altizer and Hamilton, "Preface," *RT, op. cit.*, p. xii, and dedication of book.

3. See Langdon Gilkey, "Is God Dead?" *The Voice,* Crozer Theological Seminary, pp. 4–6. Hamilton, however, describes one of Gilkey's connecting links as a "shrewd observation"—"The Death of God Theologies Today," *op. cit.*, p. 27.

4. Note particularly David L. Edwards, ed., *The Honest to God Debate* (Philadelphia: Westminster Press, 1963), and David E. Jenkins, *Guide to the Debate About God* (Philadelphia: Westminster Press, 1966).

5. There are, of course, many other aspects of the crisis theologies which transcend the fortress mold and put us in their debt. Our concern here is with the historical context of a kind of thinking expressed concisely by a Lundensian, whose militant imagery is objected to by Barth, but for all that a common platform in tumultuous times: "I am persuaded that no form of Christian teaching has any future before it except such as can keep steadily in view the reality of evil in the world, and go to meet the evil with a battle song of triumph." Gustaf Aulen, *Christus Victor,* translated by A. G. Hebert (New York: The Macmillan Company).

6. Hamilton, in an early phase of the movement he now describes as an experiment that has run its course, defines its role in similar terms as "speaking out of a community to a community." Hamilton, "The Death of God Theologies Today," *op. cit.*, p. 28.

7. David Riesman, *The Lonely Crowd* (Garden City: Doubleday Anchor, 1956).

8. See the comments of Davis, *A Question of Conscience, op. cit.*, pp. 62–117.

9. Ved Mehta, *The New Theologian* (New York: Harper, 1966), p. 164.

10. We have found the work of John Phillips, *The Form of Christ in the*

World, op. cit., 1967, most helpful in illumining the themes of humiliation and celebration, and as crucial background, Bethge's *Dietrich Bonhoeffer, op. cit.*

11. The phrase is Helmut Thielicke's found in his collection of sermons, *The Waiting Father* (New York: Harper, 1959).

12. Note Robinson's usage in *Exploration into God, op. cit.*, p. 28, and the scholarship basis in Joachim Jeremias, *The Central Message of the New Testament* (New York: Charles Scribner's Sons, 1965), chapter 1.

13. *Ibid.*, p. 18.

14. Alexander Dru, editor and translator, *The Journals of Soren Kierkegaard* (New York: Peter Smith, 1959), pp. 180–181. Copyright © 1958 by Alexander Dru. Reprinted by permission of Harper & Row, Inc.

15. Simone Weil, *Waiting on God*, translated from the French by Emma Crauford (London: Routledge and Kegan Paul Ltd., 1951), pp. 87–88.

16. Emil Brunner's phase cited by Robinson, *op. cit.*, p. 28.

17. Commentary on Anthony Flew's famous parable of the jungle explorers, the roots of which go back to John Wisdom's article "God's" in the *Proceedings of the Aristotelian Society* and the branches reach forward into van Buren's *The Secular Meaning of the Gospel, op. cit.*, pp. 3ff.

18. Aulen, *Christus Victor*, op. cit., pp. 97–109, 168–172.

19. *Ibid.*, p. 182.

20. Quoted in George Burch, *The Steps of Humility* (Notre Dame, Indiana: Notre Dame, 1963), p. 36.

21. Etienne Gilson, *The Mystical Theology of Bernard of Clairvaux*, 1940, p. 88. Roman Catholic devotional thought, classic and contemporary, deals in this idiom. For example, Michel Quoist: " 'I shall be in agony till the end of time,' God says. 'I shall be crucified till the end of time.' . . . 'I am scourged, buffeted, stretched out, crucified; I die in front of them. . . .' " *Prayers* (New York: Sheed & Ward, 1963), p. 5.

22. From "Alas and did my Saviour Die."

23. *Kirchen-Gesang Buch fur Evangelisch-Lutherische Gemeinden* (St. Louis: Im Verlag der deutschen evang. luth. Gemeinde, 1851), p. 50.

24. The last two two stanzas of "Christians and Unbelievers," *Prisoner for God: Letters and Papers from Prison, op. cit.*, pp. 167–168. The first verse is:

> Men go to God when they are sore bestead,
> Pray to him for succour, for his peace, for bread,
> For mercy for them sick, sinning or dead:
> All men do so, Christians and unbelieving.

25. This, and some of the lines of thought that follow on the suffering of God are indebted to David Jenkins' thoughtful struggle with the subject

in his Bampton lectures, *The Glory of Man* (New York: Charles Scribner's Sons, 1967), pp. 106–110.

26. Displacements as drastic as having to completely retool the concept of paternity in terms of genetic developments in man that make reproduction possible by methods other than uniting sperm and ovum from male and female.

27. Barth's distinction between Father and Son in his analysis of the Trinity.

28. Jenkins, *op. cit.*, p. 109.

29. Soren Kierkegaard, *Concluding Unscientific Postscript*, translated from the Danish by David Swenson, completed after his death by Walter Lowrie (Princeton: Princeton University Press, 1941), pp. 86ff., 345ff., 493ff.

30. See the discussion of this in Hugo Meynell, *The New Theology and Modern Theologians* (London: Sheed and Ward, 1967), pp. 117–136.

31. MacIntyre, "God and the Theologians," *Encounter* (Sept. 1963).

32. From the "Statement of Faith," United Church of Christ.

33. For the beginnings of a sober but celebrative Christian response to new developments, particularly in the life sciences, see the essays by Harold Schilling, "Science with a Christian Concern," Board of Christian Education of the Methodist Church, and "On the Significance of Science for Religious Thought," Board of Christian Education of the Methodist Church, 1964; the report of the National Council of Churches consultation, Cameron P. Hall, compiler, *Human Values and Advancing Technology*, *op. cit;* James Gustafson, "Christian Humanism and the Human Mind," reprint of essay in *The Human Mind*, Nobel Conference, Gustavus Adolphus College, Minnesota, 1967. Kenneth Boulding and Henry Clark, *Human Values on the Spaceship Earth* (New York: National Council of Churches, 1967); Kyle Haselden and Philip Hefner, editors, *Changing Man: The Threat and the Promise* (Garden City, N.Y..: Doubleday & Co., 1968); Ian Barbour, editor, *Science and Religion: New Perspectives on the Dialogue* (New York: Harper, 1968); Theodosius Dobzhansky, *The Biology of Ultimate Concern* (New York: New American Library, 1967); Harold Hatt, *Cybernetics and the Image of Man* (Nashville: Abingdon Press, 1968); Stanley Jaki, *Brain, Mind and Computers* (New York: Herder, 1969); Gabriel Fackre, "Faith and the Science-Man Questions," *Christianity and Crisis*, Vol. XXVII, No. 23 (January 8, 1968), pp. 318

34. See "The Issue of Transcendence in the New Theology, New Morality, and the New Forms," *op. cit.*, pp. 182–184.

35. In order for dialogue to be a genuine exchange between two full partners, it is necessary for the submerged party to leave no shred of doubt

in the old autocrat's mind of the thrust toward "self-appropriation," even though it may look to the receding paternal figure like an expression of hostility. This will to establish a clearcut identity so that future relationships with the white community can be genuine partnership lies at the heart of the affirmation of black identity and black power. Although often confused with, it is not the same as black supremacy, or black racism.

36. Bonhoeffer, *Prisoner of God, op. cit.,* p. 164.

37. *Ibid.,* p. 164.

38. *Ibid.,* p. 160.

39. *Ibid.,* p. 164.

40. *Ibid.,* p. 166.

41. *Ibid.,* p. 169.

6

GOD AS TUTOR

"Tutor" is a second image that illumines the response to secularization we are here sketching. The concept has affinities with Paul's characterization of the law as a "schoolmaster" that prepares the way for the coming of the gospel. We shall examine the question of law as such in the succeeding section on morality. Here we transfer the pedagogical theme from the moral to the theological in an effort to understand better God's relationship to the coming of age process.

The tutorial role has taken on special significance in the American "freedom revolution." Two expressions of it in this setting provide material for defining it in the discussion of secularization. Tutorial programs for children and youth of the ghetto came into prominence in the early sixties. They were launched by college students and others who sought to put the privileges of their academic training at the service of the educationally disadvantaged. Many who took part concluded later that the heart of the problem lay in debilitating pedagogical structures, and moved on from tutoring to work for changes in the educational system itself. Nevertheless the tutor played an important role in the attack on educational deprivation, and in many places still does.

A tutor seeks to share and review knowledge and skills that remain undeveloped in the student by the regular classroom in-

struction. He thus fills a gap left by the educational establishment. But further the tutor seeks to cultivate in the youth
charged to his care an excitement for learning so often smothered
by the futilities of slum living. He seeks as well to bestir in his
educational partner a sense of self-esteem and a self-confidence
in his own ability that will provide a momentum for the educational task when the tutor has passed from the scene. In fact the
tutor succeeds to the degree that he makes himself superfluous.

The style of the tutor reflects his purpose. As a participant in
a voluntary association generated outside the establishment and
frequently considered as an irritant to and judgment upon the
professionals, his is a marginal existence. He does not have the
authority of the classroom teacher nor the warrants of com-
pulsory education, and he does not seek them. His effectiveness
depends on his ability to win the confidence of the student, and
thus the self-starting student growth that must finally materialize
if the program is to be a success. Within this frame of reference,
the tutor often finds himself sharing deeply in the life of his
pupil as a fellow human being and a friend. Tutoring is carried
out in the posture of "alongsidedness."

A second facet of the freedom revolution fills out the picture,
although the word "tutor" is not normally used to describe the
phenomenon. We are thinking of the "pioneering-relinquishing"
pattern of involvement by various change agents. We refer here
to church participation in the struggle, although it would be
quite wrong to think of it as either the leading or critical embodiment of this style. But at its best the church does represent
a version of tutorial action, both in the present struggle for
human rights and in other expressions of its life for others. The
tutorial model so conceived can be seen at work in the areas of
housing and education.

Within the past few years congregations, denominations, and
ad hoc clusters of the concerned have pooled their resources to
form housing task forces. Either using their own funds or taking
advantage of new government financing (221 D3), the interested
unit builds or buys housing and makes it available to low or

middle income minority group tenants who are otherwise denied access to decent housing by white bigotry in one form or another. The church effort is geared to breaking the patterns of racial isolation while providing desperately needed accommodations free of rent-gouging and landlord tyranny. Its location may come in a variety of forms such as "scattered-site" housing through white neighborhoods, or in integrated housing within the ghetto.

Involvement in these efforts to melt racial barriers soon brings the participants up against a hard reality. The number of units that can be built by committed church interests is so small that the massive problem of dispersed and adequate housing is barely dented. Thus, while the church succeeds in aiding a small number of people, shattering some stereotypes in the communities in which it has a stake and lifting up a vision of what a reconciled society might look like in terms of housing, the major structural issues remain unsolved. Also, to the degree that white middle class church constituents serve on the governing boards, or as managers of housing projects, a "plantation charity" is at work in modern dress, as vicious in its own way as the white paternalism of the old South or the colonial enterprise.

When these considerations are driven home to the responsible church task force, further steps often ensue. The church group sees its role as bestirring the secular community to assume the responsibilities that properly belong to it as a whole. That means legislation that ensures the right of the black citizen to housing mobility and shatters his entrapment in an urban compound. It also means more comprehensive efforts by the whole community through both public and private means rather than the limited ecclesiastical involvement.

And again, it means that the church fights *alongside* the minority group for a decision-making voice in the execution and administration of whatever structures emerge to meet the housing plight. It leads as well to the democratizing of power through seeing to it that paternalism dies in its own models, so that finally the community which lives its life out in this housing has control over its own destiny.

Church engagement therefore passes through the rhythm of pioneering, goading, democratizing, relinquishing. It sets up a model that points to a pattern of reconciliation and ministers to it in small degree, seeks to stir the secular agents to embody the design of integration on a community-wide scale, struggles for the dispersion of power among those whose destinies are at stake, and thus finally seeks to "work itself out of a job" so that it can move on to the next area of unaddressed need. We shall explore some other dimensions of this coming of age ministry of the church in our discussion of mission. For the time being we see it as an illustration of the tutorial function.

The same dynamics are at work in the church's activity in many places in the human rights struggle in education. Thus the "freedom school" was an early expression of church (and secular as well, of course) attention to the hurt of de facto segregation, and also to the demeaning of black identity by textbook and curricular silence or caricature. Churches frequently set up model teaching situations in their own buildings in which an attempt was made to fill the voids in the public school situation. Classes and teaching staffs were integrated, and children and youth were introduced to the African heritage and the role played by the black American in history.

It soon became apparent that large segments of the school population, both black and white, remained untouched by these imaginative but tiny innovations. If a major attack was to be mounted on segregated education, it had to be done at its source, in the system itself. Out of and in conjunction with the freedom schools grew a church encounter with public education itself, including challenges to bias in curricular materials, teacher training, placement and recruitment, the quality of education in ghetto schools, racial isolation in pupil distribution within a city system or within a school itself by way of uncritical use of the "track system." Further it meant a thrust to secure black participation in the policy decisions of the school system, whether it be parent voice in the ghetto school, Negro personnel in executive capacities, or in political efforts to elect black candidates to school boards. This also was the case in its own institutional efforts where Negro leadership becomes the natural expression of pedagogy in black identity.

Thus in education, as in housing, alert church involvement has tended to live out the pioneering-relinquishing pattern. Beginning with the model-making freedom school, it moves to embody its vision of reconciliation in the public structures themselves, to struggle for the voice of the voiceless in the councils of decision in public education, and to relinquish its beach-head when its enabling role has lived out its life.[1]

The Divine Tutor and the Maturation of Man

The Father wills human maturity. But what of the anterior phases of growth? What of the time when man cannot cope by his own strength and ingenuity with hunger, disease, injustice, hatred, war and death? God comes to his children-on-the-way-to-adulthood as friend and tutor.

While it has become fashionable to scoff at the deus ex machina —and indeed, such a conception cannot be the ultimate of faith for a world come of age—Christian theology must affirm a Deity of the gaps in a penultimate sense. God is big enough to make himself small, to come to the aid of men when they have neither the will nor the way to fend for themselves, and to do it through the narrow confines of religious belief and ecclesiastical institutions. "Religion" is a pedagogical aid of the divine tutor in the time of human dependence. We shall examine this interim ministry as it expresses itself in the *ideational* and *practitioner* forms.

The Tutorial Role of Religious Belief

In Leslie Dewart's perceptive analysis of the origins of psycho-analytic theory, he points out that Freud regarded religious belief as man's attempt to render tolerable the perennial agonies of finitude. By projecting tender qualities into a divine empyrean, man was able to inoculate himself from a hostile, natural environment of sickness, tragedy and death. Dewart notes that Freud acknowledged these illusions as useful adaptations of men to their circumstances when no other way was available. Of course, when man matures to the point of understanding and being able to shape his own environment, as Freud believed he had by now, there is no excuse for continuing to entertain religious props. To do so would be regression and infantilism.[2]

To interpret God as tutor is to underscore the wisdom in Freud's observations. There must indeed come a time when man does not run to a Deity who is presumed to have control over his life, death and destiny but rather accepts for himself the mandate to maturity. We have sought to explore that theme in our discussion of a new perspective on paternal love. But it is also true that the very God who wants man to be a man—yes, who wants to be loved not for the uses to which he can be put but for his own sake—wills to do what love requires. Love is the readiness to do what must be done, to step back when *that* action is for man, and to step forward if *that* action humanizes. Because there is a time of immaturity as well as a time of maturity, compassion shows different faces. And in the context of human weakness it is divine strength which is the issue of love, the power to fill the gaps.

When man can not make it through the valleys of death and despair by himself, God comes as the Shepherd. The church offers "the comforts of religion" to man in his powerlessness and anguish. We are not speaking of pious fictions. We are talking about a God who is truly present in those structures of belief that bind up the wounded and heal the brokenhearted. The tutor does what must be done. And if it is a fragile, and in the last analysis, provisional religious belief that is available to pioneer human healing and to lift up a vision of what compassion means, then the God of healing will not despise it but use it. The God who wills to be known in the deep reaches of his being as a waiting Father, an end sought for his own sake, is yet willing out of love to be used as a means for his children's welfare. He is present incognito in the cognition of himself, a Thou who appears in the guise of an It. And his willingness to be used in the moments of human immaturity is yet another sign of his long-suffering love.

The utility of God as a religious stopgap finds expression not only in the piety of the sickroom, the counseling office, the battlefield, and the graveside; it is at work in some of the most sophisticated interpretations of faith. This is evident, for example, in the current conversation on the radical theology. A recurring refrain of the critics of the radicals claims that the denial of a belief in transcendence is destructive to man because religious belief performs important secular functions. Thus Emerson Shideler argues that "transcendental categories are an attempt to broaden the range of our perceptiveness and responsiveness."[3] He writes: "Instead of magnifying the importance of the secular world by denying any relationship with a transcendent realm, the God-is-dead theology succeeds only in denying that there are any possibilities of experience and relationship beyond those which are immediately perceived by the senses. The result is not a larger and more comprehensive view of the world to replace a divided, if not schizophrenic view, but is instead a disastrously constricted one."[4] And Larry Shiner, whose perceptive investigation of secularization was noted, can nevertheless say: "The yea-saying and the secularity of the Christian's existence derives from the desacralization of the cosmos which goes hand in hand with the understanding of God as Creator. If the Creator disappears, then the world and its powers may be on the way to becoming divinized again."[5]

While this observation shows the influence of the Gogarten thesis that modern culture is in the debt of faith for the latter's secularizing motif and historical influence,[6] it also echoes a familiar theme in our immediate theological ancestry. The dialectical theologies warned of the secular fatality of erasing biblical transcendence and thus leaving the way open for a transplantation of divine claims to the soil of finitude, which relocation issues in demonic loyalties and idolatries of nation, race, book, person, system. The other side of the coin, more explicit in apologetic forms of crisis theology and implicit in confessional varieties, was the contention that a belief in transcendence furnished a necessary ingredient for responsible living, arming one to meet the world without pretension on the one hand or despair on the other. It is not surprising, therefore, that Reinhold Niebuhr, when he assesses the inadequacies of the radical theology, does so, in part, in terms of its failure to furnish men with a perspective that enables them to function on a secular journey that requires "faith as a sense of meaning in human existence": "The human story is too grand and awful to be told without reverence for the mystery and the majesty that transcends human knowledge. Only humble men who recognize this mystery and majesty are able to face both the beauty and terror of life without exulting over its beauty or becoming crushed by its terror."[7]

Even Harvey Cox, who has significantly moved forward the conversation on secularization, in the last analysis introduces a "God of the gaps." While he has spoken of the function of belief in transcendence as insurance against the sacralization of natural and historical processes,[8] in his more recent probing of the futurological possibilities he says: "The doctrine of God would become theology's answer to the seemingly irrefutable fact that history can only be kept open by 'anchoring' that openness somewhere outside history itself, in this case not 'above' but *ahead*. Faith in God would be recognized, for our time, in that hope for the future Kingdom of Peace that frees men to suffer and sacrifice meaningfully in the present."[9]

The pragmatic value of the God of hope is a note sounded with increasing volume in the eschatological theologies that are gaining momentum. It ranges from political and sociological rationales for revolution and change to psychological support for hopeless people and times. Although there are other than functional grounds offered for stress on a future seen in Christian perspective, the argument taken up in one of the earliest modern recoveries of "hope" is repeated with regularity: "This is one of the reasons today, at a time of temptations to despair, it may be necessary to bring into view a notion of the End in which an utterly realistic freedom from illusion not only does not contradict hope, but in which one serves to confirm the other."[10]

The problem that has yet to be dealt with in all these perceptive observations on how faith can illumine man's pilgrimage is the genuine possibility of man's coping with his terrestrial needs without a transcendent referent, present or future. And more than that, there is the question of how one last card held up the sleeve of religious belief squares with a genuine celebration of man's coming of age. The tutorial framework for acknowledging the provisional pioneering role of faith as well as its ultimate rootage elsewhere is the direction we pursue here.

Thus the tutorial role of God in a world that has not yet achieved the means of its own liberation is exercised in the filling of gaps by religious succor. But our concept of tutor must be here called to mind. It is not a static phenomenon, nor is it controlled by the wishes of those served. If that were the case, the tutor would be a permanent fixture in the learning process and the learner would succumb to infantile dependency. The evil of a crutch is not its availability in time of weakness—that is its virtue—but rather reliance on it in a time of developing strength. Even while he ministers to immediate need, the tutor is laying the groundwork in his learner for independence. He builds within him the self-confidence necessary for true maturity and prepares him for the time when he must leave the nest. This future-oriented aspect of tutorship is illustrated, together with its support in present inadequacy, in the functioning of religious institutions. In tandem with the pioneering theme exemplified in our discussion of religious belief, we examine the relinquishing theme as it is seen in the dynamics of religious institutions.

The Tutorial Role of Religious Practice

Allusion has already been made to the rhythm of church involvement in the freedom revolution. The tutorial style can be seen on a larger scale in the whole gamut of welfare (including education) and justice involvements of the church. In the former case, for the social service ministries of Christianity—the care of the widow, the orphan, the aged, the young, the sick, the poor, the outcast over the centuries—the church has made available its institutional resources (regularly, too little and too late) when there was no other to do it. But when it is most alert, and when the development of social conditions and attitudes in the secular community makes it possible, the church seeks to move the larger community with its greater resources to assume its role in the human task. Man as such is called to grow up in his responsibility for his weaker brother and for the health and welfare of the common life. The Christian community works for the secularization of the ministries to those wounded in body and spirit, or undeveloped or afflicted in mind. Thus the tax which supports the secular service becomes the expression of Christian stewardship, and the struggle for medical care for the aged and poor becomes the portion of the modern Samaritan. The corollary of secularization is the often reluctant and always painful disengagement of the church's institutional hold on welfare and educational territory when the community at large has accepted its responsibilities for filling the needs of men.[11]

Welfare and educational innovation often flow toward church participation in movements for structural change. Social service points to social action, as in the alliances of those who build homes for the aged with those who struggle for medical care for the older generation, or the passage from freedom school to the struggle for an integrated curriculum and student body in the public education activities cited earlier. The very presence among the hurt, and the resulting deeper awareness of their plight, drives the church to seek to go beyond temporary and token relief to more massive surgery. However, what is true about the need to secularize church welfare institutions when the world is able and willing to handle its own affairs is equally true about social action establishments themselves. While the church may like to think of itself as the "conscience of the community," it is both possible and, from the perspective of the coming of age thesis here being developed, necessary for man to find his own ways of keeping both his conscience alive and the mandate of service before the community's eyes. The goal of the Christian diaconic mission is provisionally to raise up a corps of Christian men for others, but ultimately to generate and allow to step forward on their own simply men who are for other men.

Using "religion" in the innovative role of social service and social action, God drives toward the tutorial relinquishment of churchly pedagogy and the full assumption by man of the human task. What then are men to think of the God of Christianity if he performs no services for them through "religion?" What is his reason for being if his human functions can and ought to be secularized? We have touched only very lightly on this question in the three illustrations used so far to flesh out the meaning of tutor. We shall seek to confront it more directly in our fourth example: the maturation of a Christian congregation.

What does membership mean to the average churchgoer? Very mundane factors are often present.[12] We are not thinking here of the status-seeker, or those who join suburban congregations as a badge of middle class belonging, or the climber who could not make it in politics or the civic club circuit but who can get elected vice-president of the church council, or any of the more obvious egotisms that motivate a type of ecclesiastical joiner. Rather we have to do here with the function of the church as a "filling station." Thus the lonely find friendship in the social life of the congregation or the concern of a pastor, the sick find attention, the distraught comfort, the bereaved solace, the youth acceptance and an outlet for their energies, perhaps even a life partner, the aged a role and niche that gives some significance to their last years, and many of society's dehumanized find a face and a name in the caring life of congregation. The list can be lengthened according to the needs of a particular community and the resources and concern of a local church.

Prophetic voices have exposed the faithlessness of the congregation that exists to service the needs of its own constituency. We shall turn our attention to the indictment of the religious establishment in Part III. For the time being we want to ask whether there might be another significance to the bend inward of those who treat the church as a hospital, and another way beyond it in the light of the tutorial concept.

The understanding of the church as the filler of personal needs is the cry for milk instead of strong meat. Its estrangement from the purpose of the church consists in its infantilism; it views the church as the mother who must suckle it. But what does one do with a hungry child? The church cannot turn aside, but must offer whatever social, spiritual and psychological nourishment it has to offer. To return to our figure, the tutor will share his gifts with those who do not have them. And if the resources of religion are all that is available, then a big God will be prepared to squeeze himself into even the small horizons of the filling station congregation.

But a tutor is no tutor if he does not plant as well a burr on the seat of pedagogy. Nourishment now yes, but provisional, restless, open toward the future, a call to pilgrimage out of infancy. Parochial pilgrimage means the turning of the heart and mind of the church member away from the I, me, mine preoccupations to "the other." A living body is an *ecclesia viator,* a church growing toward the maturity of servanthood, a community learning to face around, on the way to "metanoia." A church for others is the one in which the lonely and distraught open a window to the world to see and minister to the despair of others, where the bereaved open their own hearts to those who mourn, where the affluent youth turn from their own church recreation to action in liberation of the ghetto teen, where the aged are pressed from their church-found dignity out into a struggle for the other forgotten ones of society, where the depersonalized care less about the identity they have found in the congregational community and more about the devastation done to body as well as soul in the world of poverty, war and oppression. Maturation means mission, the turning of the congregation to a life for others. The tutor stirs the learner to free himself from his dependency and to become himself a teacher.

But something more is involved in these processes of growth. We have a clue to it in the relationship that is born between tutor and pupil as a by-product of their mutual labor. A bond develops which transcends the usability of one by the other (the use made by the student of the tutor as an aid to his own learning, and the more subtle use the tutor may make of the student as a satisfaction of his own need to feel "relevant"). In visits to the slum tenement the tutor comes to know his charge on his home ground and the student learns of his helper's life on the campus, and thus each becomes aware of the other as a person in his own right outside the functional relationship of tutoring. From teacher-student ties may emerge a simple friendship that goes beyond the agendas of mutual need.

Is there a parallel to the friendship of tutor and tutored in the pilgrimage of the congregation? When the church member moves away from a conception of God as the one who exists to fill his personal and social, psychological and sociological needs, when he turns to live out a life of service to his neighbor, there appears the possibility of a new relationship to the God. Men are freed from their agendas for friendship with the tutor. God comes to man no longer in the closure of gaps, or even as the moral mandator, but as one who is to be loved for his own sake. It is in the matrix of servanthood that such friendship is born. In struggling to live out the life of neighbor service, the committed run up against the wounding love that exposes the depth of their own phariseeism and failure and the healing love of the divine forgiveness. Of such is the stuff of divine-human friendship made. We must return again to this dimension of faith. Suffice to note here that in the maturing of a congregation God embodies his tutorial life, ministering to man in the early stages of his pilgrimage, luring him beyond his own inadequacies to a life in strength of commitment to fellow-humanity, and its spill-over, a new relationship with his tutor.

Tutorial Style

We have looked at the intent and changing relationships of the tutor and attempted to see whether they cast light on the purposes and work of God in the coming of age of man. There is a further pointer to a reconceptualization of Deity in the style of the tutor. We refer again to the context of the freedom revolution.

As noted before, the tutor lives on the margins of the educational community. Not being an employee of the system, he has no formal role in the scheme of things. In fact officialdom may feel threatened by his presence, deeming it a judgment on its own effectiveness, as it is; it may see it as standards of personal attention and after-hour interest in student welfare that professional ʲeacher and administrator may have neither the will nor the way to give. Again, he comes with no state backing to compel response in his charges, and often no adequate facilities or teaching tools.[13] In short, he comes with no authority. He is "on tap" rather than "on top."[14] His effectiveness is in proportion to the dedication and skill with which he can educe response from his students.

Tutorial "alongsidedness" is an apt image for our understanding of the ways of God in the coming of age process. In his interim ministration, when man needs whatever help he can get to "make it," God is present as a resource rather than Source. He is no pedagogue that brings men into line with the whip of authority. If men are to grow in the exercise of the freedom, the tutor refuses to do their homework for them. He is a consultant who seeks to ignite in his charge the spark of self-activity even while he is available with his presence and counsel.

The same modesty in presence is manifest in the coming of the tutor as friend. God is, in Jamesian language, an "overbelief," an option that does not force itself either on world-man come of age who can solve his problems without benefit of God-talk or church-man come of age who has moved from dependency to mission. God leaves man free to choose or not to choose. But it is in this very marginality that the act of faith can be responsibly made without a divine triumphalism that cancels its very character as a genuine leap of freedom. As modesty is the form, it is also the substance. Superfluity is an expression of the God revealed on Calvary whose core reality is a power that takes form in powerlessness.

The alongsided God who does not foist himself on man is reflected in a new style of churchmanship. It heralds the end of the "Herr Pastor" who lords it over a submissive and dependent laity and the appearance of the ministerial partner who brings his gift to stand alongside others with their gifts. It suggests as well an evangelism that understands itself not as imperialism but as service in illumining with its perspective the problems of men and the dimension of reality to which it has access. It points to a pedagogy whose posture ranges from a catechetics that is dialogue rather than deliverance from on high[15] to preaching which is born in group discussion and open to "talk-back" afterwards, which is at home more at the seminar table and pulpit dialogue than in the unchallengable lecture or homiletical monologue.

A Note on Servanthood

There has been an occasional reference to the servant motif in our examination of tutorship. We could easily have employed servanthood as the second image for investigating the role of God in the coming of age process. The biblical usage and the contemporary discussion are fertile fields to plow.[16] However, there is value in working at both ends of the line of communication in finding ways to express the meaning of the word "God." By choosing the term "father" and starting our explication of it from its biblical base we get at the task of breathing fresh life into the code language of the Christian community. The points of contact in the secular family (no curse but blessing here, as we think in humiliation rather than imperialist categories) mean that the language can be a door out of the Christian ghetto.

While passing reference was made to the schoolmaster notion that gives some biblical basis for the tutor idea, we have not proceeded in our discussion of it from in out, but from out in. We borrowed language and interpretive apparatus for it from a contemporary secular setting and tried to make our way into the Christian mind by way of it. To contemporize faith and to honor the very secularity we have here under the glass means that we must work in the idiom of the time and place. Hence tutor seems a more apt handle than servant, carrying as it does the class connotations of another era. But tutor and servant are but two words for the same reality. The one who "came not to be served but to serve" and "emptied himself in the form of a servant" is the tutor who decreases so that another may increase and whose alongsided love pours itself out for man.

And we might add that while illumining different aspects of the conception of God, it is nevertheless true that "Father" and "Tutor" meet and comingle. In the servant theme this comes forcefully home. The humiliation of the Father manifest in the Son is no stranger to the self-effacement of the Tutor. In the Son, the Father comes to us as a suffering servant.

Footnotes

1. The pioneering-relinquishing rhythm of church addressment to the issues of public education in one community is traced in the monograph, Fackre, *Second Fronts in Metropolitan Mission* (Grand Rapids: Eerdmans, 1968).

2. Dewart, *op. cit.*, pp. 20–27. Freud develops the idea in *The Future of an Illusion* (New York: Liveright).

3. Emerson W. Shideler, "Taking the Death of God Seriously," in *The Meaning of the Death of God*, Bernard Murchland, ed. (New York: Random House, 1967), p. 121.

4. *Ibid.*, pp. 123–124. For the background of this position see Shideler, *Believing and Knowing* (Ames, Iowa: Iowa State University Press, 1966).

5. Shiner, "Goodbye, Death of God!" *The Meaning of the Death of God, op. cit.*, p. 209.

6. See Shiner's introduction to the thought of Gogarten, *The Secularization of History, op. cit.*

7. Reinhold Niebuhr, "Faith as the Sense of Meaning in Human Existence," *Christianity and Crisis* (June 13, 1966), p. 131.

8. Cox, *The Secular City, op. cit.*, pp. 17–37. See also the comments on Cox's conception of the need for an "anti-environment" in John Warwick Montgomery, "A Philosophical-Theological Critique of the Death of God Movement," in *The Meaning of the Death of God, op. cit.*, p. 31.

9. Cox, "The Death of God and the Future of Theology," in *New Theology No. 4, op. cit.*, p. 252.

10. Joseph Pieper, *The End of Time* (Mystic, Conn.: Lawrence Verry, 1954), p. 76. See also how eschatological theologian Carl Braaten deals with the gap motif in "Speaking of God in a Secular Age," *Context*, Vol. I, No. 1 (Autumn, 1967), pp. 12ff.

11. Fletcher's thoughtful essays on stewardship point to the public sector forms it must increasingly take in modern society. *Moral Responsibility, op. cit.*, pp. 182–214.

12. See Yoshio Fukuyama, *The Parishioners* (New York: United Board for Home and Ministries, 1966), especially summary of findings on pp. 37–42.

13. It should be noted that there are more than a few systems in which the volunteer tutor is given much more generous support and encouragement than is portrayed in this description.

14. A popular phrase in church renewal efforts to characterize an alongsided leadership style.

15. An important step in this direction is the new Dutch catechism of the Roman Catholic Church, and the new 1968 Confirmation Series of the United Church of Christ.

16. "Servanthood" had become a fighting word in the church under the impetus of such leaders and works as Hendrik Kraemer, *A Theology of the Laity* (Philadelphia: Westminster Press, 1959); Arnold Come, *Agents of Reconciliation* (Philadelphia: Westminster, 1960); *A Theological Reflection on the Work of Evangelism*, Vol. V, Nos. 1 and 2 (World Council of Churches, November, 1959); Colin Williams, *What in the World* (New York: Office of Publication and Distribution, National Council of the Churches of Christ in the U.S.A., 1964); J. C. Hoekendijk, *The Church Inside Out*, L. A. Hoedmaker and Pieter Tijmes, eds., translated by Isaac C. Rottenberg (Philadelphia: Westminster Press, 1966).

7

CONJUGAL FAITH

In our discussion of the paternal and tutorial we were coming to the task of theological reconceptualization from the perspective of relationships God sustains with man in the coming of age process. From time to time we touched on the human response to his patient, eductive love. In a final image we seek to explore our understanding of God "from below," that is, from the movement of man to God in maturation. We use a figure which Augustine found meaningful in his trinitarian exposition, one that is at home on both secular and church terrain: lover. As in the case of father and tutor, here too a voyage is made. We trace it from its "erotic" beginnings through its social bond, marriage, to its fruition in a deepening, unconditional life together, and ask how this pilgrimage illumines the life of faith in a time of secularization.

The modern relationship between lovers tends to be born in mutual self-gratification. Sam finds Jane attractive, a lively catch, a rewarding companion-social, intellectual, spiritual, physical. And Jane is drawn to Sam by similar considerations. If the spark ignites and there is thought of permanent union, further calculations regularly enter: Will Sam be a reliable breadwinner? Will Jane be a helpmate in family and work? In short it is "eros," a conditional love that develops to the degree that it benefits the lover, that is present in both the spark and the flame. We do not have to do simply with "blind love" but with with an investment of the self which has at least one eye cocked on the dividends.

While this sober description does not square with the establishment mystique and will dismay those of deeper sensitivity who rightly see in rare instances a plus factor in early courtship, conditional care can be expected to make its presence felt in a society in which pragmatism is at the elbow of most decisions. The erotic agenda of self-fulfillment is documented by the kind of reasons frequently given for divorce and the degree of marital unrest traceable to the frustrations of a relationship based on expected investment returns. Mutual self-satisfaction is a sandy base on which to build a life-long structure.

Other foundations have to be laid. A penetrating analysis of the meaning of the marriage vow by a strange bachelor whose love for a woman shaped his theological reflection gives us a clue to where they may lie:

Resolution works the miracle of marriage, as with the wedding in Cana: it first pours the poorer wine and keeps the best for last. And love is the best adornment for the beloved, but resolution is a power in the heart of him who is imperfect. So the resolution of marriage is that love conquers all. Aye, it conquers all; but verily it goes out in adversity if no resolution holds it fast; it perishes in prosperity if no resolution holds it fast; it degenerates in the daily round if no resolution heartens it; it is smothered in conceit if no resolution humbles it. Love abides, but the resolution is the abiding place wherein it rests; love is the refreshing essence, but resolution is the flask in which it is preserved. Love abides; it guides through life when the resolution accompanies it, but it loses the way when resolution does not guide; it gives life significance when resolution interprets it day by day; it suffices for the whole of life when resolution exercises its restraints; it lays hold of the eternal if the resolution has made a place for it there; it conquers everything when the resolution is present in the day of battle—and the final honor is the only honor.[1]

The vow firms the marriage bond and makes possible the journey's next stage. In an "age of faith," with its explicit transcendent reference in ecclesiastical setting, the pledge is lifted from the level of a two party contract that can be made and unmade to a three party covenant with all the lastingness that word suggests. In more secular times the pressure of social disfavor and the state's legal apparatus may furnish similar binding factors. But in both cases, the point of "wedding" is to bring two together in a oneness that is not based alone, or even preeminently, on the conditional love of the exploratory stages of the relationship. Both the church and the secular officiating agent know that the uncertainty which stretches out before the couple may take away the gifts each now brings to the other and the new ones anticipated. And there is no animal instinct on which to rely to guarantee continuing allegiance. If the union is to continue, it must be redefined in terms of an in-spite-of love that persists in the absence of mutual serviceability. Built into the center of the marriage service, and often in the counseling that precedes it, there is a vow that transmutes eros into agape. Agape in this context means the willed care about which Kierkegaard speaks, the love that ministers to the marriage partner when looks fade, breadwinning is fortuitous, and sickness, sorrow, want and worse replace health, joy, plenty and better. The public act of a willed bond before God and man fuels the fires when the wind blows the hardest.

The face of agape that shows itself in the exchange of vows is kindred to the "benevolent will" of radical morality. As Fletcher points out in his criticism of Tolstoy, love in this mode is an act of volition that is not subject to the caprice of emotion.[2] In the case we are considering here, emotion evoked by the attractive qualities of the loved one (and in this respect a different matter than the Tolstoyean "blind" love criticized by Fletcher) cannot break the bond, for the will to persist in union anticipates its fragility and transcends it in a pledge of steadfast care.

Yet this is not the only face of agape; the pilgrimage does

not end on the note of sober expectation of the worst, nor is marriage the perpetual carrying of the heavy bag of iron will. It is a light and joyful thing, the more so as it reaches other levels of fulfillment. If before, agape appeared at the altar in the profile of vow, now it comes in the face to face communion of I and Thou. It is the living together of two that have, in fact as well as in principle, become one. Now they "know" one another and accept and affirm their partner in both frailties and strengths. No longer is it the sober vow that solidifies the union in the unrewarding times but the deeper bonds of a voluntary love. Functionality has passed as the basis of the bond, and dysfunctionality is now not simply endured because of a vow born of ecclesiastical realism. Love spills out in unmerited, unconditional freedom one for the other. The lover cares about the loved simply because she is who she is and he is who he is. "I love you for a thousand reasons, but most of all I love you 'cause you're you" may be trivial lyrics and music but it has an authentic ring.[3] As human love it does not persist in pure, unbroken spontaneity but will return in its frailty to the realistic vow. Nor is it immune to frustration or unmoved by gratification. But for all the gusts and willed upturnings of the lamp, its fuel supply is undiminished and the light does not go out.

The pilgrimage of faith moves along a parallel route. We have already looked down some of its vistas in our discussions of the maturing process of a congregation. Here we examine belief as such at work in an individual. The similarity to the mystic's journey is apparent at several points, particularly Bernard of Clairvaux's description of the escalation of love. While ladder and ascent seemed natural metaphors for times in which the ascendancy-submission relationship was a framework for religious language, in an era of secular focus that has replaced the medieval verticalities of a three-tier universe, and when "alongsidedness" elbows aside divine triumphalism, the figure of pilgrimage on a horizontal plane seems more fitting.

Faith begins its voyage in company with the God of the gaps.

As in courtship the lover is drawn to the loved one by the benefits derived from the relationship, so too the believer finds succor in his God. He loves him because it helps: faith makes a difference. God is the object of an eros that uses him for the filling of needs. And God is big enough to be treated as a functional It, to be loved for what he can do for man.

In the evolution of faith, as in human love, there is a time of turning. Faith moves out of its childish incurvature and sees that it has to do with Another who has his own will and way which deserve to be honored in their own right. If the bond is to continue, it must be on a different basis. If God is to be loved in this new stage of growth, faith must vow obedience. As in the marriage vow, it also may be sealed in the church as the public profession of commitment to the Other. But it may occur as well after a long association with the faith-community in which God was assumed to have been the One who existed as the liberal distributor of favors to a believing eros. Growth in faith is the movement beyond eros to the agape of benevolent will. God is the One to whom we are bound by our pledge of loyalty. We vow to persevere in our commitment through thick and thin, anticipating the cost of a discipleship which cannot be dislodged by adversity. It is made "for better or worse."

There is a step further on the way of faith for which there is no simple analogy in the pilgrimage of human love. We are dealing with a suggestive metaphor rather than an allegory. The fresh dimension has to do with a development within the life of vowed obedience to God. The sensitive pilgrim in faith knows himself called to the life of crucifixion, but he knows as well that he is not zealous to risk all. Further, he sees a subtle self-congratulation at work in him in his moments of servanthood, the pharisaical anger toward the publicans along the way, and the ambiguity in motive and result of even his noblest acts of obedience. Can the vow be the basis for the bond with God when its substance is frittered away by lackluster follow-through?

"Wretched man that I am. Who will deliver me from this body of death!"[4]

When the awareness of estrangement strikes home, the pilgrim is on the way. The cross becomes no longer the truncheon which commands obedience and a standard that measures the degree of our failure. It is the window God opens to his forgiveness. Mercy draws from man a new kind of response that is neither the conditional love called forth by gap-filling nor the resolute love elicited by the divine command. It is not unconditional in the sense of spontaneous self-generation—only God's love is like that, as Gollwitzer has pointed out in his criticism of the *amour désinteressé* of the eighteenth century mystics.[5] While it is conditional in that it is called into being by the divine self-emptying, such a love cannot be said to rise from, or be maintained by, any benefits to man. There is no earthly "payoff" to the believer; in fact instead there is the pain of the *imitatio Christi* and no heavenly hedonism, for God's love offers no rewards but itself. Neither is there corporate, secular vindication, for while it does not violate the communal rules of the game, unlike the vowed love of neighbour, this love of God has no credentials to show the world to prove it is needed for the moral task; it is simply an overbelief. Not only is it without conditions in this sense, but it is spontaneous as well, spilling over without the heavy work of the will. It comes from no iron vow and therefore is closer to the Tolstoyan immediacy of response than Fletcher's "benevolent will." Unpragmatic, unwilled, it is a free flowing agape that reaches toward God in adoration, penitence, thanksgiving, commitment, simply because he is who he is.

How does this pilgrimage of love toward God illumine the meaning of faith in a time of secularization? There are at least four rays of light it casts on it.

First, rather than being the foe of faith, secularization is a valuable ally. It forces us out of primitive levels to see God in his own right rather than as a deus ex machina. Forms of faith that are content to rest in the early stages of pilgrimage will surely be hard put to survive in an era in which man finds ways to do many of the things assumed to be the prerogative of a gap-filling religion. That god is destined to die. Hamilton's sensitivity to the demise of this dimension of traditional faith is surely right. And Altizer's strange notion that the transcendent once lived but has passed away into the profane is also a very astute near miss in the framework of our analysis here. God is gracious enough to take the form of gap-filling in a time when there is no other recourse for men, but then he withdraws from this role and re-emerges in the coming of age creativity of man. But his presence in human virility does not exhaust his life, as in the immanentism of the radical theology, but is transcended by the marginal, suffering love that calls out to and is received by the marginal, suffering love of the believer.

In the vein of its assistance to faith, secularization also disengages faith from fixation at the stage of the vow. It is very tempting for "the church in mission" to linger here, as we shall explore in Part IV, to interpret faith essentially as obedience to God's neighbor love mandate. This is indeed a fighting word for times in which the human stakes are sky-high, but it cannot be the final rationale for the existence of the church nor the point in the life of faith. Coming of age means that man must by himself be his own moral monitor. The church that believes in his maturity will work to that end. It will seek to "put itself out of business" touching those things that man must assume for himself, including the development of his own communal conscience and pioneering the human task. Such relinquishment is only a dream in our time that cries for church involvement on every frontier of human need, but the dream does remind the church that there is a plus factor in its rationale both in the future and now. That factor has to do with the nurture and celebration of a love for God that claims man in and through, and over and beyond, the moral mandate. In the midst of discipleship, and after it, is the still small voice that speaks of another dimension of love.

A further connecting point between secularization and the lover's pilgrimage is the springboard it provides for faith. Drawing the human community's attention to the problem of living together without destroying itself, as it does by raising the stakes and making the need for reconciliation more apparent, it forces men to examine themselves and ask about their own capacity for reconciliation. When ethics becomes a passionate human concern that will spell the planet's life or death, when the demand to live a life for others weighs that heavily, men will be positioned to discover the ambiguities, self-deception, pretension, and apathy that plague the travel toward a healed community. It is in the vortex of these perplexing moral questions that faith's talk of sin and grace, self-love and divine love, come alive. As Luther learned of faith in his struggle with good works in a sixteenth century context, men in a secular age are opened to faith as they seek to come to terms with the mandates of twentieth century servanthood. One of the ironies is that the radical theology's dissolution of theology into ethics may well drive men through the kind of serious moral struggle that leads to faith.

Another alliance that faith establishes with secularization is bound up with what it has learned from father and tutor as well as lover—that God is present in the son and student's coming of age. Human ingenuity that displaces the fears and favors of traditional religion is cause enough for rejoicing. But the fact that the God of faith wills human maturity and is active in it is grounds for a special kind of celebration. We are speaking of the Franciscan mood, the eye and ear that discern a world alive for and with the praise of God. While Francis saw the stars, animals, fields and flowers lift their arms to their Maker in joy, the new Franciscan sees and hears a singing grace at work in the marvels of science-technology.

Behind the blinking bank of lights that sends up the astro-
   naut and runs the plant without people,
In laser beam that cuts the sore and steel,
Through electron path that soothes the feverish brain and
   beats the artificial heart
We celebrate your skill![6]

The "dearest freshest deep-down things" of Hopkins lay waiting
to be discovered as well in the divine creativity manifest in
maturing man.

In our quest for meaningful images to express the divine-
human pilgrimage we have explored the movement from each
perspective in the partnership. As we have spoken of God as
"Father" and "Tutor," here we point to man as "lover." The
growth of conjugal love, broken symbol that it is, gives us clues
to talk about the maturation of faith's bond with God. Roger
Mehl, in another connection, describes the kinship of such love
and such faith: "If Scripture accords to marriage, among all other
human institutions, an exclusive privilege, if it compares the
love of a man for his wife to the love of Christ for his church,
it is because it well perceives that mysterious bond between
conjugal union and the Kingdom, the prefiguration of reconciliation and the final recapitulation in this very humble, very banal,
and very impure encounter of a man and a woman."[7]

Footnotes

1. Kierkegaard, *Thoughts on Crucial Situations in Human Life,* translated
from the Danish by David Swenson, Lilian Swenson, ed. (Minneapolis,
Minnesota: Augsburg Publishing House, 1941), pp. 67–68. Reprinted by
permission of Augsburg Publishing House, Minneapolis, Minnesota, copyright owners 1941 and 1969.

2. *SE,* pp. 91–92, 97.

3. See comments by Ramsey, "Discernment, Commitment, and Cosmic
Disclosure," *Religious Education, op. cit.,* p. 14.

4. Romans 8:24.

5. Gollwitzer, *The Existence of God as Confessed by Faith, op. cit.,* pp. 103–104.

6. *Youth* (October 22, 1967), Vol. XVIII, No. 19, p. 32. Reprinted with permission of *Youth* magazine, published by the United Church Press for teenagers of the United Church of Christ, the Episcopal Church, Church of the Brethren, and the Anglican Church of Canada.

7. Roger Mehl, *Society and Love,* translated by James H. Farley (Philadelphia: Westminster Press, 1964), p. 211.

8

TIME IN THE AGING PROCESS

We have examined the radical reaction to the formulations and the sensitivities of the past. Inherited patterns of thought and the God who is said to have generated them "back when" are repudiated. The past is a would-be tyrant and/or crutch which seeks to turn men's eyes away from the demands and joys of the present.

The radical theology shares its anti-historical posture with other cultural and philosophical perspectives, acknowledged or unacknowledged, which have had their influence on theology. Consider, for example, the impact of awesome technological advance and its popular interpretation. The drastic changes it has brought about contribute to the conventional wisdom that in all things there is a radical discontinuity between past and present and that the latter has little to do with the former except to render it obsolete. Every modern knows that "horsepower" in a car is a euphemism (as was the "iron horse" of an earlier age of locomotion, as Wells pointed out), for the horse has been outmoded as a form of transportation. The cascade of new things from the technological horn of plenty that surround and control our day to day existence sets up an automatic reaction to things aged as things obsolete. It is no accident that it was Henry Ford who said, "history is bunk."

Contributing to the negative view of the past held by the innovative mind is, of course, the resistance to change by the defenders of the status quo who declare "But we've always done it this way." When the past is regularly used as a weapon in the hands of reaction, the revulsion of the change agents is predictable.

Another negative vote for the past and its constructs is cast by the variety of existential philosophies current. From Kierkegaard's "moment" to the latest Sartrian or Heideggerian, there is the call to seize the challenge of the present, free of the oppressors or dependencies of what "the others" present or past have said or done. The past is an authority figure threatening the decisive act of the "now," and hence is a cloud over one's very humanity.

The anti-past mood finds its way into contemporary youth culture from the pop hero to the hippie and the New Left. The old is the decadent and the futile, the generations that have bequeathed war, poverty and hate to the present and seek to impose their ugliness and rigidity on a free and beautiful people. This "revolution of immediacy" (David Riesman) and also the sheer excitement of the new time contribute to the phenomenon of a fading or "lost memory" about formative history, as illustrated in an interview with one of the symbols of pop culture:

"Twiggy, do you know what happened at Hiroshima?"

"Where's that?"

"In Japan."

"No, I've never heard of it. What happened there?"

"It was more than twenty years ago. They dropped an atom bomb there."

"Oh! Who dropped it?"

"The Americans to end the war."

"So what?"

"A hundred thousand people died on the spot, all at the same time."

"Oh, God! When did you say it happened? Where? Hiro-

shima? But that's ghastly. A hundred thousand dead? It's fright-
ful. Men are mad."[1]

The "now generation" is not beholden to the follies of "then"
times, nor their memories. And it should not be. The protest
movements against the autocracies of a past that seek to smother
the creativity of the present are to be celebrated. And the
vigorous challenge to the religious tyrannies and dependencies
of the heritage by the radical theology is a lively and true word.
The view from within the Christian Story gives us that picture of
the past. Let's look through two windows that open out on it.

We have found that the incarnational theme shed some light
on the relationship of God and man in our discussion of the
world's coming of age: the co-presence of divine and human
creativity. But Bethlehem and its sequels do not have to do only
with the grace at work in the earth's vitality but in its brokenness as well. In fact, strength and weakness meet on the cross
where the Son's maturity is manifest in his freely choosing degra-
dation, and the Father's power is expressed in his powerlessness.

Incarnate humiliation as it touches the question of the past
and specifically the matter of thought forms means that God has
taken the risk of sharing his life within the processes of growth
and decay that characterize temporality. Thought about God is
enfleshed, as well as God himself. As such, it is not exempt from
the process of obsolescence. The transiency of religious ideas
means that they must go through the same disciplines of updating as any secular thought pattern. Refusal to retool conceptually,
the welding of faith to the images and ideas of the past is conceptual monophysitism. It is the assumption that "grace" rides
roughshod over "nature," that God invades the human scene at
the point of thought about him with such triumphalist power
that he destroys the integrity of the human factor. What Bonhoeffer has said about the Bible is eminently true about all theological reflection: "The Bible . . . remains a book among books.
We must be ready to admit the concealment in history and thus

accept the course of historical criticism. . . . In fact it never leads to a weakening of faith but rather to its strengthening, as concealment in historicity is part of Christ's humiliation."[2]

To believe that the Word is made flesh means that God's love takes all the risks of that plane, including the passingness of fleshly forms, the superannuation of its most precious past vehicles, and hence the ever-new need for demythologizing and translation into contemporary idiom.

But we have here more than a case of inherited thought forms ceasing to be faithful reflections of reality because times have changed our angle of vision of that reality. Time changes the reality itself. Not only must we reconceptualize because of the moving historical platform from which we view Deity, but God himself will not sit still for us. It is the Christian Story's talk of the Holy Spirit that puts us on the trail of the divine restlessness.

Wherever we turn in that Story we hear of a vital, living, breathing, illumining, shattering, chastening, freeing and healing Presence. The Spirit is God in action.[3] And a special quality threads through the specific acts attributed to the Spirit, be they participation in the creation of the world, the calling of the apostle, the moving of the prophet to recall Israel to her destiny, the conception of Christ, the inauguration of his ministry, his resurrection, the birth and rebirth of the church and its participants through baptism and confession, and the fermenting action of the Spirit in the world. It is the action of creation and re-creation, the making of old things new. The Holy Spirit is the liberator from the prisons of the past. He re-forms what has gone before. To take this chapter of the Story seriously means that the believing reader must be ready to subject all the givens to re-formation. Ideational structures responsive to the renewing grace of the Spirit will be open to reshaping as well. And more, the whole self must be open to the present because the livingness of God expresses itself in the "now" of the Spirit, thus calling us to join the "now generation."

The Christian Past and its Uses

What then of the past—is it rendered obsolete and dispensable by our openness to the present? Is history "bunk"?

The answer to that question is implicit in the way we have found our route to the celebration of the present. It is our commitment to the Christian Story that drives us toward contemporaneity. Out of the womb of the "then" is born the "now." It is a happening in the past that opens our eyes to the present. Our perspective on time, therefore, is not generated *ex nihilo*, but rises from the soil of history itself. Let us examine four tough taproots sunk into the Christian past. If we are to take seriously our Christian identity, we shall have to come to terms with them in the midst of our very enthusiasm for updating, and the mandate to keep in step with the God of the present: (a) Christian existence rises from a decisive set of *historical events*. Preeminently they are the birth, life, death, and resurrection of Jesus. Inseparable from this burning point of history are the smoldering edges of Israel's pilgrimage, on the one side, and the emergence and development of the church, on the other. Interlacing this covenant history in time and space are the movements of hurt and healing in "universal history." No reflection worthy of the name Christian will do its work without serious grapple with these key historical rumbles and explosions.

(b) These events, and others fore and aft, meet us today through the medium of a great *tale*, the Christian Story of the world's inception, alienation, reclamation and fulfillment that we inherit from our forebears. In it we hear of the creation of man and his home the world by One who calls both to unity with him and with each other. We learn of the tragic wounds opened by the cantankerousness of the created partners, and the hand of healing extended to, and through the agency of, a peculiar people; its rebuff, the coming of the Physician himself, the painful surgery, the flow of new life and the promise of recovery to come. This kerygma, hammered out in proximity to the rupture and healing itself, is the heritage transmitted to the present. Set in imagery of the day in which its various parts took shape, and therefore always in need of translation, nevertheless its chapters cannot be censored in our attempt to read the present aright.

(c) The Story does not come wraithlike to us across the centuries. It's found in a *book*. This book of the Story—Story-Book— is a hard empirical bequest of the past. Subject in its form to the same temporality that characterizes any writing, it nevertheless has within it the reports of eyewitnesses to the center and circumference of the events of Christian identity. As such, it also is basic data which the most present-oriented man of faith brings with him.

(d) Another hard inheritance is the *community* in which the book makes its home, and the community's struggle with the Story. Thus, "tradition" as well as "Scripture" is an ally of faith in its addressment of the present. The "Storytellers" are companions that come out of the past, and out of the present as well, "fathers" and "brethren." These are components of Christian pastness which will find their way into responsible dealings of faith with the present.

The Style of the Past

As God enters into relationship with man, so the past makes its presence known. It does not come to dominate but to serve. Its role is that of a resource, rather than the definitive source. It is a full participant in an ongoing conversation—taking up shorter or long sections of time with lesser or greater eloquence, depending on its order of importance (a taking precedence over b, b over c, c over d)—with modesty, yet persistence. Chesterton's plea for the presence and function of tradition describes this dialogical style:

Tradition may be defined as an extension of the franchise. Tradition means giving votes to the most obscure of all classes, our ancestors.

It is the democracy of the dead. Tradition refuses to submit to the small and arrogant oligarchy of those who merely happen to be walking about. All democrats object to their being disqualified by accident of birth; tradition objects to their being disqualified by the accident of death. Democracy tells us not to neglect a good man's opinion, even if he is our groom; tradition asks us not to neglect a good man's opinion even if he is our father. I, at any rate, cannot separate the two ideas of democracy and tradition; it seems evident to me that they are the same idea. We will have the dead at our councils.[4]

The Radical Theology and the Christian Past

Does the Christian past come significantly into the radical theology's conversation with the present? As to whether Events, Story, Book, and Community are active partners in the process of doing radical theology, only those who live regularly in that frame of reference can answer. While we cannot speak here about the process of thinking theologically, it is possible to answer the question to some extent in terms of the product that emerges.

"God" either dies or disappears from the operating notions of the radical perspective. We are forced to ask, if one of the main characters in the Story is dropped, what happens to the drama? Such drastic revision does make for an interesting tale, but it is no longer the original. The rewrite is a substitute story. The degree of censorship is the measure of the excision Christian identity.

How then does the faith-community relate to the present in faithfulness to its own contemporizing Christology and pneumatology? The problem is to translate and update in continuity with the historical components, to achieve communication without accommodation. The answer we have been developing is to take the key Christian conviction about God in dialogue with man and, in the place of a censorship that eliminates Deity in the interests of human maturity, seek to find a new understanding of who God is and how he works in the time of the race's adult-hood. We have explored two concepts, father and tutor, drawing on the categories of both the past and present. Whether or not we have been successful with these particular images, we would argue that any effort of the faith-community that reaches for con-temporaneity must include the serious presence of the Story in its theological work.

Returning to our coming of age figure, we might say that the radical theology is right in wanting to avoid any fixation on the past that inhibits the capacity of a growing organism to re-late creatively to the present. Infantilism in theology is the refusal to leave behind intellectual tools that may have served at previ-ous stages but only inhibit relationship to reality at a point further on down the line of growth. But there is another kind of problem that may also impair the self's capacity to relate: amnesia. While the past must not control the present, it is its partner in the form of memory.[4] What is true of a self is also true of the Christian community. Without memory, its identity is in question. Von Balthasar discusses the role of past value in human progress, speaking of "humanity's growing consciousness of its own history, which retains in a living memory even what it once was but can be no longer, just as a man cannot reach total maturity without a living memory of his own youth."[5]

The Story is the Christian memory. It does not come to blot out the present. If it does, it is like an adult's childhood fantasy, an absorption in the world of memories which incapacitates one for living relationships. Rather, its authentic style is alongsided-ness and availability, resourceful data for coping with the present.

A Third Dimension

In the struggle to sort out the interrelationships of past and present, it is a temptation to forget that time has a third dimen-sion: the future. When the future is forgotten by those who reduce faith to either the categories of the past or present, the basic tilt of time as it is viewed in Christian perspective is obscured. Time moves out of the womb of past events through a living present, but always restlessly toward the future. Coming of age, therefore, from the angle of the "then" of Christian time, is the maturing readiness to face forward. Traditionalism is the kind of immaturity that strains backward to the security of the past. Contemporism is another kind of immaturity that prefers the security of the known present. Radical theology's mesmerism with the "realities" of the present, the things that can be "checked out" and "cashed in," the manageable and predictable, has succeeded in walling itself off from the unmanageables and unpredictables that lie out ahead. From its point of view, the way things are now is the way things really are. It puts its trust in the present agencies of discernment. One wonders whether the term "radical" is appropriate to describe its theology for, in a sense, it makes peace too easily with the present. There is no sense of the radical question mark that stands over the contemporary givens that is characteristic of future-oriented perspectives, secular or religious. It may indeed be revolutionary in regard to discontinuity with the past. But discontinuity with the future invites cosiness with and captivity to the present, as well as vulnerability to the status quo mind.

The Story's eschatological framework points it toward the future. How shall we speak of the God of the future? As the One who comes toward us out of it, casting his shadow as far as Bethlehem? Is he the waiting Father who wills us to march toward him in our freedom, but comes nonetheless with arms outstretched? Is the end towards which he beckons no predetermined design forced on man by a tyrant God, but a genuine option for us which we can make or break in our freedom, a "hope" rather than an "expectation"? Or perhaps he is the Pilgrim God who marches before us, pioneering the way toward the Land where swords are beaten into ploughshares and the wolf and the lamb lie down together? The rediscovery of the eschatological themes in contemporary idiom is fresh in contemporary theology, and we are just beginning to grasp some of its fertility.[6] While it is tempting to explore a few trails here, our task is to see rather how the eschatological bend of faith relates faith to present and past and their conceptual apparatus.

As has been indicated, the futurity of faith is rooted in the Events of the past. The wounded creation is given a forestate and promise of healing in the birth, life, death and resurrection of Christ. But further contemporizing is the continuing work of the Spirit that binds the shattered and is thus a genuine "downpayment on the future." And both past and present point beyond themselves to "the One who comes" with the gift of hope. This is the bare bones of the Story as viewed in futurist perspective. What does it mean for our uses of the past and present and their thought forms?

With the eyes of futurity, faith is always ranging over the next hill. It believes that the way things were and are now do not constitute the last word on the way things really are or will be. Therefore it does not canonize the sensitivities of past or present. A future-oriented understanding of the structures both of experience and thought will not claim that a given era has penetrated so deeply into the "really real," nor will it speak brashly about the lineaments of heaven and hell, or with equal confidence about what it "knows" does not exist "behind the scenes." An era lives within the limits of its own sensitivities, be they sacred or secular, and is no final arbiter of a restless, future-moving reality that is not exhausted by any of its particular expressions or the frail human perceptions that grope toward it. Thus a future-oriented faith is captive to the securities of neither past nor present but lives in tents with its eyes fixed on what it glimpses from afar.

Another feature of theological futurology is its style of picture-making. Its imagery must reflect its hope. That means at least two things. For one, it means that talk about God must serve as a "way-station to truth," as Rahner has put it. Ideas about God must themselves reflect faith's eagerness for the future. They must encourage men to struggle toward the maturity appropriate to it. And they must be prepared to subject themselves to rigorous testing as to whether in fact they do open the future for their believers. In short, theology must be an agent of maturity in order to earn its credentials of futurity.

For another, it means that the symbols of faith must reflect the healing that is at the core of the Christian hope, mirroring the reconciliation that is held before our eyes as the end to which we are called. Imagery and concepts must express the vision of *shalom*, the binding together of what is shattered, and themselves be instruments of it. Concepts must pass the test of opening men to each other, even as images of maturity must be catalysts of the future.

We have tried to embody the themes of maturity and love that characterize faith's final vision in our formulations of the paternal, tutorial and conjugal. By loving withdrawal the father wills the son's maturity and awaits, yet wills as well, a companionship in which the integrity of each is maintained; the tutor whose compassion seeks both to aid the student in his time of need and yet encourage a growing independence; the lover whose care for the other grows from attraction, through vow, to no-agenda affirmation.

The God of yesterday, today and tomorrow is the subject of the Christian Story. He turns towards us in the past's high happenings, is with us now, and calls us toward what will be. A theology responsive to the full arc of time will attempt to track each phase of its line and the goal toward which it moves.

Footnotes

1. Oriana Fallaci, "My Name is Twiggy," *The Saturday Evening Post*, Vol. 240, No. 60 (August 1, 1967), p. 60.

2. Bonhoeffer, *Christology*, Intro. by Edwin H. Robertson and translated by John Bowden (London: Collins, 1966).

3. See Hendrikus Berkof, *The Doctrine of the Holy Spirit* (Richmond, Va.: John Knox Press, 1964), *passim*.

4. G. K. Chesterton, *Orthodoxy* (New York: Dodd, Mead & Co., 1959). Cited by Gerald Kennedy in *SE*, pp. 136–137.

5. Hans Urs von Balthasar, *Science, Religion and Christianity* (New York: Sheed & Ward, 1961), p. 12.

6. Among the significant recent works are: Jurgen Moltmann, *Theology of Hope*, (New York: Harper, 1967); Ernst Benz, *Evolution and Christian Hope*, trans. by Heinz Frank (Garden City, N.Y.: Doubleday & Co., 1966); Harvey Cox, *On not Leaving it to the Snake*, (New York: The Macmillan Co., 1967); Ernst Bloch, *Das Prinzip Hoffnung*, Vol. I and II, (Frankfort: Suhrkamp Verlag, 1959); William Lynch, *Images of Hope*, (New York: New American Library, 1965); Edward Schillebeeckx, *God the Future of Man* (New York: Sheed & Ward, 1968); Maryellen Muckenhirn, editor, *The Future as the Presence of Shared Hope* (New York: Sheed & Ward, 1968); Wolfhart Pannenberg, *Jesus: God and Man*, trans. by Lewis L. Wilkins and Duane Priebe, (Philadelphia: Westminster Press, 1968); Walter Capps, editor, Symposium, "Hope," *Cross Currents*. Vol. LXVIII, No. 3 (Summer 1968); Martin Marty and Dean Peerman, editors, *New Theology No. 5* (New York: The Macmillan Co., 1968). The author's introduction to the theology of hope appears in the Epworth New Reformation series, Gabriel Fackre, *The Rainbow Sign: Christian Futurity*, (London: Epworth Press, 1969; Grand Rapids, Mich.: Eerdmans, 1969, American edition).

9

PARTNER, CIPHER AND
THE ONE WHO COMES

We have examined the coming of age aspect of secularization and now turn to its allied phenomenon, this-worldliness. Again we are in the debt of radical theology for forcing the Christian community to come to terms with the new land in which it must learn to live. In fact, the radical theology is one of the first courageous missionary sorties into the new secular territory of our time. By "missionary" we have reference not only to the explicit attempt to share the Christian perspective with those to whom it is strange, but also the implicit work of helping the members of the Christian community itself, shaped as they are by the language and patterns of a new age and thus foreigners in their own land of belief, to make sense of both faith and secular fact.

Radical theology's mission is expressed in its attempt to translate Christian themes into this-worldly language. Thus the man for God becomes the man for others, theology is transmuted into ethics, the adoration of the holy becomes the affirmation of the profane. Apart from whether the translation is successful, its intent at communication has a long ancestry running back to the attempt of the early church to state its case in the going intellectual framework of the *Logos* philosophies, through the medieval borrowing of the lord-serf hierarchies and the Reformation and post-Reformation penal and nation-state imagery for explaining the atonement, through modern interpretations of Jesus that have recourse to cultural imagery running from French gentility and American sales ingenuity to laboratory catalysis and human revolution. Communication means getting inside the skin of the time and place in which one lives.

That the radical theology has pitched its ideas in the key of the modern mind is borne out if one considers even the most elementary psychic impact of the science-technology that shapes our thinking and being. Man's omnipresence, particularly in the voids and places of mystery formerly assigned to God, makes it easy for man-talk to elbow out God-talk. Consider this moment. The page you survey, the ground glass through which you peer to see it, the sound of the cars outside, the plane above, the TV next door, the washing machine below, the clothes that cling to your body and the packaged food that has nourished it, even the little parcel of greenery out the front window manicured by the power mower, arranged by the city planner and discolored by the factory fume bear the mark of omnipresent man. As human thought, including theological thought, regularly follows the contours of social reality—as epiphenomenon, ideology, rationalization—so an earth shift as deep-going as the birth of the technopolitan era will have its echoes in the thought forms of men who live on this terrain. Theology, so often tardy in catching up with things, has finally produced its own seismographs. If we have not learned from the secular prophets of a this-worldly technological society—Feuerbach, Proudhon, Marx, Comte, Nietzsche, Freud—then it is about time we heard it from the missionaries of our own community who are trying to get the lay of the land.

It is not only the sheer weight of technological presence that sends our minds and hearts to this world and this time. Another component, intimately related to technology, of course, is the promise of this age. With new horizons appearing constantly, men turn their attention to the terrestrial challenges of microcosm and macrocosm. Space flight, penetration of the electron path and the laser source, the possibility of defeating the age-old enemies of man—hunger, poverty, disease, ignorance and death —cause the forehead veins in the laboratory to distend with excitement. Meanwhile the pulse of the man on the street beats faster at the speed of a car, the lines of a dramatic new building, the glow of a new synthetic, the transported images of fantasy and faraway events. It is a great time to be alive. And because that is so, talk of other and less compelling worlds, of bashful invisibilities rather than bold visibilities, pales by comparison. Death and God give way to life and man.

But it is a sad time to be alive as well. Yet that fact further fortifies men's this-wordly turn. Again the Siamese twins, science-technology, are at the root of it, or at least provide the occasion for preoccupation with the affairs of this world. The vast new power in our hands makes possible unimaginable horror as well as awesome new vistas of promise. When men rise up against one another, they are not fooling around anymore with bows and arrows. Wars bring the napalm that incinerates the village and the ultimate bomb that destroys a megalopolis.

Now we do not worry about leaping out of the way of horses or falling off bicycles. Today it is the ravage that can be done by one man with three hundred horses at his fingertips and the hundred dead in the instant of one airstrip skid that causes us to lie awake at nights. The stakes are higher, as Cox puts it, for winning *and* losing. Both the vast sorrows and joys set before men of our time drive humans to give their attention to the "horizontal" race, and that means less and less for "vertical" claimants.

Another component of the this-worldly style of our time is its trust in the *methods* of the science-technology that has produced such awesome fruits. Nothing succeeds like success. If the no-nonsense empiricism and hard-headed investigative techniques work so well in one sphere, men reason they should be applied to others. The empirical method that deals in facts as verifiable as those of the laboratory or factory order sheet becomes the instrument to review the claims of religion. Thus from the young science enthusiast to the sober language analyst there is increasing doubt cast on any visionary talk that is unwilling to confine itself to the factualities of the present.

A facet of the empirical method is the "feedback principle." Science and industry move ahead by the careful evaluation, checking and rechecking of theories and data. All grand schemes and explanations must pass muster before this kind of brutal honesty. The way of science is the readiness to "sit down before the facts as a little child." The honesty demanded by feedback plays a significant part in the radical posture, and is reflected in its very vocabulary. The radical cuts through the fog of pious verbiage to ask if we do in fact know all of the things about which we make confident statements in high-flown terms. Empirical honesty asks to see the credentials of talk of I-Thou experiences of Deity, and inquires about what has really been "disclosed" in the Christian assertions about revelation in history. There is a particular skepticism that emerges in reaction to an era of theology in which some very far-reaching claims were made about how much we knew of "the occult," written down in very big books. And when appeals are made to authority—"the Bible says" and "the church says"—the feedback mind replies, "Is that so? Let's check it out for ourselves."

This demand for verification is cut from the same cloth as the revolt against tyranny discussed earlier. The humility before fact is the rejection of the authority figure who shrouds his claims in mystery and will not take the risks of the give and take and whys and wherefores that are the currency of an empirical age.

The Grounds for Affirming This World

As a pioneering venture in communication, the radical theology has helped to teach us the nature of the new twentieth century country in which faith must live and do its work. This-worldliness is the idiom of our time, and we must learn to live in it and with it. But this is no somber trial with which the Christian community must bear with sackcloth and resignation. The verbs and nouns of the new language have a familiar ring. Faith knows about temporality from a Story that is at home in the world.

At every turn of the tale the significance of life on the earth is honored. We hear of the Creator who puts the stamp of goodness on his creation and shares his very image with another called to cocreation. Abusing his capability, the covenant partner turns his back on the invitation to coservice and brings ruin on his head and disaster to his worldly home. But the Other responds by seeking to build a showcase of his will in one strand of history and to leave reflections of it in every strand. When the case is shattered by his capricious partner, he comes himself to take form in the world to do what must be done to free man for his secular work, and does it. With this turn of events there are cosmic reverberations, and in particular a community is born that points to what has happened in Jesus, and to the hope of a healed creation that it generates. In the light of the this-worldly refrain in the Christian gospel, secular mission is categorically affirmed.

The missionary task of penetrating and building the earth is validated by the Story in the particulars of exhilaration and pain. Thus the turning of men's eyes to the vistas of conquering microcosm and macrocosm has its mandate for faith in the summons to "subdue the earth," and the word that God himself is at work creatively and redemptively in the arenas of nature and history. And the concern of a secular time with the hurts of men is part and parcel of the Story as well in its vision of a time when swords shall turn to ploughshares, and in its counsels to put aside "religious" interests for the sake of human need, whether it be ritual observances that give way to feeding of the hungry or the Samaritan's choice to "bind up wounds"—and its rebukes of the pious for otherworldly preoccupations that blind them to the needs of this world.

While it would be a pretty clear case of eisegesis to claim biblical validation for the methods of modern science, it is nevertheless true that the style of the Story is open to the honesty and scrutiny of the feedback mentality. The God of earth and history does not violate the integrity of the processes in which he tabernacles. Structures, theological, moral, and ecclesiastical, must play according to the same rules as any human form. As such, they are not exempt from rigorous inquiry or demands of honesty. That means at least three things. (1) When the church does its business it lives by responsible secular standards, whether it be the sociology that shapes its institutional patterns, the psychology to which its feeling life is subject for review, or the rules of grammar and coherence through which it must express its ideas. (2) Where religion claims insight into the nature of behavior, it must be prepared to expose its wisdom to the best testing instruments of men. We have touched on this in our earlier exposition of faith's encouragement of human maturity. (3) While faith's vision of what lies at a deeper level than the empirical, and out ahead of it, cannot be finally adjudicated by man's laboratory tests, neither can it be against what is discovered there.

The radical scouts who range over secular terrain make us sharply aware of its contours. Their missionary effort to make it habitable for Christian themes is a further lesson in the task cut out for our generation.

Missionary Problems

The long history of missionary pilgrimage has taught us some of the risks of advance over new boundaries—geographic, intellectual, sociological. We mention several in passing and will return again later to their application.

Overeager communication may mute the harsher notes. Things offensive have a way of disappearing from view. This is normally no sinister plot to subvert faith, but the desire of the missionary to make the headway he is called to do. In pursuing his translation task he may slip into the habit of taking away the stumbling blocks. To remove important themes of faith in the interest of digestibility is fatal not only to faith but to the missionary task itself. If only a baptized version of what he already knows is served up, the hearer is denied the plus to which he is entitled, the new vista which faith can open and the calling into radical question the things that must be questioned. Both faith and its listeners are cheated by chameleon tactics.

Closely related to the accommodationist stance, and often sequel to it, is the penetration of faith itself by characteristics of the field it serves. This may, indeed, be a salutary thing. The communicator discovers values in his own tradition long hidden from his eyes, or entirely new truths that are commensurate with his faith, which become visible only in contact with the new horizons on which he works. Such illumination may happen in a negative way, as when heresy, or a fragment of truth found elsewhere, forces the faith-community to lift up things too long neglected or undeveloped. It may come about positively, as when a fresh insight either latent in or relatable to faith is a seed that needs only the sun and rain of the new climate to fructify it. But there is another kind of external influence in which motifs actively alien to the Christian Story are welcomed as a result of too zealous efforts to make contact. It is about this "syncretism" we are now speaking, blends of faith which run from the idolatries of primitive society to modern nationalisms and racisms. Both faith and missionary field are the worse for these kinds of partnerships.

Another temptation that plagues the missionary task is the "oversell." The communicator discovers that one, or more than one, theme in the storehouse of Christian conviction strikes a responsive chord in his hearers. This then becomes the dominant note he sounds in practice, or the message itself may be tailored to fit a responsive audience. The monotone, however, represents a drastic curtailment and hence betrayal of faith's full sounds, particularly if, as in the case of the first temptation, it eliminates motifs that have not been heard by the listener.

On the other hand, the one note stressed may be the right one for the right time. The moment is pregnant with this concern, and the missionary responds in kind. But to be faithful to the ripeness of time is one thing; to reduce faith to only the dimensions that are at home in the *kairos* is another. The right communicative theme must indeed be bold, but the other themes also integral to faith must not be censored but only rendered bashful. Foreground does not eliminate background. And it may in fact be, as Bonhoeffer has said, that when the *cantus firmus* is strong even fuller play can be given to the melody that is right for the hour.[1] In any case faith cannot lose its full orb even while one or another section of its arc is highlighted in a given time and place.

Clues from History

To live out the missionary role without faith being dissolved in the translation process is the agenda of communication. And specifically, in this age, it involves the responsibility of relating the church's strange talk about God to a time which has man on its mind.

Although secularization puts the question to the modern faith-community in a sweeping way, it is not the first time in history that the church has had to wrestle with the interrelationships of the earthly and heavenly, human and divine. From its childhood, when it struggled to establish its identity in the Christological debates, to the anxious inquiries of a recent age when contestants fought over whether the Bible was the Word of God or the words of men, the secular-sacred poles have been much discussed. The value in checking the reports of the previous meetings brings to our attention some of the historic controversies to which brief allusion has already been made.

Who is Jesus Christ? asked wave after wave of the theology of the first centuries. The issue early became polarized. On the one hand, the Ebionite mentality held that Jesus was essentially and solely a man, the wisest, bravest and most righteous witness to the ways of God, the prophet par excellence, but there it ended.

On the other hand, Docetists, influenced by the pervasive gnostic atmosphere, argued that Christ was Deity clothed in the disguise of human flesh. He only "seemed" to be one of us but was in fact an apparition, for the glory of God could not consort in any fundamental way with the corrupt transiency of matter and history.

Variations on each theme ensued in the succeeding centuries and developed with increasing subtlety, due in large part to the conciliar and confessional rejection of earlier statements. The ancestry of Ebionism can be traced through Adoptionism, Arianism and Nestorianism, and Docetism through Modalism, Appolinarianism and Monophysitism, not with textbook neatness, but nonetheless with the marked tendencies toward one or other of the twin distortions. Thus the early centuries are a laboratory in the exploration of two considerations: (1) the desire to be faithful to the biblical reports of Christ's humanity, the conviction that he was truly one of us, and (2) the attempt to be faithful to the biblical descriptions of his divinity, the belief that in him men had to do in a unique way with Another. And together with the biblical loyalties and theological instincts we find as well the partisan interests of sundry philosophies and sensitivities that characterized the times and sought to cut the cloth of faith to fit their contours.

In the midst of the controversies that swirled around the formulas put forth by the humanizers and divinizers there emerged within the mainstream of the Christian community a perspective that contested the exclusivity of the twin certainties. By no means a serene consensus but often beleaguered, its supporters sometimes later repudiated in seesaw ecclesiastical battles, it nevertheless persisted and took form in official communal declarations. Running through the early Roman symbol and its child, the Apostles Creed, through the Christological section of the Nicene Creed to the formula of Chalcedon, there took shape an answering word about the meaning of Christ that sought to be responsible to the Story, the Book, and the research of its tellers.

Humanizing and divinizing were rejected as exercises in reductionism. In their place was put the affirmation that Christ is true man and true God in true unity. The integrity of the humanity did not jeopardize the integrity of divinity, as each lived with and interpenetrated the other in hypostatic union. Such a formula with its ragged edges and unanswered questions looks indeed like a poor alternative to the neatness and simplicities of more packaged definitions. But the church concluded that the formula's awkwardness and offensiveness did more justice to the biblical data, the Story, and the experience of the Christian community than the alternatives. And so it took its place in that circle of Christian teaching occupied by only one or two other doctrines that shares in what some like to call "ecumenical consensus."

While there is a singularity about the relation of God and man in Christology due to the once-happenedness of the event of Jesus, there are reflections of divine-human integrity and unity in agencies of reconciliation which flow from, and point to, the central Event. And the same kind of debates raged around them. In the effort to understand the meaning of the church, for example, are to be found those who view it as a sacral entity not subject to the frailties of time and space, whose institutions and formulations are divine deposits in the earth. On the other hand, there are to be found those who insist that the church is simply and solely (a) a sociological structure whose reality can be exhausted by the instruments of careful scientific analysis or (b) a gathering of the dedicated who can make or break its churchly reality by their piety and dedication or lack of it. Ranged alongside the certainties of ecclesiastical divinizer or humanizer is a more elusive third option which affirms that the faith-community is a secular institution through and through, subject to the same diagnostic and prescriptive procedures as any other historical institution, and carrying no magic potents of wisdom or piety. Yet, it is maintained, in and through its earthiness, there is a covenant relationship it sustains with Another, not by its own merits (it can claim none, for it is often in a very lackluster and rebellious state) but by his unconditional love. It is his promise and presence that makes it the Body of Christ at the same time that it is a frail and sick body of people.

Closely related to the larger issues of ecclesiology are the sacramental questions. Again we find the divinizers at work turning the rites of the church—we speak especially of Baptism and the Supper here—into sacred lumps and processes of divinity which will do their healing work on contact, as befits the power of things divine. Bread, wine, water become holy curatives, and the earthy things, their actions and administrants become treated with the reverence due to Deity. On the other hand, the humanizers deny all talk of divine luster to the things and their actions and see them in a human framework as aids to memory of the high events of the Story or anticipations of its end, or pictorial stimuli or pledges of obedience to it. Through the mist of this ongoing controversy another position becomes visible which affirms that element and action are quite human, hold no magic power and are due no holy awe, but that for all their earthiness they are tokens and vehicles of Another's love.

The polarities appear with much heat in our twentieth century exchange about the community's basic record book, the Bible. Fundamentalists contend that every word is God's own word, that secular methods of investigation constitute a blasphemous tampering with Deity himself. Modernists (at least of one vintage) reply that it is indeed only the words of men, literature investigable by the techniques men apply to their writings, albeit the greatest and most inspiring human literature of all. Yet out of the uproar there emerged a conviction by others that pleaded the humanity of the documents and total readiness to subject them to the most critical scrutiny, yet reaffirmed the belief that the word of God is spoken and can be heard with the ears of faith in and through the words of men.

Subjective soteriology shows the marks of the same polarities. A heavy predestinarianism seeking to protect the divine initiative virtually excludes the human factor in the decision of faith and life. In response the Pelagian spirit rises to defend the role of man and foreshortens the action of God. Without benefit of the logics of one or the other, a third voice is heard that seeks to do justice to both the divine prevenience and human freedom, and can do no better than haltingly echo Paul's struggling reflection "It is I, yet not I," but in so doing is faithful to the biblical data and the enigma of Christian experience.

While each of the doctrines at which we have looked hastily tends to produce the polarity noted, the two wing positions are met sooner or later by the dualities of a third option, more difficult to express, lacking in the precision and surefootedness of bolder, clearer alternatives, but for all its stammering an attempt to be faithful to the fullness of reality. We shall have recourse, implicitly and explicitly, to the lessons learned in these older debates as we attempt to come to terms with the form the question of this-worldliness takes in our own era.

Against the background of clues from history and in the light of the missionary mandate and problems we shall examine some representative theological efforts to interpret faith in this-worldly categories. As the pioneering attempt is the radical theology, we look first at it. But before we go on to work at restatement we shall also examine some other current efforts.

The Radical Theology and This World

It is worth underscoring at this point that we are not concerned to develop a detailed critique of the radical theology. We view it as an experimental response to secularization that speaks "out of a community to a community." Our question here is, therefore, what do we make of its laboratory reports? Or, in keeping with our missionary premises, does it give us some leads on the communication of faith, helping us to carry out the task of effective translation? Is the Story being both heard and told?

Christian faith has to do with a drama whose characters move from estrangement to reconciliation. If this tale is to be reported responsibly, the participants in alienation and reunion must be present in a living way in the on-going relationship. One cannot cut out a main actor without altering the plot. The word "God" in the Christian drama points to a genuine "over-againstness" with which man and his world have business to do. The Story's dynamics do not take place within the world but between the world and Another. As one of the incisive commentaries on secular Christianity puts it: "It is a truth so simple and yet so hard, that God is not the world. Nor is he man. Between God and the world, and between God and man, there is an infinite qualitative difference."[2] To withdraw "God" from the list of dramatis personae is to alter the plot. The interrelationships of wounding and healing on which the Story hinges cease to be. There is no bi-polarity on which to hang the dialectic. Dialogue has disappeared into monologue.

Our previous short trip into the history of Christian doctrine has brought us into contact with other expressions of the monological mind. The radical theology has a long ancestry of this-worldly humanizing in the Ebionite mentality in Christology and the equivalent partisans in the discussion of the nature of the church, the sacraments, the Bible and the Christian life. They represent a sound instinct, especially as they seek to correct the megalomania of otherworldly divinizers. The radical theology not only lifts up the human notes in the Story neglected by eras of theology that maximized the divine initiative (as noted in our coming of age analysis) but rightly defends the accent that should be foreground in a secular time. Nevertheless, it over-reaches itself when it censors fundamental data in the Christian reading of history.

If the radical theology has put us on the right track (its report of the this-worldly land in which faith must do its work) how can we take this countryside seriously, yet not at the price of "going native in *all* things?" We turn to some other current alternatives that are distinguishable from the radical theology, at least in this respect: they believe that "God" cannot be ex-

cised from faith but must be reinterpreted by it. Let us examine
them. While we do look at specific interpreters, we've also taken
the liberty at several points of a "thought experiment"[3] in order
to round out the typology of possible responses in a this-worldly
frame of reference.

Partnership. Partnership is a popular concept in many depart-
ments of church life and thought today: the alliance called for
between old and new forms of mission, clergy and laity, church
and world, etc. It seems natural to speak as well about partnership between God and man, particularly in a time when long
lost accents on man and this word are being recovered. There is
a growing stress, especially in institutional Christian circles today,
on the partnership theme in an effort to preserve the belief in
God while at the same time finding a significant place for the
role of man and his earth. Sometimes, in an effort to acknowledge
the precedence of Deity, it is spoken of as a senior-junior partnership.[4]

Biblical bases for the partnership thesis are found in the Old
Testament charge to man to subdue the earth and name the
animals, the teaching that man is made in the image of God and
thus given comparable creative powers, and the New Testament
call to be fellow laborers with God. Thus man and God are seen
as cocreators, companions in a common work.

The partnership motif is a welcome attempt to avoid reductionisms, human and divine, and honor the theme of over-againstness while affirming the this-worldly motif of the gospel. However, historical learnings from other debates on the relation of
divinity and humanity give us pause concerning the implications
of the cocreatorship formula. Unless it is qualified in several
important ways, there is some question as to whether the full
role of either man or God is honored. Thus it appears that the
possibilities of man are curtailed by the need of a partnership to
fulfil his task. God comes as a deus ex machina to fill in with a
power that man alone cannot generate; two are needed in the
harness rather than one. And on the other hand, the reality of

God is limited by his need for man to pull his share of the human load. In short, the partnership idea has both the same attractions and the same limitations that have characterized historic synergisms, Arianisms, and semi-Pelagianisms. In their effort to give credit to each factor by the logic of a parcelling out process, they end in *tertium quids* of one sort or another that do insufficient credit to either partner and do not do justice to the searching biblical reflection on the strange duality of divine and human. It is possible, we believe, to use the partnership imagery if it is put in a somewhat different theological context. And that we shall try to do later in this section.

The Cipher Theory. A much more drastic restatement of the meaning of God in secular terms is found in what we shall call the cipher concept of Deity. As a cipher is a symbol that denotes "the absence of all magnitude or quantity . . . a nonentity,"[5] so in the variety of exponents of the position here sketched the word "God" represents a non-objective theism in which the reality or entity customarily associated with the term disappears from view. The word "God," nevertheless, is retained as a necessary part of Christian language. It becomes an appelation for processes in the world of human experience. We utter "God" and point to "him" when we are confronted with a certain compelling configuration of events. There are a variety of nuances to, and variations on, this theme in contemporary theology. Thus "God" or its equivalent may denote the experience men have, as in the "I must" or "I may" encounters as expounded by Herbert Braun.[6] Or the term "God" may point to and drive men toward healing social relationships, as in some of Paul van Buren's more recent comments.[7] Still others speak of "God" as the expression of the conviction that the universe will not "let down" men's creativity, love, and will to truth, the belief that there is an ennobling and supportive power at work in the cosmos.[8]

The version of the cipher theory we shall here examine is that of J. A. T. Robinson, presented in a preliminary way in his *Honest to God* and *The New Reformation?*[9] and expounded in more detail in the recent *Exploration into God, But That I Can't Believe!* and the revised version of *In the End, God.* It has kinship with the formulations of Wren-Lewis, except that Robinson argues for the usage of a responsive "Thou" to the supportive dimension of reality, and in this respect says more about Deity than Wren-Lewis is prepared to acknowledge.[9]

One of the interesting things about Robinson's thought is the range of interpretation to which it lends itself, from the "What's so new about that?" yawn of an occasional traditionalist to the welcome mat of the confessing atheist. Hopefully, the more recent inquiry into the nature of God will shed enough light to avoid the odd disagreements on what is really being said.[10] *Exploration into God* makes it clear that Robinson is no conventional atheist. But at the same time there is a radical edge to his reconceptualization of God which must be respected for what it is.

In *Honest to God,* Robinson laid down the lines of his present notion by his rejection of the "God out there." Many interpreters succeeded in taming the tiger by treating this theme as virtually synonymous with his denial of the "God up there," as if it were another version of protest against spatialization of God pushed in some fashion outward instead of upward. The attack on the making of God into "an object alongside other objects" as an interpretation of his notion helped to muddy the waters, for this kind of language had become the conventional wisdom, understood usually in a somewhat different fashion as a defense of the freedom of God and an assertion of the frailty of efforts to conceptualize him, and/or the arrogance of attempts to control him.

The meaning of the rejection of the God out there, and its elaboration, becomes clearer by way of an instructive analogy developed in *Exploration into God:* the devil. As becomes a scholar who has worked with the question of New Testament demythologizing, Robinson asserts the necessity of translating ancient and esoteric talk about the demonic into modern parlance. Thus, taking the same tack as Durkheim's classic analysis of the roots of religious belief as it is put into psychological idiom by Jung, he holds that "devil" language is not sheer superstition but points to a reality that men confront in their day to day existence. It "represents the element in human experience which Jung speaks of as the dark side or the shadow. It is profoundly and inescapably real. In former times, to personify it had the effect of making it more real and more vivid. To see Satan as a Person gave him objectivity, substance, 'power of being.' "[11]

In secular times men can no longer accept the myth of a personal power identified as "the devil." If we are to retain the kernel insight of the myth, we must get behind the personal language to the experience itself. The way to obscure this probe behind the scenes of language is to continue to insist on the discredited myth of a personal devil: "In order to make people take the reality of the dark side seriously the last way would be to insist on the existence of personification . . . The way to bring evil home is to demythologize. Or, rather, it is to show the reality in human experience which the myths have been describing— and one may then remythologize, as the psychologists do, though without any suggestion that these figures and archetypes 'exist' in the psyche or elsewhere."[12]

Robinson notes that the analogy between God and the devil breaks down at one point. God is ultimate and the devil is not. The reality to which the word "God" points is totally reliable and lasting in a way that the reality to which the word "devil" points is not. Beyond that, he is comfortable with the comparison and goes on to discuss the parallel work of demythologizing that must be done with the word "God." "God" is an affirmation not of something beyond our experience or in another world but of something given in our relationships.[13] "God" is a sound Christians make to point to a "dimension of experience" or a "relationship at the heart of the universe."

To believe is to be sensitive to an aspect of the universe which makes it worthy of basic trust. To say "God" is to affirm our conviction that the world at its deepest level honors and supports the qualities of love and personhood. The center of things, reliable in its nurture of the noblest man knows, evokes from the believer the tender personal response summed up in the "Father" of faith. No one can prove that the universe does have this depth nurture; faith, in the final analysis, is leap.[14] Yet it is a leap within the framework of the functional mind of this-worldly men whose world has been depopulated of personal demons and gods. Reasonable men may not be able to "see" the "dark" side of things in the world but are compelled to admit its reality in the day to day flow of life. By the same token, the pull of the "light" side—the ultimate weight—can be felt by those who live deeply in the world, and particularly by those who have had a window opened into reality by Jesus Christ. In Christ preeminently, and furnished with his new eyes, we can discern supportive love in the experience around us, and coming in relationship to it are led with Jesus to cry "Abba!"

Robinson wants it clearly understood that the graceful reality which is encountered is not just the subjective experience of men. The experience through which it comes (subjective as all human contact must be) reaches toward an objective nexus in the world. And this objectivity is not simply human relationships. Robinson disagrees with van Buren's recent comments that "God" is a poetic word for human relationships.[15] There is an "ineffable" plus in reality itself that supports personal value and elicits from the faith the explicative, "thou."

What do we make of Robinson's reconstruction of the idea of God? Surely this is an attempt to take the thought forms of a secular time with maximum seriousness. The contemporary erosion of the sense of a world populated by invisible, personal powers that control it is woven into the very center of a reconceptualized divinity. "God" has ceased to be an entity distinguishable from the day-to-day world in which men live. But, unlike the radical theology, there is no excision of "God," but rather an attempt to redefine the term as an infra-terrestrial power, process, dimension, claim.

The basic question that surfaces has to do with our figure of missionary penetration. Is it still the Christian Story we hear in the new language? There are many impassioned disclaimers that it is, and as well a persistent relating of the new talk about God to the biblical framework, including frequent citations from the text. Let us put the communication problem in these terms: Do we have translation analogies in "God" and the "devil," taking into account the qualification noted about ultimacy? Is "God" the term that points to the powers of light in the universe —ultimately reliable and prevailing—as "the devil" points to the powers of darkness? Have we carried out a responsible act of demythologizing when we compare the two?

From the point of view of the perspective being developed here, Robinson's treatment of the devil is very much to the point. Apart from the tasteless equation of "darkness" with evil—here is a place Robinson's commitment to a sensitive demythologizing is yet to be done[16]—and the tendency to link the power of evil at work in the world with psychological data to the neglect of sociological, biological, political, etc., structures, the concern to find secular equivalents to mythical figures is an entirely legitimate and a necessary task. Its legitimacy is rooted not only in the missionary mandate but also in the coming of age thesis developed earlier. That is, if we understand Christian teaching about terrestrial reality in the pioneering-relinquishing framework, then it is possible, and finally necessary, to find secular equivalents and rational verification for all the faith-community's commentary about life on the earth. God wills an adulthood for the race in which truth stands on its own feet. Faith's talk of demonic powers is such an anticipation of secular wisdom about factors and forces in the human situation which may be ultimately described in psychological, sociological, biological and political terms. In a world come of age, it is not only possible but necessary for an adult faith to seek out the secular equivalent of its myths.

Now we come to the question of "God." Is "God" a myth whose

meaning is finally reducible to terrestrial processes also? We are not saying *human* experiences or *human* actions, as Robinson distinguishes his position from van Buren and others who speak in these terms. But while not human it is terrestrial, a dimension of one space-time world, however elusive the objective plus is that runs through and "transcends" the human experience and action that Robinson calls "God." If God were a gap-filling Deity, then indeed such a translation could and should be made. "God" would then have been a convenient symbol that served man in the childhood stages of his growth, but can be secularized in time of human maturity. We have said that this is indeed true about many of the functions of belief in God. But we have also tried to show that the sloughing off of the functional roles of Deity does not finally "put God out of business" but rather leads us toward an understanding of the God who exists in his own right. Such a God cannot be justified by the functions men attribute to him. He is not imprisoned in the primitive imageries of usefulness but is a free God. As free, he cannot be reduced to secular categories, as the "devil" can. He is who he is, and in the final reaches of his being cannot be caught in manageable categories.

This line of inquiry has two implications for the reconception of God put forward by Robinson. On the one hand, his construct is not secular enough; on the other, it fails to do justice to several basic themes in the Christian Story.

It is not secular enough, for Robinson is still holding a little territory for Deity in a world that rightfully belongs to the maturity to man. Thus he insists that important events, persons and processes are known fully when they evoke a responsive "Thou" from the sensitive participant. That which yields up the inner life of the universe, the spirit that probes to reality at its deepest level, is the act of belief. To say "God" is to point to a dimension which cannot be grasped in secular categories. The problem with this contention is that it seeks to keep men still tied to the umbilical cord of religious belief when maturity depends on its severing. Coming of age means that worldly reality must be understood on its own terms. If there is a depth dimension in the universe, if there is a process that is supportive of human value and claims our allegiance, then it ought to be open to the inspection of men and unclouded by the uncertainties of belief. Anything that is worth having on man's pilgrimage toward a healed world will not be cloaked in the nebulous. A truly secular faith will work for the total demythologizing of all religious language that has to do with the terrestrial enterprise and will not cling to residual mysteries which represent a refined form of triumphalism. The God of human maturity will not be party to the occult claims of religion to have the key to the fully human life attainable only by the leap of faith, a secret that "cannot be finally proved or disproved."[17]

Robinson's version must also be measured against the Christian Story. Does his reconception of God translate it faithfully into the language of a this-worldly land? Do we meet here the creating, calling, claiming, reclaiming, restoring Other whose dialogue with the world is honored in a way that the monologues of radical theology fail to do? There is a quality in divine otherness which invites our attention as we seek to answer this question: freedom. Let us examine two of its characteristics.

The freedom of God in the Christian Story means freedom from his creation. While the whole drama has to do with his intimate relationship with and participation in the world, its premise is that there is a distinguishable Other who is the subject of this activity. If the Story is about a bi-polar interaction, then there must be solidity to each pole. God is God and the world is the world. Relation yes, fusion, no. As noted in our discussion of the radical theology, there is an over-againstness in the Christian conception of God as it touches his relationship with the created order. Freedom means the independence of Deity.

This is the point that Helmut Gollwitzer makes about the efforts of Herbert Braun to restate the meaning of God in terms of the experiences of "I ought" and "I may." He contends that the Christian God cannot be reduced to a "cipher" that points to existential encounters. In short, encounters must have an Encounterer if they are to be responsible reports of biblical faith. Robinson agrees with Gollwitzer that there is objectivity to God.[18] Christian belief is more than a report of our experiences and commitments. We really have to do with a reality that comes through our "thou" sensitivities. There is a supportive qualitiy in the universe that is the basis for our awareness.

However, Gollwitzer is affirming more than an objective referent to existential awareness, as Robinson acknowledges in his dismissal of his line of thought as the "reaction of traditional orthodoxy," and a defense of God as a "supernatural Person."[19] In his analysis of Ernst Bloch, Gollwitzer speaks of a God who is not exhausted in his being by human or historical action outside the experiences of men. We pursue the same theme here one step further. The God of Christian faith cannot be exhausted by existential events, human or historical action, dimensions of the universe, or cosmic ferment. While he participates in the world, he is not of it. If the ennobling currents and qualities in the world would cease to be, or if the created order itself would vanish, he would not thereby be dissolved. He is free from, as well as free for, his creation. Robinson has tied the reality of "God" so intimately to factors in the created order, as the reality of "the devil" is so bound in with it, that the independent solidity of otherness is called into radical question. Without the divine freedom to be Another, it is difficult to see how the Story survives the translation.

Freedom in God means self-determination as well as otherness. The lively interaction between God and man in the Christian reading of history accords to each partner the power of decision. Man in his freedom turns his back on the divine call. God in his freedom responds in the central action of the drama of reconciliation, Jesus Christ. God's freedom to be for man as well as his freedom from man assumes that he is in charge of his own life. He is not imprisoned in the causal nexus, but controls his own responses. Can the same decisive subjectivity be attributed to the objective reality in the universe to which the word "God" points in Robinson's terminology? Here we enter into the discussion of "the personal" as it touches the doctrine of God.

Robinson makes it clear that he does not believe in a "supernatural Person." The "celestial Mikado," "invisible Superman," "divine Super-ego," "Manager," "divine Planner," etc., are offensive to the sensitive spirit who takes seriously the fact of massive evil that such a "Supreme Being" would have to either author or tolerate. But more important, in the context of secularization this projection of a big daddy in the sky is as impossible to modern secular man as is the hypostatization of a personal devil. Serious theological inquiry, however, must press past the pejoratives to the question of what really is at stake here. It is not the conception of God as "a supernatural Person." What this image calls up is either the Green Pastures deity of a spatially three tier universe, or an invisible free-floating super-good person, as the devil is an invisible free-floating super-bad person. To attribute these conceptions to responsible theology, even the "traditional orthodoxy" of theologians such as Gollwitzer and "most contemporary churchmen" ("most contemporary churchmen would regard him as valiant for the faith") is very dubious indeed.[20] Apart from the fact that theology has used the term person in its discussion of God in another context (the Trinity, in which the three persons are not usually referred to as three centers of self-consciousness, and hence cannot be a concept used synonymously with the self-determination that is under discussion), it is not a distant visible or an invisible person which we have at the center of the Story's talk about God. What is at stake is "the personal," not "a person."

We agree with Robinson that the task is "to depersonify and not depersonalize God."[21] But that is a very delicate operation. How is the personal preserved in our attempts at redefinition of God? By not cutting out that central factor of personal existence, self-determination. By this standard the patient has died in Robinsonian surgery. The personal is taken by him to refer either to the kind of response that is evoked when man is grasped by the universe's reliability, the "Thou" of the believer,[22] or to refer to the qualities which the world at its deepest level supports.[23] Nothing can be said about any "behind the scenes" subjectivity that is alleged to be the source of activities in the universe, for it is ruled out by the this-worldly style of functional modernity.

The personal is a crucial category for interpreting the God of the Story precisely because it lifts up that quality which is excised in Robinson's analysis, namely, a "behind the scenes" reality. That is the heart of personhood as we speak about it in day-to-day relationships. A person is that segment of the natural process of these relationships who juts up far enough "above" their dynamics in memory, anticipation, self-awareness, and self-propulsion to be distinguishable from them and to take charge to some degree of his participation in them. Personhood, as distinguished from other phenomena, is self-determination. When this freedom is called into question either in theory or practice, the singularity of the human is at stake. The dignity of being human is not a belief that there is "an invisible person" somehow hiding in the self. The absurdity, or perhaps we should say the schizophrenic overtones, of such an idea should not deflect us from seeing how such a misunderstanding could resurface in other contexts which draw on the analogy of personhood.

The reason "the personal"—not "a supernatural Person"—is a crucial metaphor for interpreting the Christian drama is that it expresses in the only way we now know how (there might indeed be other ways, were human evolution to produce more advanced forms of life) and that it points to the divine subjectivity, the freedom of God to dialogue with his world. As the world does not exhaust reality, so neither do its most creative processes or healing events develop sui generis. They are the expressions of the divine will, even as the predicates of human behavior point beyond themselves to their source in man's subjectivity.

We cannot prove the presence of a decisional center in the behavior of men, although the language used to describe the human phenomenon is poverty-stricken and may be virtually impossible without recourse to a deciding "I" that crops up awkwardly in the most determined efforts to reduce relationships to empirical dimensions. And there are those who make provocative charts of the landscape of self-awareness by introspective descent.[24] For all that, behaviorists reflecting the empirical spirit of secularization and reacting rightly against the rigid compartmentalizations of a faculty psychology and megalomanic forms of idealistic philosophy, still view selfhood as epiphenomenon explicable by, and imprisoned in, physiological causality. By the same token the divine subjectivity cannot be proved to the empirical spirit of a secular age. At work on a cosmic scale is the same Watsonian behaviorism which insists that functioning relationships exhaust reality, and that talk of a personal center is myth. Robinson's functionalism is of this variety. It is indeed responsive to the spirit of the age, but its openness to contemporary sensitivity is at the price of the freedom of God.

The way into the divine self-determination has other parallels to the human analogy which give additional importance to "the personal." Human love reaches out to the other in a care that passes through "the predicates" to the center of the other's being. We have spoken of this pilgrimage. While the attractions of the other draw the lovers together, there emerges in the relationship a bond that transcends their coming and going, at the heart of which is a conviction that love has really to do with a self expressing itself through the physical, psychological and sociological particulars, but not reducible to them. In a similar fashion, the subjectivity of God finding its way to man at the level of predicates leads towards a communion and life together in which God is known and loved for his own sake, a Reality that is not exhausted by his predicative relations.[25]

Two rejoinders can quickly be made to such talk of God and man. One is that it is anthropomorphic through and through, and as such unworthy of the Deity whose majesty cannot be caught in human formulas. There is, of course, an important warning against idolatry in this contention. No human analogy can finally trace out the inner being of God; in our life on earth we see through translucencies, not "face to face." But in this well-placed counsel concerning idolatry there are often some unexamined assumptions. One is that there is somehow a more accurate way of getting to divine reality than by the human metaphor. But there is no other place to go to describe any phenomenon than language drawn from human experience. All descriptions of basic reality, whether we are talking about the behavior of electrons, humans or God are anthropomorphic in this sense.[26] The problem is what anthropomorphic descriptions do most justice to the Story which gives us our identity? Does talk of anything less than the freedom of a self to be itself and to control its life point meaningfully to the God who acts in the drama of history? While God may have abysmal regions of unimaginable reality in himself, while he may be eminently more than personal, he is at the very least personal. Our anthropomorphisms that deal in freedom home in more closely than those that censor this quality.

A further word also must be said about anthropomorphisms. There is a triumphalist note borrowed from a theology of another age that comes through the diatribe against the portrayal of Deity in human categories. This "God" dwells in such majesty and is so fearful of his prerogatives that he refuses continuity with man's language. But is God such a self-possessing fortress? We have tried to say that he is not. He is a God who takes shame and humiliation upon himself in the life and death of the rejected and crucified one. It is by virtue of this participation in brokenness that human language about divine reality is validated. The very fact that God took the face of man in the incarnation has not only made human talk about God possible but has made talk of God in human categories possible. For as Barth himself notes, he came not as a star or stone or angel but as a man. In the selfchoosing life of the man Jesus the fact of God's own self-determining freedom is finally disclosed.

Another rejoinder that might be anticipated is: What does it add to believe in a subject whose solidity is distinguishable from the universe? Is it not irrelevant, obsolete, an afterthought which has no bearing on the life of secular man? Robinson speaks about the superfluity of belief in a God who is "banished to the edges of life. . . . He is on the edge of the map . . . marginal and peripheral."[27] For Robinson, God and our encounter with "him" is spoken in another idiom. We are dealing with an "ineluctable relatedness." We are "seized, held by a prevenient reality, undeniably in its objectivity . . . it comes, as it were, from beyond with an unconditional claim. . . . Obedience to this overmastering reality is what distinguishes the man who is constrained to use the word 'God' . . . compelled to say in existentialist terms, 'This is it. This is the most real thing in the world, that which is ultimately and inescapably true.' "[28]

Is God One who works by "overmastering," by seizure and ineluctable constraint? Is the style of faith for secular times one that is at home with talk of the compelling and the undeniable? We have sought to show elsewhere that neither is the case. We put it here in this way: the revision of the Story that comes in the cipher option is not only a dubious rendition of the original, but it is not a radical enough restatement to take into account the new notes of the Story that secularity help us to hear. It is too bound to the categories of the militant, the intellectual and imagery framework of triumphalism. To say that faith is superfluous, that it does not command, that is, it is subject to the deepest doubts of man—those are the credentials of a suffering God and a faith that does not draw belief to itself by the club but by a love that evokes the act of the hesitant, modest yet genuine movement of answering love.

The Option of Divine Futurity

As Harvey Cox notes, "In the coming decade . . . it will certainly be eschatology, our understanding of the Christian promise, which will require the best theological thought."[29] We have drawn briefly on some of the current themes of the eschatological theologies in our weighing of the components of time. We give more sustained attention here to Christian futurology as it touches on the reconstruction of the doctrine of God in response to contemporary this-worldliness.

Since the theological community is just at the beginning of careful inquiry into the ramifications of eschatology for secularization, we shall explore a futurological alternative to the radical theology by way of an experiment in theological thought. There is no careful exposition or defence of the position to be sketched, although there are hints of it and flirtations with it in some current eschatological commentary. Our purpose is not to attribute the somewhat awkward speculations that follow to any one theologian, but to see what such a perspective might look like in our list of options, and also to use some of its building materials in construction efforts to be later attempted.

Our theory begins with the acceptance of this-worldliness as an accurate reading of reality. In the "now" with which man today must come to terms there is no other world, other being, or other reality over against the time-space home we inhabit. Man alone must build his earth, for there is no God "out there" who controls the enterprise or even assures it of final fruition.

But even while secular sensitivities define the orbit in which theology must move, if it is faith that is to be translated, basic Christian commitments about God cannot be dissolved. Specifically, the notion of otherness and even the Story's central conviction about a divine Other who carries on a living relationship with his world must be maintained. It is possible to be faithful to this kind of transcendence and still live in the idiom of this-worldliness on the basis of two biblical themes which finally merge into one: the Hebraic framework for thinking about God, and biblical eschatology.

The Hebrew mind finds God deeply wrapped into the historical process. Such a perspective rejects the alien organ of Platonic cosmology on which the church has relied for millennia in its thinking about God. Platonism dictated to theology the necessity of speaking about God as an Other alongside the world, extending toward the world a network of invisible relationships that were, and are, more real than the world itself. This super-world is a Greek construct and is separable from the biblical Story that sees God in a different relationship to the creation.

When it is seen in authentic categories, the "different relation-ship" is cast in terms of the future. Both in the prophetic pointing toward the Messiah and its New Testament finale which looks for the "One who is to come," God is conceived as "out ahead." There is a real Other with whom we have to do, but he is the One whose claim is not from a metaphysical yonder but an historical future. This-worldly instincts are not denied, for there is no God alongside the world; the God of faith waits out ahead, beckons us from there, sets up in us a restless discontent with the givens of past and present.

Futurity makes faith revolutionary. It calls everything into question. All givens of the past and present are subject to radical change, for "what is" is always short of "what will be" which calls the status quo structures beyond themselves. The only structures that are responsible are those that are open to the future and facilitate the movement of men toward it. Further, the diversion of men's eyes to the occult doings of Deity such as characterized the Platonic conception of God is impossible, for God is not "behind the scenes." The only way to look for him and relate to him is by turning the eyes of men not "upward" but "for-ward." Obedience to him is not a retreat from the world into the invisibilities and securities of the "now"—there is no place to hide—but to prepare for his coming. And that means to be ready to give an accounting for the stewardship of the earth. That stewardship belongs completely to man, for there is no other reality contemporaneous with him on whom he can blame his misfortunes or to whom he can run for aid and comfort. He is alone in his cosmos and must shoulder responsibility for it. What happens in this world depends on what he does with this mandate to make it habitable and whole. He may indeed blow it up, or he can bring it healing. It's up to him to determine which it will be.

The urge to press toward healing comes to the community of faith through its hope. Hope is the belief in the biblical promise that God is indeed coming toward us from out of the future. His presence or absence cannot be controlled by what man does or does not do in his earth. Hope, also, is a vision of the healed world which God wills to find when he comes, his kind of world where the relations of men and creation reflect his posture. Christian hope is no guarantee of such a future; it is not *expectation* but *hope*, not an unconditional "sure thing," but conditional upon human effort. What is sure is "the One who comes."

The reflection of Christian hope is already discernible in the past and present. While there is no other Platonic world alongside creation in which Deity dwelt or dwells, there is a power at work. That power is the shadow cast on history by the One who comes. It stretches back from the end into our time to the edge of Bethlehem and further. Or to change the figure, it is a beam of light coming out of the future that has its signalling mirror in Jesus Christ. We know of what is to come, for its rays have been caught by that man. In him is the image of the One to come. And from this bent light other reflectors are illumined in human history. Thus God makes his presence felt in the Event of the past and by the gentle pressures on history of the vision of what lies out ahead. He thus does not compel history to bow the knee to him. He comes with only the power of a vision held before men's eyes which they may choose or reject. Yet he is at work even now in and through the light cast toward us from the future.

To reinterpret the meaning of God in futurist terms is a missionary penetration which seeks to translate into secular idiom by affirming (a) the this-worldly context in which men live today, and (b) the coming of age mandate that man should take responsibility for his future. But it also strives to remain faithful to the Story by affirming (a) a real otherness in God responsive to Hebrew rather than Greek categories, and (b) casting its message in the framework of biblical eschatology which, we might add in passing, is not only seen as a faithful rendering of the Story but also as another point of contact with contemporary styles of thought, in this case the future-oriented posture of many contemporaries.[30]

An Assessment of Futuristic Theology

Eschatological theology understood in the above terms is a very attractive alternative to the radical theology. Its zeal to translate faith into contemporary idiom is manifest in its willingness to accept the this-worldly reading of our experience, to call man to adult responsibility for his world and future and to gear in with a generation that has its eyes turned forward. And it represents an effort in missionary communication that seeks to do justice to the Christian Story, speaking of a God who is in futurist terms very much alive. Further, it is a reinterpretation of faith in terms of the end-point of the drama, a theme not only much neglected but of particular relevance in an era in which need for, sensitivity to, and evidence of the note of promise are manifest. And still further, the characterization of God's relationship to his world in terms of a gentle pressure is comparable to the note of crucifixion and marginality here being developed. The God of the future does not command assent but seeks to evoke it by visionary presence in the "new" and a coming in the "then." He does not appear in overriding glory to straighten out all that has been amiss but grants man the freedom to determine what will be in response to the only power he chose to invoke, the power of a sure and loving coming.

Does the position we have roughed out succeed in being faithful to both faith and modern fact? Let us look first at its reading of the Story and inquire about the nature of the God who is a participant in it.

The Christian drama reports a God who creates, reconciles

and heals. His action is manifest in what has happened, does happen, and will happen. He is the God of yesterday, today and tomorrow. It must be asked in what sense Christian futurity's God of tomorrow is also present in his livingness in the historical now and then. Can the concept of anticipation bear the weight of faith's talk about what God has done and is doing? That is, can the God whose reality consists in his coming be said to be at work in any fundamental sense in past or present creative and redemptive acts? Let us take the conviction that God is at work in the world. Translated into futurist categories this would mean either (a) God is present only in the whetted expectations of the eschatologically oriented or (b) that, like Barth's roadside reflectors, God is also present incognito in the healing events illumined by the light that shines from "out ahead" (not as Barth uses the imagery, as the light of the Word illumining the traces of divine action in the world). That is, the believer in the One who comes looks for signs in the world of what is to be, portents of the Kingdom and "King" identifiable by their healing character. Wherever men embody fragments of the vision, there is "God" at work. "God" in the present becomes therefore the ejaculation of faith, the word that denotes the processes of healing in the world. It is distinguished from either the radical theology which drops the term, or from cipher conceptions of Deity, in that there is a real referent. The difference is the referent is a reality yet to be. What is applicable in the present can be extended to the past, even to the definitive event of Jesus. In him we have the fundamental disclosure of the One to come, for here healing has broken into history in a radical way. It is from this point that we look both outward in the world to the echoes of this reconciliation and forward to their source.

As regards the first alternative, that God is present only in eschatological expectations, it would seem that the reality of the God of yesterday and today is too drastically circumscribed to be a faithful rendering of the Story. Divine grace in past and present is limited to man's cognition. But God's wide-ranging creative and redemptive action explodes far beyond the perimeter of human awareness. According to the Story, God works in and through both historical and cosmic processes without benefit of knowing subject. He cannot be domesticated in the acts of belief.

With respect to the second, God's incognito presence in healing, we must put the same question to futurist interpretations as is put to Robinson: Can the God of faith be conceived of as truly present when we point only to functions without a freedom for man which is at work in and through these functions? Will it then be objected that transcendence is not being denied? God is present proleptically; he shines in from the yonder out ahead. But we must ask, what does this really mean? His presence proleptically is not authentic if this is meant in terms of eschatological categories, for the reasons given above. Can it mean anything else? Here we face some insuperable language problems.

Futurist interpretations import metaphors from the spatial context into a temporal setting. Thus God is "the One who comes," or God is "out ahead." Now we can understand what is meant when it is said that someone waits for us on the road out ahead, or that he is coming to visit us this afternoon. This "he" is somewhere now and will close that distance between "he" and "we." But what does it mean to say that someone who *is not* now is waiting for us "out ahead in time?" It makes for giddy, and in a sense, powerful rhetoric, but in the final analysis its meaning is impenetrable.

By the same token it is possible to speak of a God who now is and who will be also with us "out ahead," for there is some analogical frame of reference (as well as some theological basis, as we shall presently argue). But there is no hook in human experience for talk of the effective presence now of One who is yet to come. None, that is, except the power of the vision of the future which so grips men that it generates new responses to the present, and in this sense it can be said that a future acts back on the present. But we have noted that this is too limited a conception of the activity of God, for God is a big God whose past and present working cannot be confined to the effects of belief in his coming. We are left with a linguistically clever but finally opaque notion of the effect of divine futurity on the present, a notion that does not seem by our speculations here, in any event, to be able to do justice to the living otherness of God that is at work in past and present as well as future.

The factor which Christian futurology so desperately seeks to avoid is the "Platonic" otherness which it believes is both inimical to contemporary this-worldliness and detachable from the Story. It seeks to restate faith without recourse to the belief that there is another Reality which lives alongside the world we inhabit. But we must ask, is it really the Platonic mind-set that is at stake here? And is it the factor that is being eliminated in the futurist reconstruction? We do not believe that either of these things is true.

The fundamental problem with the Platonic framework is twofold: (1) the conception of concurrent otherness which is held to be "more real" than the temporal flow, and the corollary counsel that salvation is to be found in removal from the corruptions and transiency of time to the placidity of eternity, and (2) the timelessness of the duality of "this world" and the "other world." Both of these themes are set against Judeo-Christian sensitivities. First, biblical faith affirms the unconditional reality and goodness of matter and history, and fought battles all around the theological circle to secure itself against sundry efforts to platonize. Second, the biblical conceptions of history do not envisage a perpetual duality of time and eternity, with sorties of the soul from one to the other. There is indeed a distinction between "time" and "eternity," but there is movement toward a point of convergence. God and man are distinguishable poles in a dialogical relationship that drives toward a goal. The Story conceives that destiny neither as collapse into finitude or dissolution into infinity but a strange transfiguration of one by the other—not the old "earth" and the old "heaven" but a "new heaven" and a "new earth," God and his world in a fresh union of time and eternity.

Platonism's bypath, therefore, is not the problem of the belief in concurrent otherness but the character and direction of that otherness. And one does no justice to the need for disengaging faith from Platonism by attacking the conception of total otherness—past, present as well as future—or by transposing it to the dimension of time yet to be. It is instructive, in this connection, to see the careful and extensive effort of Oscar Cullmann to disengage faith from Platonic categories. While pioneering an understanding of biblical at-homeness in the time framework against static Greek erosions of it, he nevertheless preserves the strong Judeo-Christian commitment to the present reality of God which he views as radically different from the Greek notion of eternity.[31]

The gist of our critique of a radical futurizing of Deity is that it cannot do justice to the historical and cosmic action of God in past and present, an action that is part of the biblical Story and not a superannuated Platonism. Indeed, the continued belief of the Christian community that reality is not exhausted by the dimension of this world may give offense not to the secular spirit of modernity which missionary faith must take seriously, but to the absolutizing of the secular sense which declares all talk of present divine otherness to be out of bounds. And so it must be if the price is the dissolution of its central drama. The missionary is doing no favor to his field by saying in a loud voice what is already the conventional wisdom. He must be prepared to risk the charge of offensiveness. It would not be the first time faith has been a stumbling block.

Christian futurology, as we have described it, raises some questions about its faithfulness to secularity as well as to the Story. They come at the point of affirming the world's adulthood. In spite of the valiant attempt to assert the competence of, and mandate for, man to seize his own destiny without the tyrannies and crutches of religion, there is a lingering triumphalism in its perspective. Why is eschatology lifted up as the fighting word of the church today? To make contact with a future-oriented time, to talk its language. Yes, and more, to help it to face its own future. That is a commendable and crucial rationale for tilting theology toward the future. However, there is in the folds of this theological good will the hint of an apologetic that says the only way that secular men can face the future responsibly without the traps that will destroy them is through a Christian perspective on the future.

The God of tomorrow and the faith he spawns prepare men to keep open to that future in a way that contemporary "isms" of man's creation cannot do.[32] If such a conviction were couched in the pioneering-relinquishing rhythm earlier outlined, it could be seen as a legitimate definition of the role of theology. However, when a theological perspective—yes faith itself—is claimed as the key to making and keeping men human, or happy, or responsible, or open to the future, we still have an invitation to immaturity. Faith may do such a work provisionally, but it must be prepared to step back, in fact it must work for the human growth that will require it to step back. Such a readiness to put belief's human work out of business "clears the deck for the God of the Bible," for faith in the One who comes in his own right and evokes the act of commitment not for the dividend of an insightful futurity but simply because God will be there "out ahead" to be companied with and served. We must now explore such an alternative, using materials which have emerged from the speculative discussion of eschatology.

Footnotes

1. *Prisoner for God, op. cit.,* pp. 131–132.
2. Smith, *Secular Christianity, op. cit.,* p. 21. See comments of David Cairns, *God up There?* (Edinburgh: St. Andrews Press, 1967), pp. 31ff., and Gollwitzer, *The Existence of God as Confessed by Faith, op. cit.,* pp. 15–51, 142–201.

3. Theological experiments are a way of taking seriously the community setting in which thought about God does its work, and a learning from the empirical method of a secular age as well. See Jenkins experimental approach to his Bampton lectures, *The Glory of Man, op. cit.,* pp. 21f., and an "experiment in thought" by Cox, *Initiative in History: A Christian-Marxist Exchange,* an occasional paper published by The Church Society for College Work, 1967, O. Blanchette et al., pp. 14ff.

4. See filmstrip "The World Come of Age," produced by the audiovisual department of the United Presbyterian Church.

5. *Websters Collegiate Dictionary,* Fifth Edition (Springfield, Mass.: Merriam, 1941), p. 182. Braun makes use of the notion in his reconceptualization of God, as does Gollwitzer in his critique of Braun. Herbert Braun, "The Problem of New Testament Theology," translated by Jack Saunders, *The Bultmann School of Biblical Interpretation: New Directions?* Journal for Theology and the Church, Vol. I, Robert Funk, ed. (New York: Harper, 1965), pp. 169–183, and Gollwitzer, *The Existence of God as Confessed by Faith, op. cit.,* pp. 82–107.

6. *Ibid.*

7. The Swander Lectures, 1966, mimeographed paper of taped presentation, Lancaster Theological Seminary.

8. John Wren-Lewis is an exponent of this position. See essay in Dewi Morgan, *They Became Anglicans* (London: A. R. Mowbray), and broadcast remarks, ATV, November 26, 1967, in Great Britain.

9. Comments on Robinson's theology by Wren-Lewis in a TV interview.

10. Perhaps this is over optimistic, for a traditional theist like the Bishop of Coventry can still say in a review of *But That I Can't Believe!* (London: Collins, Fontana Books, 1967): "Indeed it was with a growing feeling of relief that I read his latest—*But This I Can't Believe*—relief that this most avant garde of bishops could make such a clear affirmation of Christian faith." *Shire and Spire,* The Diocese of Coventry, No. 118 (September, 1967), p. 2.

11. Robinson, *Exploration into God, op. cit.,* p. 41.

12. *Ibid.,* p. 41.

13. *Ibid.,* pp. 66ff.

14. *Ibid.,* p. 68.

15. *Ibid.,* pp. 63–67.

16. The Rev. Albert Cleage sums up the deep-seated feeling of black men about the destructive pedagogy of common language: "The white man has always asserted that black is ugly. It is written into his language. Anything distasteful is black. You're blackballed in a fraternity. Everything black is vicious. So there must be a candid acceptance, if you're going to have black

and white co-existing, that black is just as beautiful as white. And as good."
United Church Herald, Vol. XI, No. 2 (February, 1968), p. 29. See also
Albert Cleage, *The Black Messiah* (New York: Sheed & Ward, 1968). The
harm done by this kind of stereotyping has been fully documented in
studies made of textbooks and school practices that reinforce myths about
both black and white. See U. S. Commission on Civil Rights, *Racial Isolation
in the Public Schools,* (Washington, D.C.: Superintendent of Documents,
U.S. Government Printing Office, 1967) and James S. Coleman et al.,
Equality of Educational Opportunity, (Washington, D.C.: Superintendent
of Documents, U.S. Government Printing Office, 1966).

17. Robinson, *Exploration into God, op. cit.,* p. 68.

18. *Ibid.,* p. 70.

19. *Ibid.,* p. 42.

20. It is unfortunate for the theological enterprise that Robinson does not
respond with more than rhetoric to the thoughtful arguments of Gollwitzer,
for the joining of the issue would have advanced the discussion considerably.
Gollwitzer's own comments on *Honest to God,* in appendix to the English
edition of *The Existence of God as Confessed by Faith* (Philadelphia: Westminster Press) are also not as clear as they might be, perhaps because the
full implications of Robinson's position had to wait upon further exploration.

21. *Ibid.,* p. 87.

22. *Ibid.,* p. 66.

23. *Ibid.,* pp. 132ff.

24. See Michael Novak, *Belief and Unbelief* (New York: The Macmillan
Company, 1965), pp. 55–106 for a sensitive mapping of this inner terrain.

25. See Gollwitzer, *op. cit.,* pp. 102–104.

26. A point made by Dorothy Sayers, *The Mind of the Maker* (London:
Metheun, 1941), pp. 17ff. See also Gollwitzer's extended discussion of
"Anthropomorphism and Analogy," *op. cit.,* pp. 142–201.

27. *Exploration into God, op. cit.,* pp. 22, 38, 111, 113.

28. *Ibid.,* pp. 66–67.

29. Harvey Cox, "Evolutionary Progress and Christian Presence," *Concilium,* Vol. VI, No. 3, p. 18. A note sounded frequently in the more recent
utterances that appear in the collection of essays, *On not Leaving it to the
Snake* (New York: The Macmillan Company, 1967), pp. 9–18, 21, 31–46,
76–88.

30. See the comments of W. A. Visser Hooft, *Christians for the Future*
(BBC Publications, 1967), pp. 21–24.

31. Oscar Cullmann, *Christ and Time,* rev. ed. (Philadelphia: Westminster
Press, 1964). See also *Salvation in History* (New York: Harper, 1967),
translated by Sidney Sowers and the editorial staff of SCM Press, pp. 17–64.

32. A familiar refrain in Christian futurology as in Moltmann, *op. cit.*, pp. 33, 41, 60, 65, 77, 93, 102, 119, 337, 338; Cox, *On not Leaving it to the Snake, op. cit.*, pp. 31–46, 85–88; Braaten, "Speaking of God in a Secular Age," *Context*, Vol. I, No. 1 (Autumn, 1967), pp. 5–17.

10

GOD AS PIONEER

In our examination of the alternatives to radical theology's response to this-worldliness, we have been building toward another option. The insights of the partnership and cipher theories provide the background, and the futurity perspective provides the jumping off point. In sketching this alternative we use the image of the "pioneer," the "one who goes before." We have made some use already of this theme in remarks about the "pioneering-relinquishing" style. We now apply it directly as a symbol of divine action.

The figure of pioneering makes contact with the innovative spirit of science-technology and a future-oriented epoch. Its biblical roots are in the moving passages of Hebrews which describe a wayfaring faith and characterize Jesus as its "pioneer" (Hebrews 11-12). And in the back of the New Testament commitment to a pilgrim style is the covenant of the God of Israel who moves through history as the One who goes before by pillar of cloud and fire.

As the God of the futurity conception just examined is "out ahead," so too is the pioneer. He sets up a revolutionary tension between what is and what will be. To keep step with him demands eyes that are turned forward and feet on the move. This tension is not a contest between time and eternity which invites flight from history but a surge forward within the historical processes themselves, calling the believer toward the horizon beyond the structures of past and present. Because he is on the move in the world, he is met and served not by standing still but by keeping pace. Faith is going toward the One who ranges before us in an open future.

While such a conception speaks of a structure-splitting opening out of faith toward the future brought by a genuine Other with whom men have to do as in our thought experiment, there is affirmed in the pioneering figure a real presence of God in past and present as well as future. The pioneer is companion to his world even as he presses forward, as the pillar went before the ancient pilgrims in their journey toward the promised land. His love is "ever-lasting," coursing steadfastly through the time plane, without interruption of past, present, or future. He is out ahead, yet he is Emmanuel, God with us.

The "pioneer" is a future-oriented image that also seeks to take seriously the steadfastness of companionship, for it lifts up the freedom of God. As such, it is an effort to correct the sub-decisional character of the cipher theory. The pioneer is in control of his own life. He is not a process without self-direction, one which may evoke feelings about the universe's reliability and the explicative "thou" in its respondents but can only be characterized by its functioning. In and through the support of value, faith discerns an objective thou, a freedom in God whose love draws men into and along the way of pilgrimage.

The companionship of a genuine Other, the coactivity of God and man, is underscored in the partnership thesis. How is it possible to restate this insight so that we are dealing with more than co-workers between whom the responsibilities of a common work and walk are parcelled out, thus providing for neither the full freedom of man or God? We have explored the historic struggles to do justice to the integrity of both divine and human action and were led to the affirmation of both copresence and copenetration. Thus here also we must speak of the pioneer who moves forward "under his own steam" and his companion, man, who is also "on his own," yet the pioneer's life is inextricably bound up with the activity of the human pilgrim.

While we are up against a genuine paradox, legitimated because of the necessity of its components to any faithful reading of the Christian Story and the fact that alternative versions do less than justice to them, there are some faint reflections in our day-to-day experiences of this strange complementarity. We have noted several in our images of father and tutor, how each can be a discrete self yet also be present in son and student. The same distinct yet coterminal quality characterizes human pioneering. The pioneer is no soloist. In the biblical setting always, and in the secular setting usually, he is part of a community expedition in living or learning. And a good pioneer, like a good father and tutor, seeks to impart to his companions those qualities which make him what he is: both the knowledge of the trail and the spirit of trailblazing. The success of the one who goes before is not evidenced by the unthinking duplication of the way that has been marked out but by the coadventuring of those who catch from him the spirit and "savvy" of a pathfinder. In our context the pioneer leads by rebirth of the grace of pathfinding in those who journey with him.

What we have been struggling to do in the motifs of co-presence of divine and human is not only to show how faith celebrates the grace at work in human creativity but to lay the groundwork for another celebrative note: the full freedom of man to chart his own course and make his own way without the God who demands fealty, lays down the law of pilgrimage, and secures its successful completion. That is why we do not want to turn the pioneer into a gap-filler who commands allegiance as the One who alone can get man on with the job of meeting the future responsibility. We want to say that the future belongs to man in his adulthood, yes, that in the final analysis man does not need the pioneer himself. The pioneer who has done his work with his companions becomes a disposable factor on the agenda of the mature pilgrim who takes responsibility for his own future. Of what use a pioneer who is no longer needed to mark the trail? Quite so. There is a kind of humor, in fact, in the behavior of one who goes before, while the company that follows is quite prepared to draw its own maps and plunge forward knowledgeably. This One who ranges before us is indeed marginal and something of an offence in his insistent functionless presence. But is not this the humiliation we have met before in other guises, the superfluous God whose only rationale is that he is there to be companied with and loved, the crucified one who comes in his powerlessness? And because he comes this way, the response drawn from us is not one wrested by the power of the proof that we need him but one that is freely given in the leap of love.

A Celebrative Faith

In our examination of this-worldliness we have been pressed once again beyond a radical theology to a eucharistic motif, a celebrative theology. Such a perspective on secularization rejoices that man has final power over his own future. As in our discussion of coming of age, so here too, there are no divine tyrannies or crutches that drive him away from the task of building the earth. Yet there is One with whom he is called into relationship in and through his construction, the pioneer of faith. This too he celebrates, the life together with Another. Respecting man's freedom for his future, the pioneer comes not to bludgeon into submission but to hold before man's eyes a vision of a reconciled world, and by the lure of this hope to draw him toward healing. And in and through that vision is to be seen the contours of the life of love that dreams it and charts the course toward it, the pioneer himself. To company with God on the way to a healed world, to meet and serve him there—that is what the Christian future holds out to the human counterpart, that is the heart of hope.

Celebration means, as well as joy at the anniversary of adulthood, the awareness that we have crossed some sort of a boundary in history when men now have the tools not only to "construct themselves"[1] but to fashion a *better* future. With the vast new powers of science-technology man can now bend his destiny toward a greater happiness, can contest the age-old enemies of hunger, disease, poverty, war, ignorance and even death. It is this fantastic new possibility that should drive the eyes of men toward this world to seize the new opportunity. With the possibility for health also comes the vaster chances of hurt. The peril reinforces the vocation of worldliness which the promise urges on mankind.

There is yet another invitation to joy. The God along the margins of our modern freedom and power makes his presence known to faith in the present ferment as well out ahead of it— the beyond in our midst. In fact if we are to find him in front, we must pass right now the way he goes. It is here and now, in the boiling, forward-pressing flow of our history, that faith moves toward its pioneer. He urges, "Never stand still; go forward with your brothers, run toward the goal in the footsteps of Christ."[2] We respond in hope, "May God in his mercy lead us through these times. And most of all, may he lead us to himself!"[3]

Footnotes

1. The phrase, Josá Delgado suggests, should replace Socrates' "know thyself." See his essay on developments in "brain technology" that move in that direction in *Human Values and Advancing Technology, op. cit.*, pp. 68–92.

2. Roger Schutz, *The Rule of Taizé* (Les Presses de Taizé, 1967), p. 17.

3. *Prisoner for God, op. cit.*, p. 169.

PART III

POST-RADICAL MORAL STYLE

11

THE DEATH OF RULE AND
BIRTH OF COUNSEL

In chapter 2 we sketched the ways in which the "death of code" morality, like the death of God theology, has gone to the barricades against the tyranny and dependency it sees embodied in the traditional concept of law. In its protest against both the club and the crutch, radical morality represents an attempt within the Christian community to come to terms with the maturation aspect of secularization. We shall try to honor its findings and at the same time shake loose from situational themes that square with neither facts nor faith. As we canvass issues and work toward an alternative ethical response we will be covering ground similar to that traversed in the previous inquiry. Rather than repeat definitions, styles, and problems—the Story, alongsidedness, pioneering-relinquishing, missionary penetration—their preliminary explanation and application in Part II shall be assumed and the task of investigating their moral meaning embarked upon directly.

Radical morality has correctly assessed the problem and identified the villain in the piece. When men are told to bow the knee to moral autocracies their dignity is in jeopardy, as that dignity is understood by both the Christian faith and the highest human insight. Moral teaching that is "handed down" as the "rule" of a "divine authority" denies to human beings the right to participate as free agents in the moral quest. A morality which "lays down the law" and treats its hearers as children is intolerable in a world come of age. Men can no longer be content to accept with docility unchallengable givens from theological and moral authority figures. It is little wonder that the concepts "law" and "rule" have become suspect. They are intimately bound up with a posture of servility.

The other side of the coin of tyranny is dependency. The bondage of the latter is as harmful to the weak as the former is to the strong. Well-meaning benevolence that comes with its supports to those who need to throw their crutch away so they may learn to walk makes for undeveloped muscles and, ultimately, moral cripples.

We can be grateful to the radical morality for its encouragement of the maturation process represented in its attack on those who would keep man a child. In particular the radical perspective has been more sensitive to the plight of the modern moral proletariat—youth—than most in the Christian community. Radical morality has, in fact, provided elements within youth culture with a fighting ideology as they struggle to throw off the authoritarian strictures that would hamper their right to be participants in the moral conversation.

Law as Target

The radical morality locates tyranny and dependency in the presence of law as such. Its solution, however qualified, is the elimination of law and its replacement by situational decision-making. In its analysis of the problem and its call for the demise of law, its position parallels the radical theology's contest with the tyranny of transcendence and its program of translating theology into anthropology. In our reflection on the latter, we have sought to show that the problem is not the fact of transcendence as such but the tyrannical and dependent conceptualization of transcendence and its implementation. There is a similar misplaced concretion in the radical morality. The problem is not with law as such but with the conception and operation of law as it is found in traditional morality. Law, understood in terms appropriate to a secular age, is neither of minor consequence nor disposable, for two reasons which we shall attempt to explore: (1) It plays an important part in the Christian Story. (2) It represents a secular wisdom that is part of responsible decision-making. This latter point is a departure from the line of argument followed in the discussion of God. The reason is that law functions as an infra-human Christian belief; as well as being an element in the Christian drama, it offers itself as a guide for man in his life on earth. Therefore it must be validated by secular methods and data and from within the coming of age perspective we have developed in Part II.

Law and the Story

Law takes form in the New Testament out of the ingredients of the old covenant's decalogue. We think here specifically of the man-man commandments pertaining to covetousness, false witness, stealing, adultery, parental care, and murder. But something happens to these mandates that are calculated to make communal life livable when they come in contact with the central act of the New Testament, the coming of Jesus. These and all other moral reflections become radicalized, internally and externally. New Testament law, defined by the life and death style of the man for others, is tightened to the last notch.[1] Now, it is not only killing but anger toward a fellow human, not only the act of marital infidelity but a roving eye that are incommensurate with the life of obedience. The spirit and the letter, the inner attitude as well as the outer act, are part of a faithful moral style. And the outer act itself takes on further strenuous proportions: law is not constituted by the adjudication of conflicting claims in a nicely calculated distribution of reward and punishment but involves the total outward movement of care for the other without counting the cost to self, yes, in abandonment of every trace of self-concern. The internal-external stretching of the covenant code is more than declamation. It is embodied in Jesus' character, direction and end. He did what he said.

As the center of the Story reshapes the meaning of the law, so does its finale. What is seen to be in one man now broadens out into a vision of a world reconciled with itself in which wolf and lamb lie down together, the child puts its hand over the asp's hole and men make war no more. The end is painted as a picture of healed relationships in which love evokes love and mutuality reigns in a new kingdom.

The center and end in our drama are the action and presence of God himself. What was, and will be, is what he is: suffering, self-spilling, caring love. As God's acts and vision, they are also man's call. We are to "be perfect" as the Father is, the Son was, and the world is willed to be. That is why love intended and embodied is "law." It is the style to which man is beckoned. The indicative becomes the imperative.

What happens when a man comes up against this new covenant code? We have a poignant record in Romans of an archetypal encounter. A decalogical mandate, read now in the light of the new center and the end, sets loose in Paul honest self-examination: "I delight in the law of God in my inmost self, but I see in my members another law at war with the law of my mind and making me captive. . . ."[2] Paul knows that the God who comes in Jesus does not covet, and thus he should not. Yet he knows that the urge to possess is in him. And further, the very awareness that it is wrong compounds the problem by stirring the desire for the forbidden. How can man come to terms with God when even the very one who "delights in the law" can only kick against it? And in so doing, man crucifies the one who is its source and enfleshment. "Wretched man that I am!"[3]

As a way to come to terms with God, the law is a route with a dead end. But to know that and to see the depth of the estrangement the law illumines, to be driven to an abysmal honesty, is to see things from a new angle. From such a precarious perch another vista opens up: the other side of the cross. The obverse of the loving law that judges is the grace that accepts. Crucifixion is gift as well as claim. God's suffering love is not only a call to like obedience which exposes our fraudulence; it is, as well, an offer of in-spite-of-care for the fraud. "God shows his love for us in that while we were yet sinners Christ died for us."[4]

The law then unfolds into something else. It is the path into the very heartland of the Story, the divine love that suffuses and gives coherence to the drama. Paul calls it a schoolmaster that prepares the way. By this reading of the meaning of the law it is an ingredient in the fundamental tale.

Although the radical morality speaks of love as the one absolute and of God as the source and ground of love, it drops the behavioral component that the biblical data associates with it. Love conceived as "intention" or "benevolent will" is indeed the fructifying core of ethical style. But the loving law we have been sketching here means also the conduct implicates, represented by the decalogue and above all the second mile, cheek-turning, coat-sharing self-abnegation lifted up in the life, teachings and death of Christ and in the vision of the end. When "love" is pared back to disposition and defined no longer even at this point in terms of radical self-giving, then it is difficult to see how either the depths of the human problem or the heights of its resolution as they are gauged in New Testament terms are adequately portrayed. We shall return to this question again in our discussion of an eschatological morality. For the time being, however, we are struggling to see how law is a companion in the Christian pilgrimage that cannot be waved away.

Law and its Role in Behavior

We want to look now at the function of law as it is seen "from below" rather than as it points and leads to the God of faith. What is the rationale for trans-situational guidelines for human behavior? The Christian community has its own conception of the role of law vis à vis conduct, and we shall seek to probe it. However, as we now touch down on the function of religion in human affairs—that is, its claim to shed light on the healing of terrestrial hurt and the ennobling of life in the world—it must pass muster before the best secular inquiry. To take coming of age seriously in moral insight, as well as the theological insight discussed in Part II, means that man in his adulthood takes responsibility for ferreting out those patterns of action that make and keep life human. As such, the pioneering-relinquishing rhythm obtains here as well, a rhythm which requires the subjection of Christian testimony about the good life to the scrutiny of a mature humanity.

When we deal with law in this context we have to do specifically with the first ingredient discussed in the previous section: law as concrete guidance for a multiplicity of situations. In the New Testament discussion above, it took the form of the decalogue. However, these mandates for human conduct neither exhaust the behavioral continuities of the faith-community nor can they remain in the form they took in ancient Israel. The Old Covenant continuities are stretched by the perspective of the new radical love and are, as well, in need of the same contemporizing as any historical formulation. By law in this setting, therefore, we refer to the day-to-day behavioral code of the community that runs from the ancient stricture against taking another's life to the latest Christian consensus that racial bigotry is a crime against God and man. (Thus we are not speaking about the final vision of suffering love in this context, for it functions in a different way, we believe, than as a prescription for behavior—as anterior to it and "out ahead of it." But we shall turn to that question at a later point.) These transcontextual commitments are the kind of law to which radical morality takes the most drastic exception. They are seen to constrict the freedom of the decision-maker and impede his ability to mate faith and facts, love and data, with ever-fresh situational relevance.

Community

The word "community" surfaces naturally in our discussion of the trans-situational. Biblical faith is a corporate phenomenon. The Story has to do with God's dealings with a mankind called to existence and fulfillment in community, with a covenant people, old and new, and its vision of a communal end and the earnests of it in history. Further, we have spoken of the role of the "Story-teller" as partner in the ongoing conversation on the meaning of faith. That no man—nor churchman—is an island is a fundamental premise of the Christian perspective.

The communal factor is honored in the work of theology when both the "fathers" and the "brethren" are welcomed on the journey. Thus the past reflection of the community in the form of its classical insights, official or otherwise, are taken as data for its labor. And the present community, wrestling in its teaching, preaching, study and action, are also co-pilgrims. Theology is not done in "azure isolation" (Barth on Kierkegaard), and faith is not conceived as the mounting of the "alone to the Alone" (Von Hügel).

As in theology, so in morality, responsible Christian reflection is corporate. It opens itself to the struggles and conclusions of the past and is in active relationship to the company working now on the issues of moment. When it confronts a new ethical question, it joins with the faith-community—and the human community—to muster reflective resources that will assist in making creative response. For example, as the new science-man questions loom on the horizon, emerging out of laboratory experimentation on the creation and control of life, the communal instincts of the Christian faith react in terms of gathering in task forces, consultations, evangelical academies of scientist, technician, lawyer, statesman, theologian and citizen to pool their understandings, looking toward finding reference points in theory and practice that will help men deal responsibly with innovation.[5] Community research data and methodology are components of the Christian moral style.

A "Story-telling" conception of theology is the effort of human beings in a particular community to think meaningfully about the events that give it identity. It is not divine deliverance from the mouth of God that is preserved carefully from generation to generation. Rather its concepts, though generated from and responsible to the Events, are once-removed, that is, produced by and filtered through the fallibilities as well as the insights of human beings. To deny this earthen vessel quality of theology is to flirt with a Monophysite mentality which, in its eagerness to honor churchly wisdom, obscures the frailty and transiency of the form and the constant need for criticism and up-dating.

Morality, like theology, is the response of humans in community to the definitive Events of the Story. It is involved in the constant development, testing, and re-testing of theses on conduct, growing out of the church's wrestle with its tale and with its world. Moral law, therefore, is not "the verbalizations of Deity himself etched with a jackhammer into some Cecil B. De Mille-like tablets"[6] but the research of the faith-community on what heals the ruptures of humanity. It is inductive in the sense that the codes develop from the combing through of human experience in order to discover what, in fact, helps and hurts man and the cosmos. It is deductive in the sense that the community examines the empirical terrain with the glasses of faith. Moral laws, as they are understood from the perspective here suggested, are the maps of life, marking both promising and perilous routes. They are charted by a laboratory-oriented community that at its most alert subjects them to constant review.

Finitude and Sin

The importance of communal ethical lore lies not only in the "no-man-is-an-island" premise on which faith is built. It is related as well to factors in the human situation which play havoc with man when turned loose in the context of an uncritical individualism. One of these factors the Christian tradition identifies as man's creatureliness.

To be a creature is to be other than self-derived, that is, to be from the Creator. It means as well an existence that participates in the givens of the created world. Finitude is rootedness in time and space. The ethical decision-maker meets each situation not from the encompassing vantage point of One who "sees all" but from an angle of vision limited by spatio-temporal location. That angle includes the biological, economic, political, social history that makes the decision-maker who he is, and thus furnishes him with the lens through which he assesses a situation. And it includes as well his physical perspective (he sees a situation from one side and not another) and his temporal perspective (he views it from within the boundaries of the "now," not the "then" of the past or future). Popular wisdom has preserved the sober awareness of perspectival limitation in its story of the blind men whose hands, confined to one or another reachable locale, describe the elephant as a tusk, a rump, or a tail. And, there is as well the common knowledge that witnesses on four corners of a street accident will tend to give four versions of what happened.

Some conclude from our finitude that what is needed is the perspective of infinity itself. Very different points of view nest in this treetop: the classical antinomian who maintains that the Spirit will illumine the situation for the believing decision-maker, without benefit of law, and the traditionalist who holds that God discloses the right course of action in an authoritative book, person, rule or system. The difficulty with these options is at least twofold: (1) they take faith out of its incarnational home, trying to make such a direct contact between God and the decision that the conditions of finitude are annihilated by an overpowering divinity. However, Christian decision-making has to play according to the same rules as anybody else, for faith has taken the incarnational risk of rootedness in space-time. (2) Both the Spirit-directed decision and the authority figure posture are remnants of the "big daddy" mentality so rightly excoriated by the radical morality. God calls a man to the freedom to participate in his own decisions, not to be at the mercy of a divine autocrat who prescribes to a servile citizenry.

While the problem of the limited perspective cannot be solved as long as men are finite, it can be modified. That is what the community wisdom is calculated to do. It represents a stretched finitude, both in time and space. In *time*, it means that other eyes and ears have reviewed comparable situations, reflected on them, subjected their findings to corporate scrutiny, sometimes formal, as in conciliar debate about moral issues (from the council of Jerusalem to an Uppsala assembly), but more often than not to the hard day-to-day informal "street" laboratories. Out of these it passes its love from generation to generation. In *space*, it means that the community's eyes and ears sit down around a current issue, formally or informally—from the evangelical academy asking the meaning of cybernation for a work ethic to the pastor called in by a couple to discuss a marital break—so that a variety of perspectives can be drawn in to see the shape of the question. Moral law, therefore, is community wisdom that has gone through the discipline of viewing the elephant and the accident from a variety of angles in the conviction that a responsible mating of faith and facts requires multi-perspective.

If finitude introduces distortion, sin compounds it. By sin, in this setting, we mean the lethal factor of self-love from which no decision-maker is exempt. This powerful bias will tend to bend the "facts" to fit the personal interests of the one viewing them, rendering dubious claims that individuals can dispassionately choose what is in the best interest of others.

As in the case of finitude, so, in the case of sin, there are versions of Christian faith which believe they have solved the problem of distortion introduced by self-interest. In addition to the two cited earlier there is the conviction held by one form of pietism which maintains that the "converted" will gaze with pure vision on the question at issue and be guided aright by his cleansed soul. However, the pietist, the traditionalist, and the antinomian lead us down dangerous roads, for they lack a deepgoing biblical realism about the self-interest which persists even where the religious language is heaviest and the heart is warmest. In fact, ethical disaster threatens here precisely for the reason that such protestations of exemption from sin blind men to the incurvatures of piety and provide an almost impervious ideological smokescreen that makes criticism and self-criticism exceedingly difficult.

In an attempt to deal with these illusory conquests of sin, the mainstream of the Christian community has spoken regularly of the need for law even in the life of faith itself, characterized as it is by "*simul justus et peccator.*" Of course, community wisdom—law—is no more exempt from sin (and finitude) than personal wisdom. However, the community has some weighty credentials. It has gone through the discipline of continuing partnership with the Story and its Book, inclusive of many perspectives, in a way that the individual as sole decision-maker has neither the sustained nor extended opportunity to do. Moreover, the distance of the community from the matter at hand, while it carries with it handicaps which we shall presently note, also has the advantage of a measure of objectivity. It is these credentials that point to the importance of corporate wisdom and scrutiny, in short, the need for communal law as *partner* in the process of decision-making.

Secularization and Law

Where does the faith community with its law stand vis-à-vis the human community at large? As one of the long-time custodians of society's moral sensitivities, and yet a steward that is forbidden to bury its treasure in its own back yard, it is called into the pioneering-relinquishing rhythm about which we have spoken before. And in the face of the coming of age processes this means a celebration and encouragement of an adulthood that seeks to understand its own moral dynamics and allow its truth to stand on its own feet. The faith-community welcomes the secularization of its law, the law that gives day-to-day guidance in the concrete questions of human conduct.

In this discussion we have not been dealing with the rationale for particular moral laws, but for law as such, trans-occasional patterns. The welcome of secularization in this context means the belief that the community at large, by secular inquiry, will corroborate the need for behavioral continuities. Thus the best biological, psychological, sociological, economic and political wisdom also knows that no man is an island, that man and his values rise from and are sustained by a communal matrix, that atomism and a rugged individualism are destructive of the human fabric. Again, work in the secular disciplines gives evidence for the faith-community's understanding of the creatureliness rootage of man that makes his view of reality a partial perspective. It assists also the understanding of the need for a "stretched fini- tude." And even the insight into the human condition that is so central to faith itself (man as a sinner, whose self-interest warps his judgments) finds secular counterparts in depth psychological probes into the self, in sociological data on the "ideology" of vested interest, and political commentary on the functioning of power. Secular perception does not, of course, lead to sackcloth and ashes. As Kierkegaard pointed out, there is a difference between understanding sin in general and sin existentially (the former has to do with the law as we've discussed it in the present context, and the latter as it touches on law in the previous context). Nevertheless, secular perception does lend itself even now to the kind of realism about decision-making that leads to an appreciation of communal continuities. It promises to do so increasingly in the coming of age process.

What has been said about the secularization of law is not very far from some conceptions of natural law. Secularized law is natural law, however, not in the sense that there is a deposit of immutable truth about the human condition which is open everywhere to the universal reason of man. We are dealing here with a process rather than a product. It is natural law in the sense that man with a developing historical reason coming of age is increasingly able to discern the moral contours of his world earlier chartered by the instincts and sensitivities of faith. And it is natural law also in the sense that faith must be ready to enter into a lively dialogue with the human community about what it believes to be the laws of the common good, subjecting claims old and new to the searchlight of responsible inquiry.

Law and Radical Morality

Radical morality exposes the tyrannies and dependencies to which the use of law has been prone, and rejects law as such as a factor in the decision-making process. While learning from this protest we have tried to show that law cannot be so easily excised from either the Story or from moral style, Christian or secular. While it is not our main concern to develop a detailed critique of the radical morality but rather to use it as a laboratory for learning and a stepping stone to reconstruction, it is worth inquiring into the validity of some other points in its case against law, specifically its position on the transiency of structures and its ontological doubts. We shall attempt to deal with structural and ontological issues in the succeeding sections. Here now, we examine briefly its attack on the club and the crutch, and the call to freedom and maturity.

While law is the culprit in the rhetoric of radical morality, there is restiveness with another factor implicit in law, the community. Radical morality is a protest not only against particular moral continuities and the concept of moral continuity but also against any abridgment of personal freedom from outside the decision-maker. To be human is to be free to mature without the frustrating tactics of tyrant or the benign invitations to an abortive security. When growing up is interpreted in terms of personal freedom and love, it is clear that the threat is seen to come from the heavy, smothering hand of the traditional community.

Although the radical morality speaks ardently of maturity and freedom, and its language is kindred to the theme of coming of age, we have to do with a different turn of mind. We hear not so much of the human race driving toward the freedom to make its own way without fear or favor as of the individual whose rights to emerge must be defended. It is no accident that the radical morality has received its most enthusiastic support from those in the culture who struggle with the issues of personal freedom. It is easy to discern why "the new morality" has become, both in the literature of its proponents and in the popular conversation, synonomous with the questions of private morality and, to a great extent, with sex morality. The fact that the moral inheritance to which the radical morality takes exception is often that prized by status quo types further solidifies its case against the corporate.

But we must ask if commitment to coming of age can be encompassed in the narrow boundaries of the press for private freedom. In fact, a rugged individualism in morality may be itself an impediment to the maturation of the race. There are important ways and times in which the communal takes precedence over the claims to private domain, as we have seen in the larger social questions of our time. The problems of private moral freedom, as also in the issues of public justice, have to do with developing a responsible balance between the freedom and dignity of selves and the public weal. It is solved neither by the dictator who smothers human dignity nor the anarchist who sees no need for corporate continuities.

A fundamental factor in the radical morality's individualist turn is the philosophical influence that helps to shape its position. While its exponents sometimes heatedly deny the connection and are at pains to distinguish their perspective from 'existentialist' ethics, the similarities are too extensive to be accidental. The father of modern existentialism, Soren Kierkegaard, inveighed both against thought patterns (preeminently speculative Hegelian philosophy) and cultural phenomena (from the "crowd" of nineteenth century middle class complacency through the "press" to the "Christian crowd") which relieved the individual of the task of the passionate subjectivity that constituted his true humanity. So too the radical morality sees the mature and human life as that in which moral deciding is done without the securities of codal prescription that cripple the moral leap.

While the existential insight has done yeoman's work calling men away from the detours around the participative act, it has also made some serious mistakes in its reading of the human situation, and therefore cannot be accepted uncritically as a guide to either the philosophical task or to the reinterpretation of the Christian faith. One limitation which bears on our present discussion and applies to the issue of community is suggested by a tongue-in-cheek comment by Harvey Cox on Sartre during a conversation on Christianity and Marxism: "Sartre's problem, I think, as Gabriel Marcel rightly pointed out once, is that he wrote his philosophy seated in the Café aux Deux Magots, without any significant relationship to any other person—people simply wandering in and drinking their coffee."[7]

In the case of both Kierkegaard and his heirs there is such a preoccupation with the individual's struggle toward identity, and such profound belief that the human other is a threat to that venture, that the constitutive, supportive and healing realities and possibilities in the communal matrix disappear from view. H. Richard Niebuhr puts the matter this way in a plea for a "social existentialism":

The existentialist problem, stated in despair or faith, cannot be phrased in terms of the "I." *We* are involved, and every "I" confronts its destiny in *our* salvation or damnation. What will become of *us?* Where is *our* whence or whither? What is the meaning—if meaning there is—in this whole march of mankind with which I am marching? Why have *we*, as this human race, this unique historical reality, been thrown into existence? What is *our* guilt, *our* hope? What power confronts *us* in *our* birth and end? . . . The existentialist question is not individualistic; it arises in its most passionate form not in our solitariness, but in our fellowship. It is the existential question of social men who have no selfhood apart from their relations to other human selves. Kierkegaardian existentialism gives up the cultural problem as irrelevant to faith not because it is existentialist and practical, but because it is individualistic and abstract; having abstracted the self from society as violently as any speculative philosopher ever abstracted the life of reason from his existence as a man.[8]

Where coming of age, maturity, humanity, etc., are understood in conventional existentialist fashion to mean throwing off the community in the interests of the personal pilgrimage, as they are in the radical morality, then the more fundamental understanding of maturation is shortcircuited, and the crucial communal theme of both faith and secular wisdom is excised. Maturation is not the self's independence from the community but the whole race's freedom for and in adulthood. And the achievement of that adulthood entails a much more drastic interdependence of selves than is envisaged by existential philosophies or moralities. We believe this means taking the communal moral wisdom summed up in the word "law" as a serious partner in, rather than as a foe of, the decision-making task.

The Style of Law

We have spoken of the need for law, and have something of its content. We must now turn our attention to law's *way* of situational entry. From our agreements with the radical morality's attack on the tyranny of law, law cannot be conceived as coming to overpower, or to call for a crippling obeisance. But is it possible to conceive of law in any other way than as a rule from a ruler, a command handed down from on high?

As we have discovered clues and figures in secular experiences that assist in the understanding and interpretation of faith, so there are similar pointers to the meaning of morality. We find one in the science community. The understanding of "scientific law" has gone through an interesting pilgrimage.

At one time a British scientific society could emphatically pronounce, "There can be no such thing as meteorites. Stones do not fall from the sky." Law in that century was conceived as the ironclad rules to which activity in the physical environment were bound. Dogmatic claims were made as to what could or could not happen in the universe based on rigorous, "proven" laws of nature.

The "natural laws" of the science community today are of a very different order. Shaken enough times by new data that upset the old rigidities, scientists now speak of law in the modest terms of "statistical regularity." Laws are working premises, open to constant verification and correction. If a phenomenon which was thought by an older interpretation of law to be "impossible" can be supported by adequate evidence, then the law must be reviewed and restated so as to include it. Law in the laboratory means humility of inquiry, not arrogant pontification.[9]

When the radical morality looks at moral law it sees iron rules dogmatically proclaimed by an iron Ruler. Traditional defenders of law have given ample cause for this caricature. However the alternative in morality, as in physics, is not to abandon the notion of law but to restate it in responsible categories. Moral law is not dictation from above but discovery from below. Christian moral law represents the findings of the faith-community as it reflects on the problems of conduct in the light of the Events. It is a summary of the regularities that establish themselves in its research. The modesty of the science community about its natural laws is echoed in the faith-community's commitment to moral law. It is a firm but open commitment.

Further, law so conceived is offered in times of human maturity in a way that befits adulthood. It does not come as a command or even mandate. It comes into the decision-making contest in the "alongsidedness' of a resource rather than as a triumphalist source. While it does not force itself on the one called in his freedom to make his own choice, yet it is a gentle pressure and firm presence in the situation. Decision-making is not a monologue in which the self talks to itself, measuring faith-love against the facts. It is a genuine dialogue in which law appears as a full participant in the conversation.

We have noted that Joseph Fletcher in his more recent writing has spoken of the need for ethicists to give thought to the concept "maxim." While this represents a move beyond the methodology used by Fletcher in his analysis and toward what we here describe as law, it has some limitations. The word "maxim" is a slippery term that can be made to mean either too much or too little. Dictionary definitions associate it with "axiom," thus allowing the impression that a maxim can be an unchallengable, self-evident truth. This claims too much for law in a world come of age. On the other hand "maxim" can refer to a wise "proverb" helpful to conduct. That says far too little about the massive communal experience at the base of law. To the degree that the radical morality has had any recourse to continuities or made use of them in its analysis, it has been in this latter, minimal way.

In the interest of moving forward the discussion of the important note struck by "maxim," perhaps we could put the difference between "maxim" and "law" in this way: A maxim seems to be community wisdom invited into the moment of decision after faith has reviewed the facts. That is, the maxim must demonstrate its credentials in order to be admitted to the context. Law, understood in its alongsided role as a communal, behavioral regularity, comes in at the *beginning* of the conversation, not the end, as in the scientific meaning of law. That is, the decision-maker enters the situation with a commitment to the communal continuities. The burden of proof as to whether there is new data that would create either an exception to the rule, or a restatement of the rule,[10] is on the particulars of the situation. Of course the one who must act, although entering the context with the community wisdom as partner (yes, senior partner), knows that partner as a counselor, not as a dictator, and as such open to review, appraisal and veto.

We have introduced two terms that find their way naturally into conversation about law conceived in an alongsided fashion: research and counsel. In our quest for meaningful language in a world come of age it is worth inspecting them.

Law is research in that it represents the inductive learnings of a community exploring viable guidelines for conduct. As it is introduced into the processes of choosing, it functions very much like the research material fed into the modern computer, data from which computations are made. Whether or not computer operations provide a helpful analogy, however, the concept "research" does express the communal laboratory findings that characterize law as it is here understood.

"Counsel" is a yet more pointed word for law. It suggests the wisdom shared in friendship, rather than the orders of a superior. It enters the situation as a servant having only the authority of a community that has passed this way before. It does its work through understanding and in dialogue with the decider, not by fiat. It evokes response by love. The word has a long history in Christian tradition of course, as in the "counsels of perfection." Its use in this setting as the crown and climax of the Christian pilgrimage yet as somehow at the same time supererogatory, not demanded of the man of faith as such, links the style of law with the theme of optionality which we have met before. In moral counsel, marginality has to do with the freedom of the Christian man, and mankind in general, in relation to the law, the chance to say "yes" or "no." Elsewhere we shall investigate the question of a moral claim "beyond the call of duty" in another sense. In any case, we offer "counsel" as expressive of the meaning of law in a time of human maturity.[11]

The Content of Law

Thus far we have dealt largely with the importance of law as a *form* for decision-making and with the *style* in which this form expresses itself. Although we touched upon the *content* of the moral law in a preliminary way in our discussion of the Story, we must now give it more sustained attention and examine it in relation to the secularization process. In doing so we will refine and also broaden the concept of law.

Law in Christian perspective has three components: (1) the will to serve the welfare of others (2) the structures in which this intention is expressed (3) the total giving of the self, within and without, which interlaces the intention to serve others. Each is a dimension of love. Together they constitute the "law of love."

(1) The will to serve the interests of others is the dimension of love which radical morality underscores. It is servanthood taking form as the "benevolent will." The intention, the care for the neighbor's needs, is the spring of Christian behavior. And that spring itself is fed by rains of the divine love. Here we are concerned to see it as the attitudinal center of the Christian moral life. It is love as benevolence, "benevolent love."

(2) Benevolence moves from within outward to find empirical expression in patterns of behavior that embody the internally willed good of others. Here the will joins with man's experience and reason to establish routes of action that serve the neighbor's

need. Again, radical morality has pointed to this blending of will and intelligence. Fletcher characterizes it in this way: "Love is discerning and critical. . . . Justice is Christian love using its head. . . . Love's calculations, which the Greeks called prudence, keeps love's imagination sharpened and at work."[12]

Viewing this mating from within its individualistic framework, however, the radical morality excises the community dimension, making definitive the existentialist qualification, *"kairos."* Thus we do not have communal reason working in partnership with benevolence, but the decision-maker's reason rendered yet more atomistic by defining it in terms of a unique moment of decision. Benevolent love must indeed exercise its right to choose the community wisdom or not as it makes the final appraisal of the situation and acts in its own freedom. But it enters the moment of kairos with loyalties to the reason and experience of the company it keeps—the counsels of faith, the moral continuities discerned in and by the life of the Christian community.

The corpus of moral wisdom runs the gamut from the ancient counsels of the decalogue, through the broad principles of freedom and justice, to the middle axioms that guide faithful action in issues of poverty, race, and peace. As the structures of community reflection on the Events' meaning for behavior, these "codes" are subject to the same processes of up-dating, refinement, enlargement and tailoring as are its structures of belief, its "creeds." Thus we are speaking here of law in the sense developed in the previous section, as the trans-occasional behavioral consensus of the community. As we try to distinguish it semantically from the other components of love, indicating the aspects of behavior, community, and experience, we refer to it in the somewhat awkward phrase, "communal-reflective love."

(3) The law of Christian love is not exhausted by intention or codal continuity (or the exceptions to codes required by intention). There is another quality lifted up time and again at the center of the New Testament tale—the life, teachings and death of Jesus—and its end in the "Kingdom of God." That quality has

to do with a life of total self-abnegation in which the self turns its attention to the need of the neighbor in a radical, uncalculating, unconditional care both in the depth of the self and its behavior. While we have labelled the ethical methodology that serves as our springboard to an understanding of secularization "radical morality," in this context the term "radical" does not fit, for radical morality repudiates this dimension. Thus in his critique of Leo Tolstoy, Fletcher takes issue with the uncalculating selflessness that spends itself on the neighbor without stint or thought of its own needs.[13] He views love instead as "calculating." If the total welfare of men would be better served by self-preservation, such a concern for one's own interests would be a more responsible fulfillment than the disinterested love recommended by Tolstoy in both theory and practice (as in his life's last act of self-abnegation for a man in need).

We have accepted the concept "calculation," but transferred it to the communal context which rescues it to some extent from the self-deception to which the most benevolent decision-maker is prone. ("To some extent," because corporate self-deception, to which communities including the Christian community are vulnerable, is a real possibility. The hope of faith is that extended life with the Story mitigates that to some degree and makes community wisdom a more reliable guide to behavior than the massive possibilities of self-fraud in occasionalism.) But it cannot be at the price of censoring a fundamental New Testament motif. That motif is the absolute of "selfless love" spelled out in the Sermon on the Mount's radical counsels of second-mile, coat-sharing and cheek-turning, the embodiment of that style in Christ's own life and death, and the portrayal of that uncalculating care as the quality that distinguishes the goal toward which history is called, the Kingdom of God. And in and through these New Testament descriptions of what was in Christ and will be in the kingdom is disclosed the divine love that pours itself out without counting the cost or the condition.

But how can we make sense of such a love as this? It seems to fly in the face of the intention to serve the maximum good of man, and is in conflict as well with the community wisdom's calculations of justice rather than uncalculating love. We shall try to find an answer to this question by exploring the relation of secularization to love.

Love and Man's Coming of Age

If the race's adulthood is to be taken seriously, we must be prepared to acknowledge and encourage the secularization of the Christian community's counsels for human behavior. That means wherever its law of love seeks to give guidance to men concerning the ways of achieving a livable and human life, it is subject to corroboration by secular instruments of insight and testing. We have said this about the need for law as such. It is true as well about the content of behavioral law.

The welcome of secularization means that the Christian thesis that a benevolent will is the healing center of human life is not held tightly to the breast, as if it were an unfathomable mystery known only to the faith-community, but is exposed to critical secular scrutiny, including investigation by its sharpest intellectual tools. And it means also that the particular behavioral continuities developed by the faith-community from its own research are subject to the same "laboratory" checks to see if they do contribute to the welfare of men. This theme is anticipated in the natural law theories that have developed in the history of the church with their assumptions that the laws discoverable by human reason coincide with the "eternal law."

The secularization of Christian moral law is an exceedingly difficult program to undertake, for it is resisted from both churchly and secular quarters. As could be anticipated, traditionalists who believe that Christians have a corner on the moral market with access to mysteries about human conduct disclosed only to the eyes of faith will resist secularization. This dangerous paternalism we have met in the guise of other autocracies. As a response to man's coming of age and to the basic themes in the gospel, it is not a creditable option.

But the traditionalist will increasingly find some strange bed-fellows. Support comes from some non-traditional sources, in fact, from those who are eager to accommodate faith to a secular age by translating theology into ethics. We are speaking of inter-pretations which fully understand the urgency of witness in the world when the stakes for human healing or destruction are astronomic and which therefore underscore the "man for others" dimension of Christian teaching.

If there is, on the one hand, a firm commitment to Christianity as an expression of truth, and on the other, "all the eggs" of Chris-tian meaning are "put in the same basket"—the basket of moral witness—the question poses itself as to how ready exponents of this position will be to welcome the secularization of the style that gives Christianity what meaning it has in a secular age. The options would seem to be: (1) Be prepared to abandon the Christian commitment when men do in fact come of age, and become in the full sense secular men who are for other men with-out benefit of Christ-talk, much less God-talk or any specially labelled Christian, communal life. (2) Be prepared to give up a particular expression of Christian commitment when men have found a secular equivalent, but move on next to unexplored ter-rain. This is the pioneering-relinquishing style discussed in Part II, and is a fundamental aspect of the Christian moral style. How-ever, if one has accepted man's coming of age without reserva-tion, there are in principle no grounds left for Christian identity but room only for a "delaying action" until man matures to adult-hood. (3) Maintain that there is a unique plus to Christian moral insight and style that no secular alternative can duplicate. This is a gentler version of the traditionalist "big daddy" mentality. As an effort to still hold some triumphalist edge on the world, it is not a genuine celebration of man's twenty-first birthday. (4) Acknowledge fully and bend one's labors to secure the right of man to grow up in his moral pilgrimage. While affirming human maturation without reservation, however, this option would maintain that the moral relationship of man to his world does not exhaust the meaning of faith. We shall deal with this alternative shortly, building on what has been said already in this vein in Part II. For our immediate purposes, however, it is enough to say that a reduction of faith to the moral witness—the option under consideration—is by definition not a persuasive option. Thus we are left with the possibility of the very sensitive moral translation of the faith either accepting the implication of final secularization, and thus evaporation as an identifiable Christian option, or an unwitting alliance with those who resist man's adulthood.

As trouble comes from the church in welcoming secularization, it also comes from quarters from which one would least anticipate resistance, the advance troops of the secular community itself. We have in mind here, for example, the "technician mentality" that is pervasive in sections of the science community. It surfaces in some of the contemporary discussion of the moral meaning of the new developments in the control of life. Scientists moving along the cutting edge of discoveries that will vest in man precisely that kind of power to fashion his destiny which constitutes secularization—in the sense of man seizing the control of his own future—on occasion take the position that it is not their responsibility to assess the moral implications of these developments. That is the job of those whose business it is to deal with morality, "the church." A similar uncertainty about man's ability to work out his own moral patterns is to be found oddly on another frontier of secularization. Thus Bryan Wilson, who develops some of the most perceptive commentary on a secular society from a sociological point of view, including a sharp attack on organized religion, can yet argue the functional merits of the religious ceremonial, and raise doubts as to whether modern society can work out moral incentives without the service of a religious establishment.[14]

In spite of the resistance and doubts from both religious and secular sources, a church that believes in human maturity must defend the right of man to emerge and take the risks of that commitment. In this case it means a readiness to test the moral grounds and meanings evolved within its community and be a catalyst of secular, adult moral patterns.

The Third Dimension of Love

What is the relation of selfless love to its two companions and to the process of secularization? Selfless love is continuous with intentional and intelligent love. Its inner direction is toward the interests of the human other (and the "natural" other, the cosmos) as in a benevolent will. Its outer expression is again aimed at the welfare of the race and its cosmic home. This is what makes it love, the turning to the neighbor in care and service.

But there is something more. Whereas benevolence is care-ful, conserving itself so that it might rationally serve what it conceives to be the neighbor's need, selfless love is spendthrift. It takes no thought for tomorrow, giving of itself without stint as it perceives the need of today. Moreover it is guileless, as incapable of envy and anger as it is of the visible act against the neighbor. And in the matter of visible acts it does not deal in the currency of calculated generosity or punishment, acceptance or rejection, according as each contributes to humanizing relationships or a just society. Instead there is a pouring out of the self far beyond the call of social duty.

Is this then the real Christian ethic that exposes all intentionalities and calculations as compromising shams? For those who interpret the Sermon on the Mount and other New Testament expressions of selfless love as prescriptions for the conduct of men, and preeminently for the disciples of Christ, this is indeed the case. The Christian pacifist, for example, lives out "nonviolent direct action" because he believes that the selfless love of Christ is a literal New Testament mandate. And it is also often held that if practiced faithfully, selfless love will in the long run, if not upon confrontation, evoke from men a response in kind, thus serving as the only reasonable basis for the welfare of society.

We cannot follow the pacifist in this interpretation. The third dimension of love is portrayed in the New Testament in eschatological perspective. Selfless love is the law of the Kingdom of God, embodied in its King. As such it is the end toward which history is called. A truly healed world is one in which men give themselves without heed to the human other and the divine Other. That is the communion for which they are made. And in such a world of total, mutual self-offering the outcome of selflessness is reconciliation and oneness. Self-giving is met by self-giving. In the perfect world of the heavenly vision, selflessness has as its companion mutuality.

But there is an important difference between this vision of what lies out ahead and the conditions for life together in the "now." A lethal factor separates earth from heaven, human sin. The presence of this "power of death" takes its toll in human relationships. When selfless love comes up against the hardness of the human heart, it does not evoke love in kind but invites crucifixion. In the central event of the Story, the cross did its work in disclosing the divine character and intent, unconditional, self-emptying care. The function of that Event and the work men are called to do in their day-to-day relationships of building a livable world are intimately related but not identical. When the heedless love of Christ is imitated in the concrete world of men, infected by its lethal ingredient, crucifixion means the real possibility of the defeat of the humane.

To put it in the simplest terms, if the Samaritan, interpreting service as literal self-abnegation, had arrived on the scene when the brigands were in the act of attack on the pilgrim, there would have been two victims instead of one, and no gracious stranger later to bind up wounds. Selfless love can only be defended as either welcoming this as the proper role of every Christian or as evoking a love in kind on the bandit's part. In the latter case the fact of human incurvature is not weighed seriously enough in the balance, a sin which exploits perfection rather than being shamed into reciprocity by it. In the former case it is possible that some are called to the act of total, selfless action as a vocation which serves as a visible reminder of the higher claim under which we stand. And further, it is true that in a moment of *kairos* the most ordinary of men may be called to witness to the final vision under which we all stand, as in the case of martyrdom. But to introduce cheek-turning love as a working law for all in the day-to-day affairs of a sinful society is to invite the slaughter of innocents. A tolerable justice that is at the basis of a responsible community life requires the presence of disciplines that are less than cheek-turning in their operation. The communal-reflective laws are just that, for they presuppose sin and seek to establish a tolerable justice in the face of this given.[15]

What then is the function of selfless love in the ethical posture here outlined? It serves as the burr and lure which never lets the partial realizations of intentional or communal-reflective love rest easy in the assumption that their stratagems are beyond improvement or criticism. Again, the rays of its uncalculating quality from "out ahead" leap to warm the moral ratiocination necessitated by decision-making here and now. Careful appraisals easily degenerate into cold calculation if not informed by something outside of themselves. And the *kairotic* saintliness that here and there is an earnest of our ultimate call serves to keep our wills bent ahead to their goal.

But when all is said and done, there can be no convincing secular rationale for selfless love. It is a work of supererogation not demanded by the needs of men living together in community who can move toward a working moral fabric in their communities by commitment to benevolent love and communal-reflective love. Its rationale is not found within the framework of the human task as such. Selfless love is part of the fabric of Christian morality—as vision, judge, and lure—because it is a faithful report of the style of the God, and the schoolmaster of faith. It must therefore live its claim to truth out of a humiliation that is unable to command assent on the basis of a niche it carves out for itself in the affairs of men. It is only an option. But it is this optionality that generates the power for the leap of Christian commitment. About that we have spoken before, and will speak again.

Footnotes

1. Anticipated in the Old Testament by the neighbor-love themes of Leviticus 19 and related concerns.

2. Romans 7:22–23.

3. Romans 7:24.

4. Romans 5:8.

5. A beginning is being made by the efforts of the Committee on the Church and Economic Life of the National Council of Churches in its three year project on "Human Values" culminating in the 1967 Consultation on Technology and Human Values, the papers and reports of which appear in *Human Values and Advancing Technology, op. cit.*

6. "The Issue of Transcendence in the New Theology, New Morality and New Forms," *op. cit.*

7. Cox, in *Initiative in History: A Christian-Marxist Exchange Occasional Paper,* Church Society for College Work, 1967.

8. Niebuhr, *Christ and Culture* (New York: Harper, 1951), pp. 243–244.

9. See Dorothy Sayer's discussion of the modern usage of law, *The Mind of the Maker, op. cit.,* pp. 2–14.

10. Rather than accepting the idea of an exception to a moral law, Ramsey has recently spoken of the enlargement of the law to include the new data. *Deeds and Rules in Christian Ethics, op. cit.,* pp. 220ff.

11. The theme is by no means new. See Keble's comments on "probability" in Newman's *Apologia pro Vita Sua* (New York: Oxford University Press, 1964), p. 20.

12. *Situation Ethics, op. cit.,* pp. 90, 95, 102.

13. *Ibid.,* pp. 91–92, 97.

14. Wilson, *op. cit., passim.*

15. See Niebuhr, *Introduction to Christian Ethics,* and *The Children of Light and the Children of Darkness* (New York: Scribner's Sons, 1960), for the development of the thought reflected in these paragraphs.

12

THIS TIME AND
THIS WORLD

The issues of morality point to a somewhat different ordering of analysis than that followed in the investigation of a theological response to secularization. We shall examine next, therefore, temporality and this-worldliness. This-worldliness, as it is posed in a moral context, belongs more fittingly in the discussion of the temporal spectrum than in a separate treatment, so we shall deal with the questions of "time" and "space" in tandem.

The Insights of Radical Morality

As in radical theology so in radical morality, the past is viewed with suspicion. "Law" calls up the picture of a moral anteriority that is offensive in at least three respects. First, as a *method* of decision-making foisted on the present by the ancestors, law denies the contemporary decision-maker (who is in a better position to know his own situation than the man who lives in it?) the freedom to cast his own vote and shape his own life. "Men who are now dead made the old tradition; let men who are now alive make the new."[1] Freedom from the law means, therefore, freedom from the heavy hand of the past that seeks to throttle the choice that can only be authentic when it is unfettered and made in the context of the "right now."

Secondly, in *style*, the inherited law is dictatorial and paternal. It comes as an authority figure with its commands and threats. Law in its pastness is an exercise in arrogance which again smothers the creativity and freedom of the present. And finally, the *content* of the ancestor's law is obsolete. Its formulas may have been germane to another time with its different conditions, but "circumstances alter cases." In any event, what took rise in another historical context, relevant or not to that context, cannot be imposed on new times radically discontinuous with what has gone before. Moral constructs, to the degree that there are such, and certainly moral decision, must be contemporized. The realities of the present provide the data for choice, not the laws of the past, whose prefabricated solutions run roughshod over the persons and facts that are the moral data of the here and now.

The radical morality has made an important contribution in each of its attacks on the tyranny of the past. Let us look at its telling points. Together with, and as an expression of, the historical sensitivity of modern man, the radical morality understands that conceptions of value are relative to time and place. Hence its legitimate suspicion of inherited law, and its readiness to come to the aid of the now-oriented. And it has good reason to be wary of the damage law can do, for it has seen the defenders of law at work. Whether it is the "hatpin" brigade that worries Hugh Hefner, or the legalisms impeding the work of the Galileos and Darwins, traditionalists have constantly hamstrung the business of living and learning. Moral law has been a club used to thwart advance and to drive to submission. Moral dictatorship is an offence to God and man.

As the radical morality has shown, there is a serious case not only against the form and the spirit of inherited laws but also against its content. This applies not only to those clearly superannuated moral judgments that even the traditionalist politely acknowledges as such, e.g., the historical conditionedness of the Old Testament command not to boil a kid in its mother's milk, apparently of some sanitary value in ancient times, or Paul's views on women's wear. Central moral commitments about work and play, marriage and the family, life and death, are on the way to obsolescence. Consider a few striking examples.

Technology makes it possible and likely for cybernated agents to "man" increasingly large segments of the work process, opening up new vistas of both productivity and leisure. Thus the "puritan work ethic," with all its biblical rootage, that served an earlier generation is not only an anomaly but may well be a disaster. To insist that men work in order to eat, to impute dignity to labor and associate leisure with sin, hobbles us for living in a society in which only a fraction of the work force will be needed for production. Citizens must both be furnished with a means of livelihood apart from the productive role and learn as well to find dignity in leisure and participate in it meaningfully. Again, in a time of high infant mortality, low life expectancy, and underpopulation, the mandate "be fruitful and multiply" had its place in the conventional moral wisdom. In overpopulated countries today and on a world scale tomorrow, literal obedience to this moral law could spell doom for the planet. And as if these present dilemmas were not enough, we are on the edge of new developments in the life sciences that touch on the creation, extension, direction and perhaps even destruction, of life ("death management") before which our inherited moral wisdom leaves us helpless, not because it represents out-dated ideas but because it has not even anticipated the moral options now surfacing in the redefinitions of man that loom before us.

While some will acknowledge the obsolescence of particular laws derived from the past, the basic act of neighbor love which they spring from and must be judged by is seen as a constant. How could the role of Good Samaritan be put into question? Yet even this central thesis, as literally conceived, is manifestly obsolete in some modern settings. A bulletin of the Automobile Association of America notes that in some places it is considered not only immoral but also illegal for a car to stop on a major turnpike to aid a stranger in distress. The technological setting of a super-highway is such that the course of action appropriate to a first century rural road becomes inhuman today. It risks the lives of others using the thoroughfare who might run into the well-intentioned modern Samaritan weaving across the lanes on his mission of goodwill and parking as an obstruction on the road shoulder.

Radical morality exposes the dangers in the pastness of law's form, style and content. Is the past then dead? Are living men to make their own moral way on the basis alone of the data of the present? The elimination of the past is not the only way to deal with its megalomania and remain loyal to the present. The problem is not the past as such but its abuse in those ways so correctly pinpointed by the radical morality.

Why find a place for moral inheritance? We have covered some of the ground in the previous chapter. Moral law in the Christian community is the three-faceted gem of benevolence, research, and selflessness. The radical morality does not take issue with the perennial relevance of intentional love. Here there is agreement. From the perspective being honed in these chapters, intentional love can be corroborated by the best human inquiry as the value necessary for man's survival and development. Selfless love is a counsel of the faith-community which has another justification, its fructification of all moral endeavor, but even more its consonance with the Christian Story as it deals with man's most profound relationship to God. However, it is not these theses which come under the indictment of obsolescence. The stumbling block to healthy decision-making is seen to be the communal-reflective heritage.

We have spoken of the need for a readiness to bring under the searchlight of contemporary experience all formulations of behavior born out of the community's wrestle with faith and facts. And we have noted several examples of the antiquation of moral mandates having to do with work and birth. It is an easy step from the premise of historical relativity and some dramatic exemplification of it, to the declaration that all the moral givens developed in another time are by definition obsolete.

There are at least three serious problems with this sweeping judgment. The first is that it violates the empirical spirit of a secular age. Responsible securality will seek to be faithful to the research modesty of the science community. It proceeds step by step, case by case. And from careful and lengthy testing it builds its theories and "natural laws." To reject the morality of the past out of hand without the careful, corporate scrutiny of the premises that have a history of meaningful service to the human community is a carelessness that makes it easy to "throw the baby out with the bath." The route new moral insight must take is the way of the hard-nosed inquiry of economic, political, biological, psychological, sociological disciplines. That is the path the work ethic and birth ethic are going through in their process of overhauling. And if the faith community makes a new judgment its own, it must attempt comparable research involving conciliar dialogue and public articulation.

The second problem, implicit in the first, is the assumption of radical, temporal discontinuity. Here again ideology tends to control reality. A situational morality with its roots in the existentialist perspective struggles for the freedom of the moment, and in doing so calls into question learnings of the past that are seen to threaten it. Most of all, an era of hurtling technology creates ideologies of change, and of unspoken and unquestioning cultural belief in its ubiquity, that predispose men to question any historical continuity. However, responsible morality will not have its pace set by ideology or cultural instincts. It will subject its inheritance to the tests that ascertain whether a given thesis of the past is or is not still germane.

A third problem brings us again in range of the Christian Story. The excision of the moral past in the interest of the present is a captivity to one segment of reality that is intolerable to a faith not imprisoned for its data in any single slice of the time spectrum. The God of yesterday, today and tomorrow appears "around the clock." And because that is so, the past may have a wisdom the present needs.

Threading through these various difficulties is an ideological captivity which, in its well-meaning resistance to the tyranny of the past, plunges into a new despotism that refuses to let the ancestors be heard. Moral decision-making is difficult under any circumstances. To deny it the benefit of counsel from any source, especially that which has emerged in its own faith-company, is a narrowing of the range of data that makes for poor research.

To illustrate the continuing light past moral judgments shed on the present, let us take two other communal-reflective continuities that seem anything but obsolete. They represent, in fact, two categories of the moral heritage that differ from those heretofore discussed. One is the long-standing community judgment against taking human life. When all the qualifications are made—that it has been honored in word but not by deed, and the tragic exception in which it may be the lesser of two evils—few if any in the Christian community would declare that time has so radically altered circumstances that this moral continuity developed in ancient society is now antiquated. Thus, there are some givens that survive even without alteration well into the most contemporary situation. In fact, the horrors of war as it is carried out by the new technology are such, and the inhumanity of former exceptions to the rule such as capital punishment are so manifest, that the sensitive modern conscience presses more powerfully than ever before for the implementation of an aged code rather than its extinction.

Another example of relevant moral directive from the past is the biblical care for the "weak things of the world" which made its way into the church practices of the early centuries, and into the institutional life and style of the church since. The mark of this concern for the orphan, the widow, the poor, the slave, the aged, the sick, the stranger, is its compassion for the dysfunctional and/or powerless. The helpless, aided by the early Christian communities, had "nothing to offer" to society, the slave excepted, who was nonetheless still an offscouring. But faith's conviction that God loves men in spite of what they are, whether or

not they are "useful" and can contribute to his plans, found expression in a love that reached out toward the "useless" and
"nobodies."

The church has increasingly come to understand this concern
for the "refuse" of society not only in terms of care for the
dysfunctional in its own community but also in the wider society,
and not only by way of benevolent institutional programming but
also in the struggle of the voiceless and powerless for a voice and
a power that will establish their dignity. What is happening in
this widening perception of the counsel rooted in the character
of God himself is an illustration of a second kind of debt we owe
to the past. In this case we have a kernel insight—the Christian
stands by the defenceless—that goes through a process of deepening, refining and up-dating according to the new situations
through which it passes and to which it must learn to speak. This
is neither obsolescence, nor is it the persistence of an ancient insight unchanged except for its application.[2]

Thus when we speak about the moral heritage, we are talking
about a variety of past sensitivities, some of which must be rejected, some maintained, some up-dated. Simplistic rejection of
the past is as debilitating to the moral task as uncritical captivity
to it.

The Moral Memory

In our discussion of coming of age, the images of "research" and
"counsel" came into use as describing the style of the law in its
dealings with adulthood. There is another image for moral wisdom that comes naturally to mind in our analysis of its function
in the time sequence: memory. As noted before, amnesia am-
putates the past and as such takes away our identity. What we
were defines in basic ways what we are. Yet memory, when it is
functioning properly, does not preside over our day to day existence. When it does, when a man "lives in his memories," his
capacity to relate to reality is crippled. Memory plays out its

proper role when it serves as a resource to the self, as the self encounters the present.

The moral memory of the Christian community serves a comparable function. Without it the task of decision-making in the present is seriously maimed, for the reference points of our identity are missing. On the other hand, a memory of who we were and what we did that controls the present is as debilitating as moral amnesia, for it blots out the contemporary reality with which a person must deal and crushes the fresh data of immediacy. A working moral memory draws into the conversation with the present the past's learnings, yet is not so strong a claimant that it denies the vote to the now. It lives in partnership with the present as a resource for decision. Christian moral memory goes one step further. It not only is open to the present; its action and direction open out toward the future.

The Future and the Intrinsic

In its missionary attempt to state the meaning of morality in this-worldly terms, the radical perspective commits itself to an empirical approach to value. Moral decisions are made "from below." They take their lead from a rational survey of the facts in a situation, by intentional love. Thus the method of the radical morality reflects the secular posture that has little use for moral deliverances from above, be they philosophical or religious.

Wound into this methodological commitment to empirical inquiry is the assumption that there can be no pontification from on high because there is nothing "up there" or "out there" which can pass judgment on the rights and wrongs of human conduct. We have examined its attack on the "intrinsicalism" which locates value in an ontological standard outside the context. By denying the existence of such an exterior norm the radical morality aligns itself with a generation suspicious of the occult and content to base its moral judgments on conclusions drawn from data in its time-space world.

There is a basic agreement between the radical morality and the position being developed in these pages that the methodology in ethics must be "from below." Accompanying the theological premise that the paternal release for, and tutorial encouragement of, human maturity is the moral corollary that man must finally establish his own patterns of responsible behavior by his own lights. And that means the probing, inquisitive, testing spirit and techniques of empiricism. We have gone further than some of the proponents of the radical morality to assert that intentional love, as well as communal-reflective love, must pass in review before the best of human inquiry. Whatever touches on the things that make for a full life on earth are the business of man in his maturity, however important tutorial religious insight may be at earlier phases of growth.

What of the anti-intrinsicalist thesis of the radical perspective? Is it a solid building block for a theology and morality of secularization? We are faced by an immediate problem in answering this question. There is some doubt whether the radical morality in its present form holds consistently to its rejection of intrinsicalism.

While the radical morality clearly parts company with the hypostatization of value in the forms of communal-reflective and selfless love, it presupposes another kind of reification, an intentional love that becomes an intentional Love. Insofar as benevolent will has, for the radical morality, its ground in the will of God himself, value is located ultimately in a reality distinguishable from the extrinsic relations of men on the earth. For Joseph Fletcher, it does have this ontological rootage, as we noted, in the divine agape. To the degree that the radical morality maintains its conviction that we have to do with Another distinguishable from human relationships (although intimately involved in them, of course), and traces its attitudinal posture on behavior to that source, it cannot reject intrinsicalism as such, only the forms of intrinsicalism which it finds inimical to its thesis.

While there is no explicit acknowledgment of this qualification on the disavowal of intrinsicalism in the writings of Fletcher, there are statements that move in that direction. Thus when it is asserted that there is no absolute but one, love, there is an implicit acknowledgment of a rootage in something more than the extrinsic complex of persons and events.

Robinson, who follows Fletcher's line of argument with some faithfulness, might seem to be a more likely candidate for a consistent radical morality in the matter of rejecting intrinsicalism. Since he does not accept the reality of a divine Other, he cannot speak about a divine intentionality in the same sense as Fletcher. However, as we have seen, Robinson pleads for the objectivity of a "God" who cannot be reduced to human relationships, as in his disagreement with van Buren and his assertion that there is a quality in the universe that makes it supportive of value. Thus while the cipher theory depersonalizes Deity, it does not deny the reality of a source of value in some sense "external" to man and hence "intrinsic" in nature.

A theological position which could house the radical morality with no inconvenience would be the radical theology. While Fletcher has noted the connection of "new morality" and "new theology," there seems to be little indication of movement toward this more hospitable environment, and only slender systematic work in ethics has yet been done by the radical theology. The linkage with the anti-intrinsicalist note is apparent. The radical theology has no place in its constructs for a reality over against man and his affairs, and as such has no need to argue the rootage of value in transcendence.

In working toward an alternative response to secularization in its this-worldly expression, we shall look in another direction for the meaning of intrinsic—"ahead" rather than "in" or "out." The theme of the future provides grist for the mills of reconstruction. It furnishes us with materials for a Christian morality that is less captive to the givens, less esoteric, interiorized, and conservative than the radical ethical posture. We shall touch on these limitations in the radical morality in passing, as we attempt to discern the contours of an "eschatological ethics."

The Ethics of the End

The Kingdom of God which has come, is coming, and will come, is the framework for New Testament reflection on conduct. The definition of the moral life is given in the vision of an end which is already at work in Christ and his world. That vision is of a cosmos at one with itself, a world in which leopard and kid lie down together, the child puts its hands over the hole of the asp, men beat their swords into ploughshares and perceive one another with the eyes of angerless, second-mile care. Thus the goal God holds before man is a world in which nature is reconciled with itself, man with nature, man with himself, and man with man. It is *shalom*, wholeness, healing. There is no more rupture in creation; it is a New Creation.

This vision of what will be is the hope in the heart of the pilgrim God. As such it is the map of those who follow him here and now. This image thrown on the screen of the future is the point from which pilgrimage bearings are taken. As "out ahead," it is an intrinsicalist morality, for it is separable from the moment of decision, standing as a lure and guide for choices, and judge upon those that fall below its standards. Its intrinsicality is further rooted by the past actions and present reality of the God who bears us toward the future.

However, because of its rich cosmic texture, its concrete images of human and natural behavior, its portrayal of healing in terms of transfigured secular relationships, events, persons, processes— no more pain, crying, death, shattered swords, new cities, fertile crops, stilled seas—it breaks out of the cramped quarters of interiority, human or divine. The ground of ethics is not in the narrow passageways of the intentional self, or in the elusive depths of the divine mind. It is in the broad ranges of a transfigured world. The Christian is not only called to a good will that reflects the divine benevolence and then to make his way as best he can to enfleshing will in fact. He is beckoned also to a kind of behavior and a kind of world whose lineaments are sketched in the vision of biblical hope. Morality at its very center has to do with what makes for healing in nature and history as well as in intentionality. It puts into the category of absolute not only a good will but a good world.

Of course, that remade world of the Christian vision is couched in the language of another age. It was an era when the mending of nature was dreamed of in the symbolism of wolves and sheep, plagues and harvests. And the reconciliation of history was described in terms of primitive tools and weapons. Translation and implementation may mean for us the healing of the strip mine scar, the harnessing of the atom for peace, the fashioning of man and his environment for undreamed of possibilities, the passing of nuclear war, racism, poverty, dehumanization, the coming of joyful and creative play, the sparkling and serving secular city. But through the new notes will be heard the same motif, *shalom*, a reconciliation whose horizon is no smaller than man and the cosmos.

To be caught by such a vision of God's design is to be wound up tight with the restlessness of futurity. Because this hope is the point from which the Story's teller takes his bearings, a profound tension is set up between what is and what will be. Things in the status quo which smudge the mirror turned toward the future must be wiped away so its reflection can be caught. Hope generates revolutionaries, as eschatological theologians have been at pains to point out. It drives toward the embodiment of what is anticipated.

One of the problems of the radical morality is that its imagery and framework do not press unambiguously toward action that calls into question the social givens. The thesis that the only absolute is a good will is a flirtation with an interiorized piety. Although none of its better-known interpreters fall prey to this, it would be a short step to such an interpretation, as the kinship of radical morality to existentialism indicates. The logic is amply illustrated in the subjectivizing of ethics by Kierkegaard, up to

his controversy with the social and religious establishments of
Denmark, and even then in the rationale for more visible forms
of discipleship.[3]

The fundamental problem with the radical morality as touching the question of time, however, is its contemporizing reductionism. In the zeal to do justice to the this-worldly focus of a
secular age, it takes the empirical now too seriously. The givens
bulk large in the radical moral equation, faith plus facts equal
love. Too large, for the tension toward that eminently non-empirical reality, the future, which is productive of genuine radical-
ism, is missing. There must be another component in morality
if it is not to slip into a "servility before the factual."[4] That ingredient is the future which is neatly excised by the preoccupation
with the data of the present in radical morality. Christian eschatology does not necessarily have the only view of the future which
generates a creative disaffiliation with the present, although it
may well have a crucial role to play in a time that is beginning
to grasp the significance of futurological considerations, and to
do it in its pioneering-relinquishing style. The human community
must ultimately discover how to conceive the ethical function of
the future in a secular fashion. But the radical morality in its
this-worldly thesis has accommodated itself too easily to the
sensitivities of the age to be of help to a future-oriented secular
morality.

While we earlier suggested the image of "memory" as a way
for morality to include the insights of the past in its calculations,
it is appropriate to consider "anticipation" as the figure for
ethics' future. As Augustine reflected on the meaning of self-
transcendence in terms of the self's retrospective and prospective
capabilities, the moral task here is viewed in terms of the resources of the past and the future that come to the aid of the
decision-maker as he confronts the present. As memory, so anticipation too does not so mesmerize the responsible self with the
dreams of what will be that he cannot see the data and demands
peculiar to the moment. He must not import the future neatly

packaged into the present. This is the problem of the utopian who wrenches the ethics of heaven from its moorings out ahead in order to be re-settled in the present. Not so. Eschatological ethics functions best from its location on the horizon as lure and judge. Like memory, anticipation is a resource that must be tailored to fit the present, not a source that rides roughshod over it. But it is there, nonetheless, with its gentle pressure from beyond rounding out the partnership of yesterday, today and tomorrow that composes responsible decision-making in this world and this time.

Footnotes

1. Mary Jean Irion, "Confessions of a Mumbler," *United Church Herald*, Vol. XI, No. 1 (January, 1968), p. 51. See also Mary Jean Irion, *From the Ashes of Christianity* (Philadelphia: Lippincott Co., 1968).

2. As, for example, the church's current participation in efforts to "give voice to the voiceless" by way of the independent community newspaper. For information on how church and secular groups have combined to print the news and views of the poor, black, young, and other minority groups, see *The Lancaster Independent Press*, 120 S. Queen St., Lancaster, Pa. 17602.

3. On the former see *The Gospel of Suffering*, translated by Marvin Swenson (Minneapolis: Augsburg Publishing House, 1942), *passim*, and on the latter, *Attack on Christendom* (Boston: Beacon Press), *passim*.

4. Bonhoeffer's phrase, *Ethics*, translated by Neville Horton Smith and edited by Eberhard Bethge (New York: The Macmillan Co., 1955), p. 198.

PART IV

POST-RADICAL MISSION

13

GOD AND MAN IN CHURCH
AND WORLD

In reviewing the troops along the radical battleline, William Hamilton glances to the right at the "soft radicals." In contrast to his own "hard" line, "Soft radicals tend to have difficulty not with the message but with the medium through which the message should be passed. They worry about adequate institutional embodiment, the problem of communication, hermeneutics, secularism, and modern man."[1] Elsewhere he describes the institutional revolutionaries as "ecclesiastical radicals" who "say critical things about the present form of the institutional church. Members of this group write study books for the student movement and speak about secular, worldly, and non-religious theology. (They are often confused with the theological radicals for this reason.) New strategy and new structures may well be forthcoming, but we should probably not expect new theology in the strict sense."[2]

The proponents of a new missionary style and revision of the doctrine of the church are indeed "soft radicals." They tend to affirm biblical motifs, and show the continuing influence of neo-orthodox and ecumenical theological themes, and even evince an interest in "Christian formation" and devotional style, however contemporized.[3] Whatever our nomenclature, it is worth asking what constitutes radicality as we make comparative notes on the sister movements under consideration, and particularly as we try to assess the significance of radical missiology. What seeks to go to the roots, to change the direction of life in a fundamental way?

Marxism is something of a laboratory in which the meaning of "radical" has had some testing. In Marx's critique of the "left-Hegelians," he says these "critical critics" are like the fellow who "had the idea that men were drowned in water only because they were possessed of the idea of gravity. If they were to knock this idea out of their heads, say, by stating it to be a superstition, a religious idea, that would be sublime proof against any danger from water. His whole life long he fought against this illusion of gravity, of whose harmful results all statistics brought him new and manifold evidence. This honest fellow was the type of the new revolutionary philosophers in Germany."[4]

For all their hectic attack on religious belief, Marx felt that the Bauers, Max Stirner, and Feuerbach were "head revolutionaries." Their proposals for change were rooted in the Hegelian assumption that human improvement lay in the task of reordering men's ideas. Even social reformers of the stripe of the "true Socialists" relied on conceptual engagement as the way of change. About the formula of one of them, Grün, Marx comments: "'Preach the social freedom of the consumer and you will have true equality of production. . . .' That is an easy matter! All that has hitherto been wrong has been that 'Consumers have been uneducated, uncultured, they do not consume in a human way. . . .' The prophet's doctrine is in every sense a sedative. After these samples of his Holy Scripture [Kehman as well as Grün] one cannot wonder at the applause it has met among certain drowsy and easygoing readers."[5]

Marx's assessment of the Hegelian premise that underlay both thought-reactionaries and head-revolutionaries is summed up in his famous thesis on Feuerbach, "Philosophers have only interpreted the world. The point is to change it."[6]

It is interesting to note that the program of today's "hard

radicals" to eliminate the "occult," to turn talk of God into talk of man, theology into ethics, is anticipated by, and in debt to, some of the same members of the Hegelian left that Marx excommunicated from the circle of genuine revolutionaries.[7] Surely the effort at ideational up-dating cannot be dismissed as peremptorily as it is in Marxist commentary, a line that is much more deterministic in over-eager disciples of Marx than in Marx himself.[8] Nevertheless, it may well be that those who see our task as altering social and institutional patterns are more seriously radical than the intellectual reformulators. And it may also be true that, insofar as insightful reflection itself grows only out of firsthand involvement, authentic responses to secularization will have to put their major efforts into the nitty-gritty work of structural and historical change. To date, most of the attention of the proponents of new mission has been directed to the socially existential questions. There is evidence, however, that the institutional radicals are pushing their inquiry into the area of "new theology" and "new morality" as well as "new forms."[9] If the thesis of this inquiry is right—that God is met in, with and under the ferment in world and church—the most valuable insights on Christian response to secularization may come from those working on the boundaries of church-world involvement.

We have noted in our canvass of the radical mission position its rejection of the visible church as a mother figure. The assertion that healing can come only through this vehicle—*nulla salus extra ecclesiam*—is replaced by the commitment to the worldly work of Christ. Counterposed to the teaching that the institutional church is saturated with a divinity that guarantees its uniqueness and saving power is an ecclesiology which asserts the church to be an event defined by the act of being for others. In its more modest expression only those namers of the Name who are "for man" qualify. In bolder terms the church exists *wherever* there are men who are for fellow-humanity. In all shades of radical mission there is a call for the servant-style manifesting itself in such ways as the retirement of the clergy to the role of assistant to the laity, withdrawal of church-state ties, and the stress on a listening rather than a telling church posture. Threading through the new ecclesiology is a protest against the tyrannies and dependencies of Mother Church and a commitment to a world come of age.

Agreements with the Theses of Radical Mission

The ecclesiastical matriarchy that smothers human initiative with its benevolent control is rightly challenged by radical missiology. Adults must cut apron strings. The members of the Body of Christ are offspring indeed, but no breast-fed "children" (nor infants bounced on the knees of sundry "fathers"). "Christ's men" are found in the world as well as the church. Radical mission is a blow struck for maturity in ecclesiology, both in content and in style.

Ubi Christus, ibi ecclesia—where Christ is, there is the church —is a classic Christian teaching. Viewed through the lens of Matthew 25, the Christ who is at work in the human actions of neighbor love gathers the church to himself. As he is truly present in the struggle to humanize, so those who participate in healing action for man are "in the church" in a fundamental sense. What that sense is, and how it is related to lovelessness in the community that bears his name, we must yet explore. But the crucial witness to the presence of the worldly Christ in human ministration, both within and without the visible church, is a welcome corrective to the domestication of Deity in traditional enclaves.

We go one step further to affirm the active adult role of man. Whereas the traditional maternal teaching held that there is no salvation outside the visible church, it is more correct to say there can be no salvation *within* the visible church (or outside it) in the absence of the Christic grace at work in human love. It is not the matriarch that finally determines healing but the worldly Christ present in the work of his brothers. Faith must be active in love to be saving faith. And if it is not, there is damnation.

The role of the human act is once more underscored in the fact that by its absence the church brings judgment upon itself. The mother cannot go it alone without her sons of commitment. We shall examine this in more detail presently.

Finally, the human factor makes itself heard among the proponents of radical mission by the content of their ecclesiology, their understanding of the church as a sociological entity. The church is not the agency of a divine power that steamrolls through history unresponsive to or uninfluenced by the human structures, persons and events that compose it. A humiliation-Christ takes the risks of temporality. He makes his pilgrimage in a body, not a soul. The body, like all historical bodies, is subject to sociological vicissitudes measureable by sociological instruments and even beholden to sociological wisdom. It is humbling, if not shocking, for some to think that the church must have recourse to a human partner, sociology, for *aggiornamento*. But the claim of exemption from the rules of historical contingency is a relic of triumphalist thinking, whatever the piety or the theological pedigree of the claimant. To take the humiliation of Christ seriously is to be prepared to speak of his vulnerability to, and presence in, the things of man.

In style as well as in content, the radical ecclesiology makes some telling points about autocratic conceptions of the church. For one, it calls into question the sacral temper of traditional mission. Desacralization means the passing of ecclesiastical control over secular terrain. We welcome the coming of age of sectors of the human community that are throwing off church domination and penetration, and a theology that declares for both secular autonomy and a church that offers itself as servant rather than master, that is ready to listen to its partner, the world, rather than deafen secular ears with its orders. The separation of the fingers of control from the reins of the state, its disavowal of special privilege, its readiness to serve and learn, are marks of the self-emptying Christ.

And in the doing of household chores, the radical missiology's call for the end of the "big daddy" figures and habits is a word to be celebrated. The claim of clerical monopoly on the wisdom of the church's faith and over the decision-making processes of its life has been long overdue for challenge, as have the questionings of all benign and/or high-handed methodologies and premises within the life of the faith-community.

The sharp indictments and proposals for redirection of the religious establishment by institutional radicals have taught us much about mission in a secular age. Their insights are the building blocks of a new style of mission. However, the same kind of sweeping diagnoses and prescription characteristic of its sister movements hobbles the effort of radical missiology to work out a viable alternative to traditional constructs. We must deal with these pitfalls along the way to reconstruction.

Radical Mission and the Story

One of the mighty acts of the Christian drama is Pentecost. As part of the unfolding Story, a visible community is spun off from the divine-human action at the center of history. We are not speaking of "an extension of the Incarnation," a groove made in time in simple continuity with the appearance of Christ. There is no "perfection of natures" in the church comparable to the once-happenedness of Jesus, no hypostatic union in simple equivalence to the person of Christ. The church is a company of sinners; whatever they are or have is by virtue of longsuffering in spite of Love. But for all their imperfection and discontinuities with the happening, this fragile community is nonetheless called into a special relation. Upon it is laid the claim to tell, celebrate and enact the Christian Story. And the One who calls this company into that covenant promises that he will not desert it. Through all its stumbling and bumbling, he will be "where two or three are gathered" in his name. This strange love denominates a very ordinary body of people as the Body of Christ.

As it is a community of *memory* of the Events that give it

identity, it is also a community of *hope* distinguished by the quality of its anticipation. The church is the visionary people whose journey through time moves toward the goal of a world at one with itself. But that vision is not only in its mind. Its Herald and Embodier is the Head of the church. By virtue of this bond, the vision is already at work in the present. The celebrating community which looks forward to the coming of God with appetite whetted for the reconciliation of the world is, by dint of his presence, a downpayment, a "firstfruit" of the kingdom which comes.

Does radical missiology find a place for these themes in its conception of the church? It is much more difficult to deal with the issues of the Story as they relate to radical mission than to the companion movements we have examined. Steeped in biblical data, closely identified with the Christian company by participation in the ecumenical discussion, explicitly committed to the Story, it represents no private adventurism in theology. In fact the position can be expressed in the same biblical language and can make its peace with ecclesiological definitions that leave room for a variety of interpretations—the church as firstfruits of the kingdom, for example.[10]

However, if we take the formula God-world-church in either of the meanings assigned to it by radical mission—that God forms the church out of those committed to his worldly work apart from naming the Name, or God forms the church only where those who name the Name are doing his worldly work—it appears that the divine life is so rigorously tied to the act of human service that the Story's report of the freedom of God, and his promise to be with the covenant community, is called into question. But that is a fundamental theme of New Testament reflection on the visible community—God can choose to share his life even among the base things of the world, and does. To the squabbling, incurved Corinthians whose moral standards were lower than the pagan community outside,[11] Paul could say "You are the Body of Christ,"[12] and to the "wretched, blind and

naked"[13] Laodiceans can come the announcement of the presence
of the knocking Christ.[14]

It would seem that the Story is striving to preserve the freedom
of God to act in his own right, unbound to the "by your leave"
of human goodness. And further, it is telling of the enactment
of this freedom in the covenants he makes with consistently
cantankerous peoples. Most crucially for the Christian, it speaks
of the bond he establishes with "Corinthian types" and their
successors. Surely this is a central tenet of faith, God's love for
the unlovely, a care that makes no bargains with its recipient, a
compassion for those who have no moral credit cards to display.
A showcase of that unconditional love is the Christian community
itself, *simul justus et peccator.*[15]

The factors that evoke the protest of radical mission are apparent to anyone caught up in the renewal movement. Again,
as in radical theology and radical morality, the chief blame for
its reductionist response falls on the faith-community's own faithlessness, and judgment must begin with our own household. The
failure to enact the Story it tells and celebrates, to make the
human response called for in its own covenant, brings it under
the deserved indictment of prophetic voices.[16] Traditional church
life has been as turned inward and resistant to structural change
as the keen eyes of institutional radicals have portrayed it. And
its monolithic claims to divine custodianship do fly in the face of
the Christ at work in worldly creativity and commitment. Is it
any wonder that a "death of church" mentality surfaces alongside
a death of God theology? Here the popular watchword might
well be "big mommy is dead" in partnership with "big daddy is
dead." A possessive Mother Church is as dubious as an autocratic
Father God for men come of age.

But the death of Mother can be no more a final solution for a
reborn church than the death of Father is for a reborn theology.
The murder of the mother figure means not only the excision of
the freedom of God for his broken, visible community witnessed
to in the Story. It represents a new triumphalism that binds God

to the work of man. Like a genie that materializes and disappears at the beck of Aladdin, so the divine work is seen to come and go as moral heroism rubs its lamp. One difficulty with this assumption is that human servanthood cannot bear the weight of this claim, for no act of man is that clear a reflection of the divine, suffering love. That is the nub of Christian teaching about God's unmerited agape, which does not, cannot, wait upon the never-to-come human credentials. The related problem is the entrapment of God in human action, the questioning of the freedom of God to be God and to express his life where and when he will.

A doctrine of the church that seeks to do justice to the role of man's power—the human and worldly action of God—to which such powerful prophetic testimony is made in radical mission, must do it not in the idiom of the church's demise but in fresh understanding of the role of the human in, and alongside of, the visible community. We shall attempt then to move beyond the death of mother mentality to a new conception of maternal companionship in a world come of age.

God and Man in the Visible Church

In our endeavor to move beyond autocracies old and new, we shall work at a partnership understanding of the divine and human action in mission, exploring its meaning within the visible community. And we do it with the aid of perspectives borrowed from the long history of sacramental discussion.

Conceptions of the sacraments have tended to polarize. On the one hand, there have been points of view that stressed so heavily the power of grace in the transactions at font and table that the reality of the earthly elements and human actions—as through and through earthly and human—is called in question. The divine penetrates so deeply that it infuses the terrestrial vehicles with its own glow, in a way comparable to the representation of the divine presence in the person of Christ by the Monophysite Christology. Traditional transubstantiation theories, and the popular piety associated with them, lend themselves to this over-divinizing interpretation. The grace in elements and action is treated like a pill that, upon ingestion, works on the spiritual system much like aspirin on a feverish body. It does its work without benefit of the will's activity or, in more careful formulation, if no major impediment is put in its way by the receiver. And accompanying this kind of understanding of sacramental action is the treatment of the consecrated elements and those who dispense them with an awe, an esteem, appropriate to the holy. In short, the humanity of the sacrament evaporates.

The form that critical response to this conception takes is the predictable divesting of the elements and actions of all direct divine import. Thus the administration of bread, wine, and water becomes an "ordinance" whose chief function is to point to events in the Story—as a memory of the first supper or the sacrifice it represented, or as anticipation of the heavenly banquet, or as acknowledgment of the rich communal bond of Christians round the table, or their mandate to embody unity more perfectly in both church and world, or as a pledge of renewed loyalty by the guests to the Host (or any of these in combination, or all together). The heart of the sacramental event is the human action that remembers, anticipates, rejoices in, points to, and pledges. Its benefits and rationale have to do with the believers' activity, not an overpowering Presence doing its healing *"ex opere operato."*

While it cannot be said to enjoy ecumenical consensus, there is another perspective on the sacrament that is widespread in the Christian community. The third option affirms that Christ is truly present in action and element, yet in a fashion that does not violate their integrity. The earthy processes and ingredients are not transported to another realm of being, nor do they act medicinally without human attitudinal response. That response does indeed play a critical role in what happens in the transaction, determining, in fact, its outcome. But it does not materialize or volatilize the divine love offered in the sacramental action.

Christ comes to the people gathered in his name as he promises. But *how* he comes is determined by the free act of the receiver. Love, met with hostility, burns, according to Paul. Applying his conviction in the vivid imagery of I Corinthians, he maintains that impenitence and faithlessness take their toll at the table.

This interpretation of the sacrament speaks of an unconditional, promise-keeping love which is not dependent on human loving or lovability, and thus represents a "high" view of what transpires—the real presence and action of Christ. Yet at the same time it views grace as efficacious, as healing rather than judging, only to the degree that man as a full partner in the action shapes its destiny. In this respect it is a "low" view of the sacrament which stresses the human role.

As the church is, in a sense, "the sacrament of God,"[17] the sacrament writ large, historical reflection about one illumines the other. As through bread, wine and water the divine promise is kept, Pentecostal election draws the visible community into the orbit of divine action. The steadfast love of God in Christ continues in this fellowship of men, not by their merit, but by his longsuffering.

But this divine presence does not mechanically transfigure the community in which it makes a home. There is no power exercised to guarantee the virtue of the church constituency or the wisdom of its pronouncements. Christ does not overwhelm the members of his Body. Men may accept or reject his call and claim. The freedom of the human component is not obliterated by a divine steamroller. The risks of this freedom touch the sociological as well as the moral dimensions of its humanity. As noted before, the church is not exempt from the demands to keep pace with the sociological facts of life, requiring the same restructuring and up-dating as any other institution that must make its way in the world.

Men's faithful "yes" or faithless "no" to Christ in his company determines their destiny. When there is "yes," Christ comes as healer. When "no," men bring the coals of love down on themselves. And what do "heal" and "hurt" really mean? They are the "punishment" and "reward" that comes to every institution as it lives within the rules of the ethical and sociological games, the laws of life. The ethical rules, the law of love, apply pre-eminently to the community called to be one of its custodians. When the community lives for itself, it sets in motion the processes of self-destruction that work in self or society when men live for themselves rather than for the neighbor. The "love or perish" mandate is maximized in the potential of the self-hate that comes from the church's knowing violation of its professed identity. Also, failure to bring its life in line with the sociological processes—the most pressing current one being both the internal reconstruction of the local denomination congregation and its external reorganization in ecumenical, functional, and regional terms commensurate with the new sociological lay of the land[18]—will also take its toll as "some get sick and others die" who balk at structural faithfulness.

While there are hard visible consequences for the narcissistic and status quo community, the meaning of both "heal" and "burn" is not exhausted by these categories. Christ's love has a personal depth that cannot be measured empirically. The knowledge that self-centeredness breaks the heart of the divine love is the profoundest punishment that comes to the faith-community, as it is to the individual believer. To bring the church under the indictment of wounding love will not drive it to final penitence in the same way that awareness of its empirical self-destruction might cause provisional penitence and an urge to reconsider its institutional incurvature. But final penitence, like authentic faith, can not be clubbed into existence. It is only born in the freedom which, faced by what is only a possibility and not a time-space "sure thing," takes the leap across the abyss of uncertainty to a humiliated love that does not "seek its own way."

We have examined the work of God and man in the visible church with the aid of the sacramental analogy, attempting to

see how "partnership with," rather than "exclusion of," is key to
the relationship of divine and human. While our comparison has
focussed on this "withness," there is another dimension of the
third option. Sacramental terminology speaks about a grace that
is "in and with" or "in, with, and under" the elements and human
actions. Talk of "in" and "under" is an attempt to speak of the
commingling of divine and human that is companion to the integrity and partnership of each. In the church at large, as in the
sacrament, the human act of response to God's electing presence
is, parodoxically, the work of God himself. Viewed in the perspective of the actor, it is his own free choice. Viewed from the
angle of Deity, it is God's. We can no more sort out this strange
phenomenon in the canons of Aristotelian logic than we can
render intelligible the profession of the physicians who speak of
the discovery of anaesthetics as the work of man for which we
give thanks to God.[19] We meet the same paradox in the freedom
of man in the church as we do in the coming of age of the world.
The best we can do is to say it does more justice to the facts of
Christian experience and the turn of the tale than simplistic
reductionisms. The divine love is in, with, and under human
love in the constitution of the church.

While we have struggled here with the divine and human in
the visible community, there is another area of related inquiry
to which we must turn to flesh out the God-man interrelationship in church and mission: the relationship of God's work in
the visible church to God's work in the world.

The Church and the World

Christ comes to men who tell and celebrate his Story. He is Head
of his body, inseparable from it even in its most confused and
erratic movements. Does this then mean that to confront Christ
men must enter the visible community of faith? Have we rein-
troduced the old imperialism which claims that there is no
salvation outside the church?

It is impossible to go back to the maternal ecclesiology of the tradition. Radical missiology has helped us to see that Christ is not domesticated in the household that names his Name. He is alive wherever men are for other men, and in the cosmos wherever mutuality is at work. But how is it possible to hold together these two motifs which seem to lead to very different ecclesiological expressions?

There is a clue to understanding the relationship of Christ to church and world in a biblical report of a dual relationship that Christ sustained with his friends. It is found in the incident on the Emmaus road. The story tells of the post-resurrection meeting of Jesus and two of his disciples. As they walked together to Emmaus "Their eyes were kept from recognizing him."[20] On arriving at their common destination, "when he was at table with them, he took bread and blessed it, and broke it, and gave it to them. And their eyes were opened and they recognized him."[21] Incognito passed into disclosure.

Do we not have here a paradigm of the two bonds Christ shares with his "disciples" today? Perhaps we can call them the two "faces" of Christ. He is truly present in the flow of neighbor love in the world. His secular footfall is heard wherever men are for the neighbor. This worldly presence is a bashful reality that does not yield up its identity. It happens in and through the actions of those who may know little or nothing, and care less, about the Name. It is a secular presence through and through, but for all that utterly real, for it is truly Christ with whom we have to do in the feeding of the hungry and the clothing of the naked. Those who participate in this ministry are his companions.

But the relationship to the incognito Christ in the church invisible does not exhaust the bonds men can have with him. In "the breaking of bread," the One who is unknown becomes known. The Christ who ranges alongside of men on the secular roads now turns to reveal who he is. Before he was "in profile," as the alongsided companion in a common walk and work in the world. Now he comes to us "face to face" in the personal self-disclosure of word and sacrament. Here lies the significance of the visible church. In and through its Story-telling and celebrating, Christ reveals his Name, who he is. To "know" him is more than an intellectual exercise. It is the meeting of an I and a Thou.

To unfold the Emmaus clue we have introduced Buber's terminology. But it must be refined in order to avoid some popular misunderstanding which are made possible to a degree by some of the overtones of Buber's own development of this powerful symbol. For one, while Buber acknowledges that the I-it relationship is a necessary one, there is the sigh of disappointment that accompanies the recognition that I-thou must pass into I-it, and hence an assumption that one is superior to the other.[22] The use to which Buber's commentary is put regularly assumes the former to be salutary and the latter a misfortune.

Harvey Cox has helped to press for a reexamination of the simplistic understanding of the I-thou theme, stretching the typology to include the third relationship of "I-you," less-than-intimate but a fundamentally important non-personal relationship in a complex urban world that would exhaust itself by constant attempts at depth intimacy.[23] While there is some value in experimenting with other formulae, it is still possible to use the Buber framework if both relationships are viewed contextually. For example, when a surgeon is about to perform a delicate operation, a deep personal attachment to the patient is not the best perspective from which to enter the operating room. Emotional involvement may incapacitate him for the work he is called to do. Responsible surgery requires a cool dispassion capable of viewing "the case" with objectivity, narrowing for several critical hours a human being into the confines of "an organ." Again, some may protest the depersonalization represented by the treatment of the aged as "just a social security number," or the young as "data for computers," but without this transformation of persons into statistics there is no income for the old that arrives regularly at the mail box and perhaps no ob-

jective grade on the young's comprehensive test. In short, the
I-it relationship, depending on the context, may be the only way
in which life can be made human. The impersonal *becomes* dehumanization when it is the controlling and/or only relationship.[24]

The I-thou of knowing, and the I-it of doing, are comple-
mentary bonds and as such illumine, through the Emmaus tale,
the church-world question. The non-personal incognito relationship of Christ with his people in the world is no less important
in its setting than the personal meeting of Christ and his people
in the telling and celebrating of the visible community is in its.
In fact to universalize either is to play havoc with the relationships appropriate to each setting. When at the barricades in the
encounter with human issues, a faithful response attends to the
matter at hand, and the Christ "in profile" is served as a comrade.
On the Jericho road the Samaritan does not hold a worship
service or a seminar in theology but binds up wounds. As Bonhoeffer notes in his own commentary on the integrity of the
secular, "To long for the transcendent when you are in your
wife's arms is, to put it mildly, a lack of taste, and is certainly not
what God expects of us. We ought to find God and love him in
the blessings he sends us."[25] There is a time and a place for
everything. And as the Christ of the Emmaus road meets us in
the *incognito* acts of service, so he wills to be *known* in the
tenderness and devotion of a faithful life together of those who
speak of and celebrate the Story.

Are these airtight compartments? Are some favored with one
relationship and others with another? Is Christ divided? The
question answers itself. It is the one Christ who comes to stranger
and acquaintance. He calls secular and community disciples to
know him in his fulness. Let us see what this can mean.

To those in the visible church who are offered the Name of
Christ comes the invitation to join him in the world. Whoever
wants to "come after me must deny himself, take up his cross
and follow me" onto the secular roads. If any one says he loves

God in cozy ecclesiastical relationship but does not love his worldly brother and neighbor, he is a liar. "He who does not love his brother whom he has seen cannot love God whom he has not seen. . . ." Where there is no love there is no saving faith. Where there is no commitment to the worldly claim of Christ, the One who comes to meet the people who know the Name in bread, wine, water and word is despised. To make oneself an enemy of Christ is to suffer the consequences of alienation, to know a burning love. Thus there can be no full and healing response of faith in the visible community unless it be a faith that is active in worldly love. The member of the visible Body has chosen a dangerous place to be. With the knowledge of Christ comes the expectation of service. "To whom much has been given, from him much will be required." In the language of another era of theology, transposed to this ecclesiological setting, "it is a fearful thing to fall in the hands of the living God."

What of those who live alongside the worldly Christ, who relate to him "in profile"? For their discipleship to find completion they too must know who it is with whom they have to do. Without the acknowledgment and celebration of their companion from within the faith-community, their relationship remains aborted.

What is it they "gain" from this knowledge? Here we must part company with those within the perspective of radical mission who, while disavowing proselyting, yet claim that there is a special quality that the church brings to the world which the world requires for its fulfillment. This represents the residue of *deus ex machina* thinking. There is no final card the church has up its sleeve to demonstrate its relevance and assure its place in the human enterprise. While it most certainly has a pioneering function, the sharing of insights and resources for the work of man, the church must ultimately be prepared to relinquish its beachheads on human terrain. Therefore it cannot be said of those outside the visible community that they require the face-to-face relationship with Christ in the same sense that those who know him in the breaking of bread need the bond with the worldly comrade, that is, at the price of ethical and sociological damnation. Here lies the truth of the attack on high-powered proselytism that seeks to club its hearers into the kingdom. Because there is nothing the church knows about the laws of the good life that the world cannot by itself come to know, the church cannot deal in the currency of "need" and "imperative." It can make no ironclad case for its offering. Its gift is supererogatory. It is "only an option" and cannot command the attention of secular men who may well lead happy and human lives without the Christ who comes in the breaking of bread. In fact that secular citizen may well save himself a lot of trouble, not only by avoiding all the internal strife and confusion of the "all-too-human" institutional life of Christianity, but also the pain that comes from living under the vision of a selfless love. But for all that the other face of Christ looks toward us in its patient defencelessness, waiting to be known and loved for its own sake.

May we speak of the incognito relationship as participation, in some sense, in the church, or is that description only possible for those who are part of the visible faith-community? If we are to take seriously our commitment to the multi-dimensionality of Christ's love in church and world and read it in the light of the classic conviction, *ubi Christus, ibi ecclesia*, then it must be said that those who company with him in the world are also in a fundamental way in the church. But how can this be so?

Sometimes the dual reality of the church is described in terms of latent and realized, or the "unconscious" church is treated as a "preparation for the gospel." The difficulty with these characterizations is that they are hierarchical figures which do not honor the integrity of the secular church nor the delicate interrelationship of the two communities. Let us explore another way of acknowledging each and describing their bond. We build on the classic figure of the marriage tie: Christ is related to the faith-community as bridegroom to bride. Here there is a depth of communication described biblically as "knowing." It is a tender, personal communion, a self-disclosure of Christ within the faith-community as an I to a thou. Knowledge is not only "wisdom about," it is a profound "acquaintance with" and celebration of the One who comes.

"Bride" and "bridegroom" are descriptions for the roles of human beings. They do not exhaust the reality of persons who live them out. A bride may also be a student, a mother, a scientist, a writer, a skier. A bridegroom may be a steelworker, a philosopher, a father, a church school teacher, a trumpet player. And a single bride or bridegroom may be all these things, depending on the perspective from which he or she is viewed. Each "wears many hats."

The Christ who comes to join himself to the faith-community in the intimate knowing of bridegroom to bride cannot be domesticated. He ranges in freedom through the manifoldness of his world, "accommodating" to men in the richness of their existence. While his worldly work and the partnership he sustains with worldly men cannot be described in the "knowing" marital communion, it is no less real in its "doing" relationship. Might we say that his co-workers are members of the "doing church" even as the participants in the faith-community are members of the "knowing church"? And we must speak about the incompleteness of each, as much as of their integrity, in the light of our discussion above of the full relationship with Christ.

To further explicate the duality of the church there may be some value in reexamining a concept that has fallen into some disrepute, that of the "invisible church." Translated into fresh terms, the invisible church is constituted by those who do not "know" Christ but nevertheless do his worldly will. They company with the incognito, the invisible Jesus. The visible church is made up of those who relate to the known Christ, "seen" and acknowledged in the language of faith.

It may be asked, which is "better"? The answer is found only in context. There is a time for knowing and a time for doing. On the Jericho road Christ traced the lines of a grace that bound up wounds rather than gathered men around a table of communion. And there was that moment when he celebrated the spilling of the oil of worship (Matthew 26:6–13). That men choose to live in one to the exclusion of the other is his agony. In both knowing and doing, Christ and his church come into their own.

Footnotes

1. Hamilton, "The Shape of Radical Theology," *op. cit.*, p. 1219.

2. *RT*, pp. 5–6.

3. For a strong plea for the importance of "the inward journey" from one of the frontiers of renewal see Elizabeth O'Connor, *Journey Inward, Journey Outward* (New York: Harper, 1968). While not representative of the renewal Left, as such, the 1967 "Parish and People" conference in Great Britain illustrates the struggle of world-oriented mission with the questions of spirituality. Eric James, ed., *Spirituality for Today* (London: SCM Press, 1968).

4. Karl Marx and Frederick Engels, *The German Ideology*, Parts I and III, (New York: International Publications), p. 2.

5. *Ibid.*, pp. 163, 193.

6. *Ibid.*, p. 34 Marx's comments on Proudhon are in the same vein as in "Letter to P. V. Annenkov," in *The Poverty of Philosophy*, C. P. Butt and V. Chattopadhaya, eds. (New York: International Publications), p. 160.

7. See the connections drawn by Robinson, for example, between the task of reconceptualizing God and the groundwork laid by Feuerbach and Proudhon, *Honest to God, op. cit.*, pp. 41, 49–53; *The New Reformation? op. cit.*, p. 112; *Exploration into God, op. cit.*, pp. 36, 132.

8. See the illuminating comments of Engels: "Marx and I are ourselves partly to blame for the fact that the younger writers sometimes lay more stress on the economic side than is due to it. We had to emphasize the main principle in opposition to our adversaries who denied it, and we have not always the time, the place, or the opportunity to allow other elements involved in the interaction to come into their right." "Letter to Joseph Bloch," *Selected Works*, prepared by the Marx-Engels-Lenin Institute, Moscow, V. Adoratsky, ed. (New York: International Publications, 1939), Vol. I, p. 383.

9. See Williams, *Faith in a Secular Age, op. cit.* Also, "Report on the Enlarged Meeting of the North American Steering Committee" (October, 1967), Washington, D.C. Missionary Structure of the Congregation Study.

10. See the "passionate debate" surrounding the meaning of this phrase and its context in *Concept*, Vol. VII, *op. cit.*, pp. 3–21.

11. I Corinthians 5:1.
12. I Corinthians 12:27.
13. Revelation 3:17.
14. Revelation 3:20. See the comments of Trevor Huddleston on this passage, *The True and Living God* (London: Collins, Fontana Books, 1964), p. 94.
15. For efforts to do justice in ecclesiology to this duality see Lesslie Newbigin, *The Household of God* (New York: Friendship Press, 1960), pp. 55–57, 66–68, 110–112, and more recently, *Honest Religion for Secular Man* (Philadelphia: Westminster Press, 1966), pp. 100–122; James Gustafson, *Treasure in Earthen Vessels* (New York: Harper, 1961), pp. 49–112; J. Robert Nelson, *The Realm of Redemption* (London: Epworth Press, 1951), pp. 79, 166, 168; Hans Kung, *The Council, Reform and Reunion*, translated by Cecily Hastings (New York: Sheed & Ward, 1961), pp. 12–36; Gabriel Fackre, *The Pastor and the World* (Philadelphia: United Church Press, 1964), pp. 43–45; Langdon Gilkey, *How the Church can Minister to the World without Losing Itself* (New York: Harper, 1964), pp. 75–77, 105–127; Richard Moore and Duane Day, *Urban Church Breakthrough* (New York: Harper, 1966), pp. 15–19; Huddleston, *op. cit.*, pp. 73–83.
16. We mention here a few of the indictments which our narrow selection of data in chapter 4 omitted: Peter Berger, *The Noise of Solemn Assemblies* (New York: Doubleday, 1961); Martin Marty, *The New Shape of American Religion* (New York: Harper, 1969); Gibson Winter, *The Suburban Capacity of the Church* (New York: Doubleday, 1961); Colin Williams, *What in the World*, *op. cit.*; Pierre Berton, *The Comfortable Pew* (Philadelphia: J. B. Lippincott Company, 1965); Stephen Rose, editor, "Who's Killing the Church?" (Chicago: Renewal Magazine and Association Press, 1966); Colin Morris, *Include Me Out* (London: Epworth Press, 1968); Malcolm Boyd, editor, *The Underground Church* (New York: Sheed & Ward, 1968); Arthur Herzog, *The Church Trap* (New York: Macmillan, 1968); Rodney Stark and Charles Y. Glock, *American Piety* (Berkeley: University of California Press, 1968).
17. See the reflection by E. Schillebeeckx on this conception in *Christ the Sacrament of the Encounter with God* (New York: Sheed & Ward, 1963).
18. For data on the toll taken and to be taken when the church does not restructure in terms of the sociological realities see David Bell et al., *Ecumenical Designs*, The National Convocation of the Church in Community Life, 1967, *passim*.
19. See plaque on wall of Museum of Science and Industry, Chicago.
20. Luke 24:1b.
21. Luke 24:30–31a.

22. Martin Buber, *I and Thou* (New York: Scribner's Sons, 1958), 2nd. ed., pp. 16ff.

23. Cox, *The Secular City, op. cit.*, pp. 48–49.

24. See Will Herberg, *The Writings of Martin Buber* (New York: Meridian, 1956), p. 22.

25. Bonhoeffer, *Prisoner for God, op. cit.*, p. 86.

14

THE PILGRIM CHURCH

We shall explore the function of the time dimensions in ecclesiology from the perspective of the "pilgrim church." As the
basic purpose of our study is to examine ways in which the
faith-community can function meaningfully and responsibly in
secular society, we shall be primarily concerned about "church"
in its empirical sense, the "knowing" community. The word "pilgrim" suggests that its frame of reference will be a journey
toward the future.[1]

Radical mission provides valuable data for a reconceptualization of the visible church as a future-oriented community. We
shall try to follow this lead, expanding and turning it in terms of
current eschatological reflection and some of the themes on past,
present and future developed earlier in the volume. The double
grounding of the Christian future is the pioneer God and the
vision of the end which he projects on the screen of tomorrow.
The God who moves out ahead toward his goal calls men to
keep pace with him. What are the ecclesiological ramifications?

For one, the church which sees the vision of the healing to
which the world is called is drawn to set up signs and pointers.
In the imagery of the radical missiology the end is *shalom*, the
healing of the wounds that cripple the world. That vision tells of
the wholeness for which the world is made: the laying down of

arms between man and man, man and nature, nature within nature and man within himself. It is a *secular* hope, as millennial expectations in the history of the church have demonstrated time and again: Papias and the dream of new crop fertility, Justin and the rebuilt city of human togetherness, Irenaeus, Tertullian and Hippolytus and an earth renewed in natural and human splendor, the radical reformers and a world free of oppression, injustice and war.

Those who have the eyes to see are moved to do. The visionary gripped by his hope presses for its embodiment in the world in which he finds himself. The restlessness induced by the vision is such that he cannot bear to live in a world with less than the vistas that have opened up before him. He longs for the Lord and cries Maranatha! But his urge to be with the Lord in his kingdom is no leap into the invisible future, for the future cannot be taken by storm but comes only in its good time. What is man's to decide, however, is the present. So the one who sees the pioneer God, and dreams his dreams after him, seeks to set up signs in the now to what will be.

The vision takes hold in that circle which tells its Story, the faith-community. Do men live in love and communion in the end? Then in this circle of life there must be neither Jew nor Greek, slave nor free, male nor female. Do the offscourings and dysfunctional of this world receive a name and a face and a new humanity in the world to come? Then in this little flock there shall be care for the prisoner, the orphan, the widow, the aged, the slave. Do all the hurt and helpless find fulfillment in hope? Then here and now in the community of faith the hungry will be fed, the naked clothed, the sick and dying cared for. Is there a life of sharing and self-giving? Then here in the Christian community possessions shall be shared, credit unions begun,[2] no one shall lack and all shall give of themselves.

There is more than one small mirror in the present to reflect the rays of the future. The Christian future takes root in the present, not only among the "little flock." It is the *world* that is made whole in the Christian hope. And it is in the world now that signs of the end are called into being. As the kingdom is a vision of a new commonwealth, a polis made whole, so it is to political embodiment in the present that Christian eschatology points. Mission that grows out of hope, hope in action, includes the "calling of the nations," the claim upon the principalities and powers to bear witness to their Lord and end. Secular mission is the ordering of the structures of society in the light of the healing of hope.

As we have seen in our discussion of ethics, the final vision cannot be neatly transplanted from heaven to earth. It is scarred by the filter of sin and evil through which it must pass. And Christians weep. But though it suffers in translation it is the same message that can be heard, resisting all accommodations that would remove its glory and sting.

As the vision provides a measure and lure for the content of mission, it also illumines its form. The restlessness with the shape of the present applies as well to its structures. The reference point for the church is out ahead. The pilgrim is always far from home. The pilgrim church therefore can never let its benediction rest on what is. And more than that, it is always restlessly pulling what is toward what the divine wills to be. The pilgrim and stranger to this world calls into question the givens and works for their conformation to the vision. In this respect it shares with radical mission the readiness to question all inherited structures. And more, it does not place its hope in "new forms," for hope alone is commensurate with what lies in the future. From its eschatological angle of vision it places a question mark over both past and present, committed alone to what lies beyond. The history of Christian apocalyticism has born witness to the revolutionary edge of future-oriented faith.[3]

There is another component in the Christian vision. *Shalom* as it is understood in a biblical framework is not uni-dimensional. The narrowing of healing into the horizontal plane is an understandable gesture of Christian communication in the radical missiology. Men understand our deeds better than our words. And more, the terror and promise of the human questions, maximized by modern technology, cry for our attention. Secular mission must be the tip-point of the church's ministry. But there is more to an arrow than its head. The final mending of the earth includes the healing of the wounds between God and man as well as the ruptures in man and creation. Can there be *shalom* without "divinization" as well as humanization? The Story's vision tells of a praise lifted by the whole creation to its source and end, the overcoming of the alienation between man, the cosmos, and God.

Radical mission draws back from talk about God in its acts of penetration not only because of its missionary desire to be understood without the barriers introduced by either the offensiveness of or the misunderstanding about its code language. It also has a well-placed suspicion of those who have specialized in God-talk, privatized, incurved, oblivious of time, history and the secular commission. Joy in God calls up a picture of a retreat from historical existence to "timeless adoration." If some of the keenest spirits in mission mute the vertical notes in the Christian message, again we have nobody to blame but ourselves. But does the echo of the praise of God around the heavenly throne have to mean retreat from secular mission? Can it not be a song raised from the very center of the participative act? That celebration can take place in the midst of humiliation we most firmly believe, and shall explore in the last chapter. For the time being we simply note that the full range of *shalom* and its embodiment in our now includes life with the pioneer who calls us to company with him as well as with his vision.

The Present

Eschatology, while taking its point of orientation from the future, deals in the currency of "already" as well as "not yet." It speaks not only about what will be, and therefore what ought to be, but also about what is. It is in the biblical image of "firstfruits" that the activity of the future is nailed down in the present.

The visible church is a firstfruit. Because the pioneer God who leads out by pillar of cloud and fire is also a present companion, his pilgrims live in a special relationship on the journey. We have explored this theme in the previous chapter in images of knowing. However, the I-thou formula must be broadened into historical and cosmic categories. Firstfruits in the church mean not only the singling-out love of God in Christ within the faith-community but also his corporate visible activity.

Christ had promised to be where two or three gather in his name. He also is the prophet and embodiment of a new mankind and new cosmos. He keeps his promises and fulfills his prophecies. Where he is at present, he brings with him signs and seals of his renewing power. As he is present in the midst of his community it becomes the object of his restorative grace. As dismal as is the picture of the faith-community at times, the promise-keeping Christ will not sever Head from Body but will breathe new life into dry bones. Renewal can happen. That is the faith of those who believe that the church is a downpayment of things to come. Firstfruits show themselves in a bloom here and a bud there where the walls of division have been torn down between Greek and Jew, where the offscourings of the world find their humanity, where ministry to and with the oppressed and the hungry and war-torn becomes a reality. To look at the faith-community in all its tawdriness with the eyes of hope is to believe in the resurrecting power of the pioneer in those with whom he keeps company.

But it would indeed be "ecclesiastical positivism" to see the possibility and reality of new blossom alone in brambles of the visible church. As the future has broken into the present of the church, it also establishes a beachhead on secular terrain. Men are not only called to do what will be; they are called to discern what already is, the lively signs of *shalom* in the world. One of the great contributions of radical mission is to call our attention to the evidence of his coming in the theater of history. To discover, to leap into the midst of and to celebrate those living foretastes of the end, is the task of a pilgrim church. And more, to work to shape new, present structures of mission commensurate with the persons, powers and problems that plead for ministration. The commitment to the worldly present and its missionary tasks is one of the contributions of radical mission to a pilgrim church.[4]

The Past

The end of eschatology is the future, its middle is the present, but the beginning of the Last Things is in the past. Neither the Christian future nor present, therefore, can dismiss what has taken place before their time, although they always must put a question mark over it. But the source of that very mark is a strand of the past, the event of Jesus Christ. And on the borders of Bethlehem, Galilee, Calvary and Easter morning is Pentecost. The birth of the church is part of the central drama of the Christian Story. From its participation in the saving events the faith-community receives its election to special service, the telling and celebrating of the Story. And with the mandate goes Christ's promise that he and his Spirit will be with it through thick and thin.

This root and promise mean that the church in its pastness, from Pentecost to the threshold of the present, cannot be ignored. When the Book it brought to be—and by which in turn it measures itself—is honored, through that esteem also is honored the community from which it was born. While other communal action and reflection—conciliar judgments, the best thought of its theologians, its liturgies, codes of behavior, social forms and style of worldly witness—do not enjoy equivalent status, nevertheless because they emerge within the stream of telling and celebrating they are important data for the work of the church of the present and future. They tell us how the Spirit helped the covenant community meet the challenges peculiar to this era as well as the mistakes the church made in its search for relevance. We learn from skill and failure alike. But as the past is not a series of discrete events, our bequest is more than an operational savvy that gives us clues to work in our own isolated time slice. There are things that persist through the changing, developing witness of the visible church. It is no easy matter to locate these factors, but each generation the community returns anew to rediscover them, viewing its data each time in new perspective. But return to the past it must do, however it may alter its inheritance, for the Spirit brings it new buds out of seed long sown.

Because faith works out of a three-dimensional eschatological perspective it has a freedom from the ideologies that wave their banners on one or another of these corners of time. It is not so captive to the past that it cannot be open always to present and future. And because the reverse is true, it can even be open to the possibility of the fresh significance of the past itself. This fact is of special importance in the quest for fitting missionary structures for our own time. The radical missiology, when it is captive to an ideology of the present, will reason from the premise of the relativity of structures that the historical givens in church life are by definition obsolete inasmuch as they were formed in an age other than our own. This a priori judgment, clothed sometimes in very sophisticated sociological argument, lacks one important thing, a posteriori reality. To be free from ideology is to be prepared to "test the spirits." For example, to what extent is the local congregation as a form obsolete; in some respects, in all respects, in no respects? What varieties of local congregations do in fact exist, in what varieties of social situations? In what respect is the form obsolete in one or all or some of these settings? Answers to these questions can only be given by careful scrutiny of particulars and cautious generalization from this research. This kind of procedure is only now being explored in depth in pioneer missionary work on structures. And there is some evidence that the overhasty a priori judgments of radical missiology were very wide of the mark.[5] To consider the possibility that the past may have something to offer to the present is to have the kind of credentials for openness necessary for such research.

The inclusion of the past as a partner in mission means as well the chance to avoid the closure mentality regarding the possibilities for harnessing the institutional givens themselves to mission, however antiquated they may be, and thus to resist the temptation of adventurism. Only a very naïve missionary will ignore the resources in the network of parish life the past has bequeathed to us. As "hic et nunc," as Abbé Michonneau reminds us,[6] it is a failure in stewardship not to use this gift of the givens. While structural aggiornamento is no easy task it is not impossible, as some church-wide renewal efforts are beginning to give evidence.[7] In fact there are strong signs that the early polarization of "new forms" and "old forms," "swingers" and "squares" is developing into a partnership in mission among renewal centers, congregations, and supra-parochial agencies that hold the promise of yet unanticipated structures which express the vital elements of each in new organisms.[8]

The heated debates between past and present come into perspective when they are seen as ventures along the way of a pilgrim church which has final eyes for the future. Drawing on both but captive to neither, it listens to the word, "Go forth to him outside the camp. . . . For we have no lasting city, but we seek the city which is to come."[9]

Footnotes

1. See especially Moltmann, *op. cit.*, pp. 304–338 on the "Exodus Church" and Gerald Jud, *Pilgrim's Process* (Philadelphia: United Church Press, 1967), on "The Pilgrim People of God," pp. 23–35.

2. See James Luther Adams, "Exiles, trapped exiles, in the Welfare State," Rockefeller Chapel, University of Chicago, (August 21, 1966), pp. 2ff.

3. Rahner's phrase. See his recent eschatological reflection, in *Theological Investigations*, Vol. V, translated by Karl H. Kruger (Baltimore: Helicon

Press, 1966), pp. 135–153, and *The Christian of the Future* (New York: Herder, 1967), *passim*.

4. See particularly George Williams, *The Radical Reformation* (Philadelphia: Westminster Press, 1962), and Ernst Benz, *Evolution and Christian Hope, op. cit.*, pp. 51–63. Behind much of the recovery of interest in the left wing of the Reformation and its relation to eschatology is the work and teaching of James Luther Adams. See Max L. Stackhouse, "James Luther Adams: A Biographical and Intellectual Sketch," *Voluntary Associations, op. cit.*, pp. 347ff.

5. For evidence of the possibilities of the local congregational form see Harold Fray, *Conflict and Change in the Church* (Philadelphia: Pilgrim Press, 1969); Wallace Fisher, *From Tradition to Mission* (Nashville: Abingdon Press, 1965); Robert Raines, *Reshaping the Christian Life* (New York: Harper, 1964) and *The Secular Congregation* (New York: Harper, 1968); John Fish et al., *The Edge of the Ghetto* (Chicago: University of Chicago Divinity School, 1966); Richard Moore and Duane Day, *Urban Church Breakthrough* (New York: Harper, 1966); Elizabeth O'Connor, *Journey Inward, Journey Outward* (New York: Harper, 1968); Stephen Rose, *The Grass Roots Church* (New York: Holt, Rinehart and Winston, 1966); Gerald Jud, *Pilgrim's Process, op. cit.;* James Dittes, *The Church in the Way* (New York: Scribners, 1967); Grace Ann Goodman, *Rocking the Ark* (New York: Presbyterian Distribution Service, 1968); David Marshall, editor, *Creative Ministries* (Philadelphia: Pilgrim Press, 1968); Gabriel Fackre, *Secular Impact* (Philadelphia: Pilgrim Press, 1968).

6. Abbé G. Michonneau, *Revolution in a City Parish* (Westminister Md.: Newman Press, 1959), p. 13.

7. See *The Local Church in God's Mission:* the 1968–69 United Church of Christ Emphasis (New York: UCC Executive Council, 1967).

8. See Fackre, *Secular Impact: The Promise of Modern Mission* (Philadelphia: United Church Press, 1968), on "The Church in 1984."

9. Hebrews 13:13–14.

15

CELEBRATIVE HUMILIATION

Radical missiology responds to the this-worldly sensitivities of our time in its functional definition of the church and in its conception of secular mission. As we concentrated on the former in the preceding chapter, we shall address ourselves here to the second answering quality.

We noted in chapter 4 that the *outward* momentum of radical mission, the places and times when it penetrated the secular community, is understood essentially in terms of humanization, that is, the service of, and participation in, the movements of *shalom* in the relations and structures of society. But we must say "essentially" and not exclusively, for there is the note sounded on occasion that the world needs the interpretation of secular healing in Christic terms for its own sake inasmuch as faith illumines the problems of the world, thus preserving it from self-destructive meanings. However, operationally, the code language of faith comes to the foreground not in the public square but in the catacomb life of the faith-community, when it gathers with those who have broken its code and find meaning in the archaisms of the Bible. It is at the *gathering* pole in the rhythm of dispersal and return that talk of God goes on in radical mission. Dispersal talk of God is in another idiom: "Secular talk of God occurs only when we are away from the ghetto and out of costume, when we are participants in political action by which He restores men to each other in mutual concern and responsibility. . . . Speaking of God in a secular fashion is thus a political issue. It entails our discerning where God is working and then joining his work. Standing in a picket line is a way of speaking."[1]

While there is no shortage of code language, and of God-talk in particular, in the "ghetto" literature and life of the kind of radical mission we have been examining, it is worth noting a current development within the ranks of radical mission. Sensitive to the questions raised by the companion movement of radical theology, some parallel issues are raised, as we have noted before, in the American conversation on mission with the question being asked "Should we declare a moratorium on God-talk?" What this means is not yet clear for the mainstream of radical mission. It is fairly clear what it does mean for the kind of "revolutionary mission" that is under the influence of radical theology. The interpretation of prayer by van Buren gives us a clue, as the transcendent reference disappears and secular prayer becomes either contemplation and reading or the action of neighbor concern.[2] At the left end of the spectrum of mission, worldly language and act either define both poles of withdrawal and return, or mission is reduced to its secular pole of involvement.

Humiliation

What is the alternative to either radical or revolutionary mission for those who both refuse to migrate from the secular land which they choose to call home and feel nevertheless the pull of a "homeland" out ahead? How and when can we speak of God in a country that does not seem to understand this language?

We affirm here the rightness of the radical thesis that secular mission must be in the foreground of the church's witness. The towering possibilities for evil or good that technology has put in man's hands can mean either the literal end of the human pilgrimage or a fresh beginning. "On the Jericho road, the Good

Samaritan did not hand out tracts." Our cosmic-scale journey to
Jericho is a mission whose central thrust is "binding up wounds."
Humiliation is sharing the sorrows of the world. It can be nothing less than a profound identification with the hungry, the
thirsty, the stranger, the naked, the sick, the prisoner, and their
struggle for a human world.

While the secular accent is bold, there is another theme that
is bashful. Here we pick up that small strand in radical mission
that speaks about the world "needing" the church and its Story,
but we give it a somewhat different turn. The world "needs"
faith, but only in the sense of the pioneering-relinquishing pattern. The church has no final claim to superior wisdom about the
nature and destiny of man on earth, but it may have insights that
illumine human issues at a given point in the pilgrimage toward
maturity. Because this is so, the faith-community must bring its
God-talk into the streets. And not only in the secular dress of
this-worldly deed and word but also in the code language itself.

The secular role of religious talk is illustrated in the part the
church may play in the developing science-man questions. On
this frontier, one of the dramatic expressions of secularization
itself, the honing of tools for man to change the direction and
definition of life itself makes talk about God seem awkward
indeed. Yet if the faith-community has in its theological research-
files some data on the ethics of the manipulating of man and of
nature, then it is called to share in the emerging dialogue on the
morality of steps anticipated by the introduction of electrode
implantation, genetic surgery, and computer operation of human
behavior. While it will translate its talk about the dignity of man
and the honor yet utility of nature from the Storybook talk of
"image of God," "Creator-creation" etc., these themes will be very
present in the mind of the translator. And out of respect for the
honesty of responsible disclosure, these cards will be laid on the
table for what they are, insights that grow out of faith itself.

But Christian talk about God in the public forum is humiliating. If it is responsible, it is not an exercise in one-upmanship in

which Christians parade their winning wisdom before the secular losers who are presumed to have no chance of seeing as deeply into the nature of things. No, the pioneering-relinquishing style confesses its marginal meaning as a gap-filler that will and must be finally retired. Serving the secular scene means the grace of humility-relinquishment when one's time has come.

It is humiliating in yet another sense. Precisely because religious language is archaic to the modern ear, and worse, is the carrier of all sorts of unworldly connotations given currency by the zealots of unworldly religion, it is exceedingly difficult to be heard by secular ears. The option, therefore, to stop talking in this ghetto language is inviting. However, commitment to a "humiliation-Christology" must decline the invitation. God has taken the risks of temporality in the incarnation. He hides himself in the ordinary and ambiguous. He evokes the struggle of faith to penetrate the disguise, for its reality is in the leap generated by the ambiguous, and not in the calm assurance of the self-evident. There is a certain irony in the possibility of God disclosing truth about his world behind the very veil of religious language. For pious language, mass-produced in the factories of fundamentalism, has indeed shrouded the meaning of the very biblical tale it claims to tell. The task of the missionary is not to run from that language but to confront it, use it, and sweat over its translation for secular man. God is a big and free enough God even to take on the humiliation of disclosure through language abused by a false piety.[3] Misunderstanding and the titter of secular laughter that sometimes attend even modest talk about God is small cost compared to the divine humiliation of incarnation and crucifixion then and now.[4]

Humiliation means as well life on the margins. In this sense the characterization of the church as "postscript" is entirely correct. Here we intend it in the sense that whatever is shared in the street and forum is done in the servant style. Faith does not come in the spirit of gamesmanship, nor to collect scalps, nor to hand out authoritative statements on the way things "really" are.

It foregoes triumphalism in mode as well as message. It listens, is open to learn, and shares what it has in modesty that befits its *paroikos* status. A hard thing to do in the heat of passionate inquiry or action, but this is the posture of a faith which sees itself as resource, not source, in the conversation and concerns of secular men.

But does faith come into the secular circle with its modest and halting God-talk only to illumine the issues that agitate this-worldly men? No, there is another reason as well. Though the words may stick in his throat, and the times seldom come when it is right to say a meaningful word, the man of faith cannot still the Story. It tumbles out with a certain awkwardness in a moment of *kairos*, not only to shed light on secular matters but simply because the one saying it believes it is true. As surely as the humanist, the Buddhist and the Black Muslim are driven "in the wee hours of the morning" to the roots of their commitment and will uncover it, so too the Christian will speak about the things that make him what he is. Mission to the world includes these moments of *kairos* in which faith speaks about God, not only in pragmatic terms, not only because his wisdom can illumine and make human, but because God is God.

What strange talk indeed. That may well be the response of those for whom the limits of language are the limits of human experience. To their ears "God" sometimes evokes a yawn, sometimes comes as an offense, sometimes is the butt of ridicule. Yet it would not be the first time that the language of faith was found to be a "stumbling block" and "foolishness." Perhaps secular mission will entail along with its deep involvement in the human issues and idiom the readiness to live out the role of the clown. As Peter Berger observes in regard to the role of the minister:

If one combines the idea of absurdity with that of vicariousness, he can think here of a striking analogy: that of the clown. This analogy is not an insult to the ministry; on the contrary it points to the profound significance of the clown, who dances through the world incongruous in the face of the world's seriousness, contradicting all its assumptions—a messenger from another world, in which tears turn to laughter and the walls of man's imprisonment are breached. In this role the clown carries out a vicarious action: it is for *others* that he is clowning. I think that one can speak of the clown, without exaggeration, as a sacerdotal figure. In absurdity and in vicariousness the two figures meet. The clown ministers and the minister clowns.[5]

Our odd and awkward talk of God to secular men who could not care less, and do not hesitate to tell us so in all understanding and good humor, is yet another dimension of the meaning of missionary humiliation.

Celebration

In secular mission the naming of God is bashful. But there is a time and place for it to be bold. The full-throated sounds of faith are heard within her own community. Of course the members are also secular men. They can resonate to faith's notes only if heard in their own auditory range. That is what our quest for new images and themes in this study is striving to find. But the faith-community is composed of those who have cast their lot with the code language, and that choice legitimates the display of the Christian Story in this circle of life without apology.

To "fling the faith in the air" (Monica Furlong) so that it may be seen in its joyful fulness is celebration. It is no accident that the word has become synonomous with the central act of Christian devotion, the Eucharist, and as well a description of worship as such. Worship is the occasion in which men of faith move through the horizontal (not around it) to the vertical, the confrontation with the beyond in our midst. The celebrative act is attention magnetized to the One through the medium of the many, the One out ahead through the facilities and events of the here and now. In worship the final loyalties, the end commitments, come home.

Because the celebrative mood is not halting and tongue-tied in its praise to God and talk of him—in contrast to the awkwardness and modesty in the secular setting—it makes a bold claim to time and space. Attack on the gross immorality of establishment practices in worship is indeed doing important iconoclastic work. The sickening overinvestment of institutional Christianity in its buildings and appointments while bodies wither and die and crucial humanizing movements want for lack of funds deserves every blow of the prophetic lance. The proposals either to eliminate the tabernacling of faith in buildings or locate it in the tents of mobile and temporary quarters is fully understandable. The church ought "to get out of the real estate business." Telling also is the critique of a worship that wastes time as well as space that could be spent in worldly mission, a critique which substitutes a style of devotion "on the run" or redefines work itself as the whole of worship. The well-placed protest against institutional givens of time and place are less on target in their proposals for new options. It is helpful here to take a leaf from secular "spirituality."

In discussing the alternative to prayer we noted earlier that van Buren cites the role of reading and personal meditation. In this sense the daily journeys of Marx to the British Museum to give shape to *Das Kapital* were the "spiritual exercises" that brought a world-shaking movement to self-consciousness. And the cult life of the Communist cell has been a well-known phenomenon since, down to the daily times set aside for reading, discussion and contemplation of the sayings of Chairman Mao in China's factories and offices. The father of modern sociology, Auguste Comte, understood very well the need for sociological forms that give body to and assure the continuance of ideas. He gave expression to this insight in efforts in the spiritual formation of the disciple of his "religion of humanity," with its secular saints, church calendars, worship services, buildings and professionals. For the nourishment and perpetuation of basic commitments there are required segments of time and space.

On these secular grounds alone Christian celebration must have some room in the world for the cultivation of its perspective and the training of its members. This will mean more than "prayer a-go-go" and an anti-building ideology. It will involve the dramatization of the Christian Story done with the same care and sensitivity and time that Marxist or humanist take to ritualize and nourish their commitments in cell or laboratory. And while the day is long gone for British Museum-style settings or university-scope complexes for the formation of faith, there will be visible structures, ranging from the rented storefront quarters of the renewal center to the urban "Central House,"[6] where celebration in its many forms literally "takes place."

But place-taking, for all its necessity and the fullness with which it is lived out, cannot be imperialist. It must be immodesty of God-talk in modest setting, celebrative humiliation. Bonhoeffer says a helpful word in his occasional reference to the *disciplina arcani.*[7] With roots in Alexandrian Christianity, and possibly further back in the strong New Testament language about "casting pearls before swine" and Christ's own incognito ministry, re-examined in detail by the Oxford Movement,[8] the understanding of a hidden discipline may once again be a resource for faith now in a secular era.

God-talk, unobstrusive in the world, is celebrative in the faith-community. But the faith-community is itself unobtrusive. Occupying time and space, it is nonetheless marginal time and space, a hiddenness that befits its postscript character. While there is a tendency to interpret the hidden discipline in terms of the solitary life of prayer,[9] the corporate cannot be excluded, and this for both secular and Story reasons. As indicated above, every ideology requires social rootage and nuture. And further, Christian faith is by its very nature social. Thus celebration lives a catacomb life. It does not make a great to-do about its symbols, demanding their exposure in the public places—be they public square, school or legislature—but does its praying in the closets of modern society. Strangely enough those communities which sociologist and reformer find to be increasingly marginal may well be the catacomb centers of the faith-community: local congregations. While local congregations will increasingly be changing their character as they grow more ecumenical and become only one in a pluriform of Christian gatherings, thus moving toward the central house or "cathedral" or "theological park" shape,[10] they represent that location in which the Christian Story is told and celebrated for the vast majority of its present constituents, and where a new generation is introduced into the stream of faith.[11] But whatever the social form celebration takes, it must be that of an "underground church" that does not intrude its symbols noisily in either its secular mission or its general behavior but lives out its celebrative life in modest alongsidedness to the world.

Worldly Celebration

There is always the risk in talk of celebrative withdrawal that the "closet" may suggest insulation from the world outside, and may in fact lead to it. That spells the end of authentic worship. Responsible withdrawal is no retreat to a quiet pool of Siloh in order for the alone to commune with the Alone. It is respite and reorientation on a riverbank in full view of the rapids and in preparation for reentry. The shattering of all tendencies to insulation happens, in the very character of responsible celebration, in at least three ways.

The worship route to the pilgrim Other is through the sorrows and joys, the particularities, structures, and issues of this world and this time. Michel Quoist has given powerful contemporary expression to this kind of devotion.[12] Prayer rises from a confrontation with persons, things, events and processes; a bald head, a brick, a swing, a telephone conversation, are lifted up before God. The great public issues and the need for structural changes in society—in housing, war, industry—are unfurled and struggled with as well, not in glittering generalities but in terms of concrete names, faces, and movements. The worshipper cannot escape into a never-never land, for his prayer must take form from secular history, the same history in which Christ took form and from which his prayers rose.

What Quoist does in individual idiom is represented in corporate worship by the freshest winds blowing in liturgical reform in the Catholic and Protestant wings of the church. While translation into common language and architectural and appointment changes are part of this sensitivity to the secular, further breaks through liturgical ghetto walls have come in content, style and location of worship. Early pioneers include the Roman Catholic priest-worker experiments, the worship patterns of the Iona Community which early sought to bring the bread of holy table into conjunction with the bread of the world,[13] the Anglican house church celebration of Ernest Southcott[14] and the polis-oriented worship of the East Harlem Protestant Parish.[15] Currently, world-drenched innovation is finding its way into denomination-wide structure in the revision of worship forms,[16] or ecumenical inquiry, as in the Missionary Structures Study[17] or recent cross-denominational British exploration.[18]

One of the most dramatic new forms of celebration that seeks to take the world seriously in term of contemporary language, content, format, and beat is found in the *Risk* hymnal produced by the Youth Division of the World Council of Churches. Containing music and verse in folk idiom which attempt to relate the Christian Story in meaningful images to the modern world and the issues of war and peace, poverty and abundance, love and hate, it roots worship in the historical and bends it toward its goal. Albert van den Heuvel, writing in the introduction of the collection, sums up the need for the kind of worship to which all these aforementioned trends point:

It is senseless to speak about the secular city, but to keep singing "O come, Thou Key of David, come and open wide our heavenly home". . . . Where are the hymns which speak about the humanization of the structures of our society? . . . Where are the hymns which express hope, not in heaven, but on earth? . . . Wherever something happens people start to sing. In the racial conflict, in the struggle for independnce of the southern hemisphere, songs flourish. . . . I would have thought that the Christian community could only learn to sing again if we were to find the *kairos* of our history, the pregnancy of the times in which we live.[19]

If the content of celebration is worldly, so must be its style. As befits an empirical age, modern worship is at its best when it is "inductive," rising out of the raw experiences of the community from which confession, petition, intercession, praise and thanksgiving find their reality.

While there must ultimately be some continuities in the worship of the faith-community, as in its ethical style, it is also true that these must develop from genuine research in real situations. This is particularly so in a time when old forms have demonstrated their inadequacy, and the ad hoc laboratory moves to the foreground in an effort to discover clues to a new style. Thus in the movement to renew congregational life in the United Church of Christ, worship is placed in the context of a "planning process" —identity clarification, situation definition, self-study, action, evaluation, celebration—in which a task force in the congregation seeks to catch the pulsebeat of a congregation in mission and shape its worship so that it expresses the life of that congregation at that particular time and place.[20] Secular style means, in this case, a worship that is built on the "feedback principle." It is celebration that not only makes use of the secular content but also of the process of soundings and of the inclusion of this particular community, with its particular data, in the formation of its own celebration. To come full circle the new learnings must be shared with the larger community of faith outside a given particularity, so that fresh reference points in worship do not deteriorate into a rugged individualism but are both stewarded for the whole people of God and corrected by learnings from that community.

A very visible symbol of a new worship style is the increasing use of the guitar. It can and already has in some places degenerated into an imitationist fad. That fact should not obscure its significance as a sign of new times in celebration. In a brainstorming vein, might we not ask if the guitar is to the organ as humiliation-celebration themes are to a triumphalist and otherworldly theology? The folk singer is part of the stigmata of the protest movement, whether it be in arenas of race, poverty or war. He provides the music for worldly mission. Further, the folk singer, at least in Movement setting, is a modest singular presence, bearing one slight instrument, whose music is frequently developed ad hoc out of the immediate political events. This is in sharp contrast to the sonorous and overpowering tones of the organ and its massed choirs with their carefully rehearsed oratorios. As a symbol of the world, and the kind of a world in which modern men find themselves, the folk idiom, or something like it that embodies the secular style, should increasingly find its place in the life of celebration alongside other forms.

Another point at which the secular is brought into range of worship in terms of style is in the symbolical movements of the worshipping congregation. The reorientation of the priest at the altar facing the people in Roman Catholic reform is such a gesture. We must ask in what further ways the worldly and coming of age foci might be adumbrated. Does not kneeling in prayer suggest a theology of patriarchal obeisance? What might be the physical counterpart to a theology of maturity—standing prayer? And as the theology of dependency is reflected in the bowed head and closed eyes, might not the address to God the Partner and the visible world in which he is at work be better expressed by a prayer with eyes open to the world and a face forward? It may well be that the working out of these seemingly minor issues will cause more explosions within institutional Christianity than all the ruminations of radical theology, morality and mission, for they impinge directly and painfully on long-established mores. That in itself would be a sad commentary on church life if the

scaffolding of faith matters more than the building itself and its
life and death issues. However, there are plenty of pitfalls in easy
formulations of maturity and worldliness too. One thinks of the
"new form" of worship proposed to American visitors by Reichs-
bishof Müller of the "German Christian" church in the Nazi era.
Caricaturing traditional Christian (and Jewish) worship by his
own gestures of grovelling and words of whining, he then strode
across the room in brisk goosestep, clicked his heels at attention
before the bust of Hitler, and saluted "Ich bin Deutsch!"[21] The
bowed head and lowered eyes of traditional prayer at least reminds us that there is no claim to moral or spirituality maturity,
and no god but God. In any case we need honest conversation in
the churches as to how faith can develop a secular style in its
catacomb life.

The most fundamental way in which the secular makes its appearance in Christian celebration is in the living context of the
worshipper and his congregation. Authentic worship is a life
toward God dug into the hard earth of contemporary events.
Those who live in the currents of *shalom* are the ones who will
recognize *shalom* when it comes to them in worship. And those
who are not immersed in the struggles of men to heal a broken
world will know at best a burning love.

Worship in the context of involvement may, of course, mean
community celebration "on location," as in the priest worker
model. However, as E. H. Wickham has pointed out, the simple
physical interpretation of involvement worship has its drawbacks,
for it may divide Christians from others on the factory floor at
precisely those places in which they should be one, and this from
a faith that pretends to affirm unity.[22] Moreover, the fundamental
expression of worldliness in worship is not the physical location
as such but the genuine involvement of the persons and the community in the struggle to make and keep life human. That is what
gives basic secular roots to celebration.

While we have been speaking about the "new" secular content,
style and commitment in worship that protect it from the tempta-

tions of insulation, there is a very old theme implicit in all that has been said. The character of Christian worship has, since its inception, always had a secular flavor manifest in the early use of the service of communion as an occasion of assistance to the poor and hungry. In fact it is in the use of ordinary elements of bread, wine and water in its most revered communal actions that worship is grafted into the body of the world.[23] As God became man in Christ, he comes to men again and again through sacramental vehicles that drip of matter and history. As such, the components of worship are silent missionaries themselves, pointing the Christian community to the matter and history in which the Body belongs, if it is to be faithful to its Head. All Christian worship is therefore celebrative in this sense as well—eucharistic, a grace that is at work in, with and under the events and processes of the world.

Joyful Celebration

Celebration is worship, it is eucharistic worship, and it is as well joyful eucharistic worship. How so? Can we talk of joy in this kind of a world at this kind of a time? Can there be joy in a world in which war has become the slaughter of innocents, when the poor and the black struggle to find their humanity and are answered by the cattle prod and the suburban shotgun? Only an insane Galgenhumor or ruthless insensitivity would dare to crease a face with smiles before these and countless other secular horrors.

What makes our back arch in anger and our eyes fill at the sight of the great miseries of our time, and what bolsters our will to plunge into these crises to do what feeble little we can? The magnitude of the horror. And that magnitude is in direct proportion to the advancing technology that makes possible the destruction as well as the ability to see and feel it first hand in our global village.

But there is another side to the new technology anticipated

already in the media that makes misery so tangible. It is the possibilities it opens up in history, as well as the impossibilities. The very human power to destroy with such omnipresence also holds the promise of healing. And healing on a scale that so far men have only dared to project into eternity itself—the overcoming of disease, ignorance, hunger, poverty, and death. To have the power of life and death over man and his cosmos that men once thought belonged to God alone, that is what it means to come of age. And because within that new power lies the possibility of yet undreamed of *shalom,* we celebrate this twenty-first birthday of man. Within the very signs of new levels and nuances of the death man can and does bring are new tokens of life he can bring, yes, and even now does bring.

Faith needs new sets of Franciscan eyes that can roam over the vistas of human adulthood and hymn what they see through the smoke and travail that all eyes can see. In a world come of age, the new Franciscan's sight ranges beyond the flowers and animals and sun to catch a glimpse of the laser beam that can build new cities, the genetic surgery and transplant that can build new bodies, and the computer that can build new minds. And could it be that his horizon includes as well social sciences that finally teach men about the hate that only destroys society, and psychological sciences whose lesson is "love or perish"? As long as men are men, with some measure of freedom, and not reduced by their new playthings to automatons themselves, sin will continue to infect even the bravest new world. But that does not mean its effects cannot be made tolerable and human life livable. The hymns of the new Franciscan, therefore, celebrate the strange and fearful maturity that God has given man, and rejoice in the possibilities that are not yet obscured by the impossibilities.

But he will not gainsay the latter while he celebrates the former. And more, he will be sober enough to know that the maturity in process is by no means an accomplished fact. Life is still four score years and ten, and far less than that for the vast majority of men; the cure of all disease is still blue sky expectation, and for billions even the present curative resources are not accessible; nor are the things that remove the blight of mind or hunger of body within reach. Franciscan worship therefore will have its sober underpinning of petition and intercession to the God who is big enough to close gaps in unknown and perhaps odd ways for a world which cannot close them itself. And it will never be far away from a confession which must make its home even at the last stages of the human pilgrimage toward adulthood.

But the capstone of worship in a world come of age is joy. Joy for the new juices flowing in the human organism. And joy in the God who sets them loose. Joy in God not only because the eyes of Franciscan sight see evidence for new possibilities in the world. But because the eyes of Franciscan *faith* see something as well. It is the pioneer God whose contours they discern on the horizons of history. It is this pull from the new future that is the final anchor of hope for a celebrative faith, the anticipation of "things not seen." And this God evokes a very special kind of joy. Not only a thanksgiving for the maturity that is aborning and the promise of the future that is to come—but also there is to be found in faith a love for that One only because he is God, an adoration of He Who Is, and He Who Will Be.

And who will listen to such strange talk in a secular age? Few, perhaps, except those who live in the catacombs. That is why such talk is bashful and secular mission is bold.

Yet it would be an unfinished tale of our time if we did not leave one small footnote on its sensitivities. While the empirical spirit and this-worldly mind call the age's tune, there is a certain disquietude increasingly manifest among those who have chosen to dance with gusto to the secular music. What is this hippie talk of "eucharistic experience" and visions of God, this cultic urge to "drop out, turn on, tune in" and transport from the technological trap that kills bodies and spirits into a world of love and Love, this pilgrimage of the pacemakers in the swinging worlds of modern song and film to the Himalayan monastery for contemplative passage to new levels of "sagacity"? Self-deception and a clever new escape from responsibility for a hectic future? Perhaps. But might there not be in these strange defections from our trim and manageable common-sense world a judgment on the empirical limitations our age confidently places on reality? Herbert Marcuse puts it this way in his reflection on the range of data declared in bounds by some practitioners of linguistic analysis:

But whether or not they are integrated into science, philosophic concepts remain antagonistic to the realm of ordinary discourse, for they continue to include contents which are not fulfilled in the spoken word, the overt behaviour, the perceptible conditions or dispositions, or the prevailing propensities. The philosophic universe thus continues to contain 'ghosts,' 'fictions,' and 'illusions' which may be more rational than their denial insomuch as they are concepts that recognize the limits and the deceptions of the prevailing rationality. They express the experience which Wittgenstein rejects—namely, that 'contrary to our preconceived ideas, it is possible to think 'such and such'—whatever that may mean.' [24]

Odd talk of God and the non-empirical reality and pull of the future may, after all, not be so odd to some, even some who have drunk deeply from secular cups and remain unfilled. But when all is said and done, faith and hope, and love as well, do not rest their case on whether they fit the assumptions and sensitivities of this time or any time. In the last analysis celebration is scandalous. It does not violate the best of human plans and hopes and instincts, but the final reaches of its joy cannot be slipped into by easy deduction from the way things are or by the "constraint" of its answers to the world's questions. It wells up in the heart of a man who looked at a marginal option and in his freedom has leaped to meet it. He is "surprised by joy."

Footnotes

1. Cox, *The Secular City, op. cit.*, p. 256.
2. Van Buren, *The Secular Meaning of the Gospel, op. cit.*, pp. 188–190.
3. It is interesting that Cox, who has spoken forcefully about the kind of God-talk that *is* secular action and the need to leave the ghetto language

behind in the public square, read biblical passages (from the Song of Solomon) during "An Evening with God" whose leadership ran from Dick Gregory to Timothy O'Leary. For Bonhoeffer on the "Song of Solomon," see *Prisoner for God, op. cit.,* p. 144.

4. *Fact* magazine pulls together current jokes about God in Warner Brown, "A Funny Thing Happened to God on His Way to the 21st Century," *Fact,* Vol. IV, No. 2 (March–April, 1967), pp. 35–37. The interpretive subtitle says, "He died. And one of the subtle symptoms of His fatal illness was that for the first time, people began laughing at Him."

5. Berger, "Letter on the Parish Ministry," *The Christian Century* (April 29, 1964), p. 549. Copyright 1964, Christian Century Foundation. Reprinted by permission.

6. See Rose, *The Grass Roots Church, op. cit.,* pp. 109ff.

7. *Prisoner for God, op. cit.,* pp. 123, 126, 140–141. See Phillips' review of Bonhoeffer's thought on the secret discipline, *The Form of Christ in the World, op. cit.,* pp. 225–237.

8. See particularly Tracts 80 and 87.

9. See Ronald Gregor Smith, *The New Man* (New York: Harper, 1956), pp. 104–105, and *Secular Christianity, op. cit.,* pp. 202ff.

10. *The Grass Roots Church, op. cit.,* pp. 97–119, and *Secular Impact, op. cit.,* "The Church in 1984," pp. 118–125.

11. "Letter on the Parish Ministry," *op. cit.,* p. 550.

12. Quoist, *Prayers, op. cit., passim.*

13. See *The Abbey Services of the Iona Community* (Glasgow: Iona Community Publishing Department).

14. E. W. Southcott, *The Parish Comes Alive* (New York: Morehouse, 1956).

15. George W. Webber, *The Congregation in Mission* (Nashville: Abingdon Press, 1964), pp. 92–112; *Concept,* Vol. I, pp. 13ff.

16. United Presbyterian Church, United Church of Canada and United Church of Christ are a few in which significant changes are under way.

17. Western European Working Group, *The Church for Others, op. cit.,* pp. 41–43.

18. *Spirituality for Today, op. cit.*

19. A. H. van den Heuvel, "Preface," *Risk: Hymns for a New Day,* Youth Department of the World Council of Churches and the World Council of Christian Education, 1966, Vol. II, No. 3.

20. *The Local Church in God's Mission, passim,* pp. 42–45.

21. Story related by James Luther Adams.

22. E. H. Wickham, *Encounter with Modern Society* (New York: Seabury Press, 1964), p. 120.

23. A theme much emphasized by the Iona Community. *We Shall Rebuild, op. cit.,* pp. 23–90.

24. Marcuse, *One-Dimensional Man, op. cit.,* p. 196. On this point and related themes, see Peter Berger's intriguing *A Rumor of Angels: Modern Society and the Rediscovery of the Supernatural* (Garden City., N.Y.: Doubleday & Co., 1969). Note also Ernst Bloch's comments on daydreaming in "Man as Possibility," *Cross Currents, op. cit.,* pp. 273–283.

CONCLUSION

This study has dealt with "themes" in theology. It has attempted neither an extensive critique of the radical perspectives examined nor a new overall structure to replace the old. Those tasks are important. Whether their time has yet come—or perhaps is past —is another question. What does seem clear is that Christian reflection must move beyond the phase in which it sees its job as "raising questions," or developing extended diagnoses of the ills of church, world and its theological ancestry, or piecemeal reconstruction. We cannot yet claim rounded "answers" for all the well-worked questions. But we can speak about the material for an answering theology. We call these materials themes, and focus on two that thread their way through the three areas of Christian thought and action here explored, humiliation and celebration— crucifixion and resurrection. Humiliation: the divine powerlessness that takes the risks of temporality alongside men in its suffering marginality, and the faith that follows. Celebration: the divine power that expresses itself in the creativity of a world come of age, and the faith that leaps in joy to the side of the God who waits out ahead. They are not formulas to "conquer" the doubts of secular men but options that have learned to breathe the secular air and are, in fact, nourished by it.

The themes have found their way into our inquiry by way of a set of pictures, some new, some old but refurbished: father, tutor, lover, pioneer, counsel, research, pilgrim community, profile, face to face. There surely are others, and better. If the inquiry evokes them, it has served its purpose. The study does not choose to die at the barricades of one variety of imagery but to push forward the quest for a new language of faith and new styles of action which are meaningful to citizens who make their home in both church and world. And we do not pass hastily over the citizens of "church" country. Not only because they are also secular men who struggle as much as the next man for clarity in their faith. There is more than this personally existential concern at stake— laid, incidentally, with all the traps of self-concern that have plagued those who only see issues as invitations for private identity struggles. Because the faith community has a charge to steward and share its treasures wherever it is placed, it needs to carry on the missionary labor of communication. And it must be prepared to live under the special call of special times. That means, we believe, deep participation in the human issues of a secular age with a straining forward in future orientation, and doing it as a minority that may increasingly be greeted with the benign smile of those who know they do not "need" faith and have yet to discern another dimension of reality than the functional.

If theology is to move forward to a new set of themes and images, it must settle accounts with the radical scouts of secularity. We have attempted to honor their reports and go on from there making our own maps. The theology of tomorrow can neither ignore their findings nor uncritically accept them. The way is through radical theology, morality and mission; it is not around them, nor does it stop at them.

The modest work in themes and images opened up some paths that cry for concentrated exploration. For example, the problem of evil. If God has genuinely freed man for his own future—yet is in, with, and under human decision—what does this say to the long-standing agony over the reality of both God and evil? Does the suffering God in some sense allow man to take the risk of freedom in the interest of maturity—thus evil is a real possibility —yet also work through human effort to cope with it? How much new thinking needs to be done here. And then there is the whole field of eschatology that sings out to be planted and reaped.

These are the great areas of theory. But the practical work is even more imperative. All the talk of celebration will come to naught if men do not learn to master the god-like power to destroy as well as to create life. War is the Damocles' sword that hangs over all our whetted expectations. It is the top priority in mission of today and tomorrow. And there is the other side of the coin, the new power of science to control and redefine life itself. If we can achieve a tolerable peace, then these issues will rise to the top of our agenda.

Can faith really be stated meaningfully and lived institutionally in the alongsided style? That is the real question the churches have to face in the years ahead. The problem is not the sundry obituaries announced by radical thought. God, counsel, and community have a resiliency which are regularly underestimated. But so does the real enemy of faith in a secular age, autocracy. Triumphalism dies hard. It takes on new disguises, even radical ones. Will men—and churchmen—be able to understand talk of a God who really has nothing to offer except himself, law that is not rule but counsel, church in the form of crucifixion? It's hard to lose face, to go out of business gracefully, to withdraw to the sidelines, to be "only an option." But that is the style of faith in a secular age. God calls us to live it out, alongside him, today and tomorrow.